**Library at the Bridge**
1000 Westerhouse Road
Glasgow G34 9JW
Phone: 0141 276 9712 Fax 276 9711

This book is due for return on or before the last date shown below. It may
be renewed by telephone, personal application, fax or post, quoting this
date, author, title and the book number

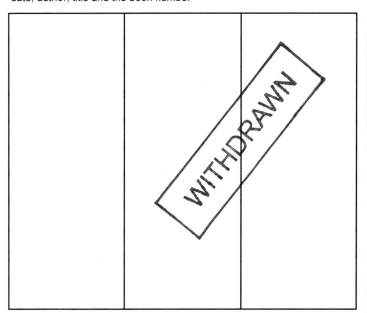

Glasgow Life and its service brands, including Glasgow
Libraries, (found at www.glasgowlife.org.uk) are operating
names for Culture and Sport Glasgow

LOST
ARGYLL

ARGYLL'S LOST HERITAGE

Marian Pallister

ORIGIN

*To St Columba, whose path
I keep crossing – please pray for Argyll.*

✳

This edition first published in 2018 by
Origin, an imprint of Birlinn Ltd
West Newington House
10 Newington Road
Edinburgh EH9 1QS

www.birlinn.co.uk

First published by Birlinn Ltd in 2005

ISBN 978 1 912476 35 0
eBook ISBN: 978 1 78885 164 0

British Library Cataloguing-in-Publication Data
A catalogue record for this book is available
from the British Library.

Design: Mark Blackadder

Printed and bound by
Gutenberg Press Limited, Malta

CONTENTS

INTRODUCTION

To call this book *Lost Argyll* is a little misleading: this is a county of Scotland in which buildings, industries, modes of travel and even the very lie of the land itself have not so much been lost but treated as jigsaw pieces to be taken from the box, pieced together, reshuffled and created anew. Since the first settlers roamed this western seaboard some six thousand or so years before the birth of Christ, shelters have been thrown up, defences built, monuments erected, tools made, artefacts crafted, tracks trodden. Artists and religious leaders have made their mark. The politically and the fiscally powerful have created and destroyed. The landscape of Argyll, as ancient as landscapes come on this planet, is now enhanced by a rich patina of the presence of the past. Like lichens of many shades, the evidence of Argyll's heritage cloaks the county and invites the curious to scratch a little at the surface to uncover the layers beneath. Because this is a predominantly rural area, the architectural heritage is very different to that of a cityscape. Because of its exposed position, it has acquired an abundance of forts and castles, duns and brochs. The lairds and the runrig farmers have left their mark. Industries have come and gone. For some, this has been the centre of their universe; for others, the very remoteness has been a catalyst – or a repellent.

Argyll – in its historic rather than modern political concept – has been accommodating to them all. A gentle giant offering up the detritus of one generation for the benefit of the next. In the 21st century we tend to want to live in aspic: to preserve, to conserve, to protect, to enclose in Perspex. We fight against new industry because it will spoil our view. We fight for the preservation of buildings which have long outlived their usefulness. Our ancestors lived for their moment. They cannibalised the broch, the fort, the chambered burial cairn, the big house too expensive to run, the draughty, rheumatism-inducing cottage emptied of its tenants by a greedy landlord – or even one benevolent enough to build a new, watertight cottage with floorboards and a tiled roof.

Industries have been welcomed because they meant work in an area where farming and fishing have not always filled bellies or clothed children. Sometimes those industries have snatched lives, sometimes they have simply been a footprint on the sands of time, washed away without profit for the owners or adequate wages for the workers. Technology, ancient and modern, has also changed the face of Argyll. In recent times, the most dramatic losses have been due to the quick succession of new modes of power – and their demise. Steamboats and railways came and went, leaving memories of an Argyll packed with people who either came to see the county for themselves or were en route by the quickest means possible to other destinations. (Hard to believe now that Inverness was a destination most quickly reached from Glasgow by steamer to Ardrishaig, a journey through the Crinan Canal, another steamer to Fort William and a final sail through the Caledonian Canal).

This book cannot pretend to be encyclopaedic and all that could be described as 'Lost Argyll' cannot be catalogued – or indeed, this would become a catalogue rather than a book which seeks to place the 'lost' in its context. And as with humans when we mourn the passing of the very old but concede that they have had a good life and their time has come, so too we grieve with a degree of shock the departure of the young. Aros Castle was bound to pass into the mists of time: why did an art deco railway station in Appin have to be axed by Dr Beeching? The beehive cells on Eileach an Naoimh could be expected to merge back into the landscape from which they rose: did monuments to Victorian prosperity like Poltalloch House in Mid Argyll have to be slain on the sacrificial altar of exorbitant 20th-century rates? And couldn't the vernacular houses throughout the county have been conserved and upgraded to offer affordable homes to new generations? Armies, sheep and sitka spruce have changed the face of Argyll down the centuries. Christianity was cradled in Argyll but now the cells of saints crumble in bracken on remote hillsides and schools which saw the foundation of a universal education system are no more than folk memories.

But lost? No: we must simply look a little harder. Scratch the lichen and ten thousand years of history will come alive. In 1790, the minister of Kilmartin Church wrote in his report for the First Statistical Account that there was nothing of note in his parish. By the late 1990s, Kilmartin House museum was showing the world that Kilmartin Glen was one of the most important archae-ological sites in the UK. Sensitivities change. There is now a will to conserve the best of the past but that must not be at the expense of future generations. Protection, not petrification, will keep alive the spirit of Argyll – a county which has always existed in its own time.

ACKNOWLEDGEMENTS

I would like to acknowledge the great help of Murdo MacDonald, the Argyll and Bute Archivist, for his encyclopaedic and quirky knowledge of Argyll; Eleanor Harris for her help with documents and illustrations; and Michael Hopkin and Duncan MacMillan for their great patience and generosity in sharing their collections of illustrations. Duncan's *Memories: Past Images of Old Argyll* can be accessed through duncan@cuilfail.fsnet.co.uk.

I would also like to thank:

His Grace the Duke of Argyll and his Estate Factor, Mr A. Montgomery, for kind permission to use a number of illustrations from Inveraray Castle and Estate documents;

Argyll and Bute Library Service for providing access to images from their postcard collection;

Maureen Bell, Drumlemble, Alan Miller and Archie Smith of Tighnabruaich, Dr Alastair MacFadyen of Newton, Neil and Marie Kennedy of Campbeltown, James and William Wallace of Drumlemble, and Sheena Carmichael of Ford for access to their collections of photographs. Catriona Bell of Craigard Holidays, Islay, for help with illustrations;

Hamilton Currie for granting permission to use Minerals of Scotland website material provided by D. Green and D. MacCallum on a site constructed by Mr Currie, whose help has been invaluable;

Michael Davis for making material accessible.

Christine Roberts of Melfort Village for photographs and access to the gunpowder factory site.

Geoff Waters of the Scottish Council for Archaeology for access to his own and Council for Scottish Archaeology Summer School photographs;

RCAHMS staff for their help.

CHAPTER 1

NORTH ARGYLL:

BOBBINS, BROCHS AND BEATERS

Agnes Torrance had gone to bed at 11 o'clock on a chilly July night. She had been sitting by the fire in the kitchen for half an hour or so to let the embers die down and she'd been glad of the rest. It had been a long day, what with the steamer coming in to take away a consignment of bobbins and her being left in charge of the young lads who worked in the little factory at Salen in Ardnamurchan. The manager, William Davidson, was away overseeing wood-cutting at Drimnasallie near Lochshiel and the foreman, Duncan Mclean, left with the bobbins on the *Maid of Lorn* because he was sick and was off to Glasgow to see the doctor. When the steamer had gone, she'd got the boys to work in the garden, but they were like any other boys in their early teens – turn your back and they were in the mill swinging on the machinery and melting lead to make a fishing weight. Not that Mrs Torrance had been too sure what the boys were up to at the time. She had other duties to attend to. She was the housekeeper at the mill and it was the three boys – Thomas Donald, Robert Stewart and James Colquhoun who were supposed to look after the mill. They were responsible enough in their own way. On the Monday they'd cleared out the mill and the machine shops and packed the 'pirns' into bags, all by evening.

The 'pirns' or bobbins were for the Clark's thread factory in Paisley. The Clarks were important people – they'd had a mill in Seedhill in Paisley since 1813 and now there was a grandson, John Clark junior, in charge. Their clever ways of making thread had turned Paisley into the manufacturing town it was in the 1850s. In time they would amalgamate with J. & P. Coats but now they had come to Ardnamurchan in Argyll because it was a good place for larch wood. They built a mill and a house for the manager and a wooden hut at the back as a bunkhouse for the young lads who worked there. Mrs Torrance, a widow, was Mr Davidson's housekeeper and she lived at one end of the dwelling house in a kitchen and bedroom. The other end of the house had a parlour and three bedrooms. There was a fireplace in one of the bedrooms and one in the parlour, as well as in the kitchen and Mrs Torrance's bedroom. In the centre of the house there was a milk-house and pantry. There were windows in the gables and skylights in the roof. Mrs Torrance scarcely needed a candle that July night, even though it was 11 o'clock when she went to her bedroom. Night is a stranger in Ardnamurchan in July.

The wheel of the mill was next to the gable on the parlour side of the house and a large pole ran up through the roof of the mill into the parlour as a support for the trows and the waterway. There was no getting away from work for Mr Davidson – unless, of course, he went off to get more consignments of wood. The mill itself was divided into two – the one under the kitchen was the saw shop, where there were saw tables, circular saws and benches. Beyond a stone-and-lime partition wall was the machine shop on the south side of the building. It was directly under the parlour and three bedrooms. Three bobbin machines and other pieces of equipment were fixed in the machine-shop. There were also wooden boxes for the bobbins as they fell from the machines. The room had a fireplace and there was a wooden press fixed to the gable where oils and other articles for the mill were kept. Next to the press was the other pole which ran into the parlour and through the roof. There was a door on the west side of the building into the machine-shop and one in the north gable into the saw-shop. The whole mill was lit with large glass windows which opened to give the workers air. At the north end of the building there was a shed with a wooden roof and on 18 July after the *Maid of Lorn* had come into Salen early in the forenoon from Glasgow, the shed was still full – there were two stacks of squared larch all ready-cut the right size to be turned into the next assignment of the long, thin bobbins used in the Paisley mills. One stack was against the gable end and the other was at the opposite side of the shed. Outside there was still more wood, stacked but uncovered.

The wooden cottage to the back of the mill had a wooden roof covered with tarred canvas to keep out the rain, although there had been little of that for a week or two and that was why the mill was so idle and the men could afford to go off elsewhere. There was no water to turn the mill wheel. After the steamer left Salen at two o'clock, the boys were left to their own devices. Mrs Torrance tried to keep them occupied in the garden but she was almost sure they were swinging with one of the leather bands between two of the pirn machines. She admitted she didn't go in to check – it wasn't her territory – but the noise stopped after about eight o'clock anyway. At nine o'clock, Robert Stewart, Thomas Donald (who was just 15) and 16-year-old James Colquhoun went off to the cottage to bed. Mrs Torrance milked the cow and shut the pigs in their pen and got some kindling to light the fire next morning. She locked up and put the key through a broken window onto the inside sill. There was no sign of a fire in the machine-room grate and nothing amiss. With a clear conscience she read her Bible in the parlour for half an hour or so, or, as she said later, 'for as long as I could see'.

She was feeling lonely when she went to bed later and she was restless. She put out the candle then heard a cat crying 'piteously' and she went to the kitchen to see if she could find it. There was no sign of the cat but it was still crying somewhere and Mrs Torrance just couldn't sleep. Eventually she did fall into a doze but woke up to the sound of breaking glass. She went back to the kitchen again and found it full of smoke. By the clock in the lobby it was one o'clock in the morning and not only was there smoke in the kitchen but in the lobby as well and there were flames over the roof. 'Naked' as she had risen from her bed, she went to knock up the three boys in the cottage and they all saw that the mill was alight. Mrs Torrance made a dash to get some clothes, almost getting trapped in the process. She grabbed some underclothes and a blanket and got out in time to see the flames above the parlour roof and the roof falling in.

Dugald MacNaughton, the inn-keeper in Salen, came rushing over with his brother John, a lad of just 13. They turned water on the fire but to no effect and as sparks fell onto the cottage and the wood shed, both buildings were consumed by the flames and all the stocks of bobbins were destroyed. Mr MacNaughton left at three in the morning. At daybreak, there was nothing left but the walls of the mill. The wood was burnt away, the machines damaged, saws and benches destroyed and the cottage gone. Mrs Torrance told the local justiciary on 21 July that the furniture in the house was also destroyed and she had lost all her personal possessions, including £11 in cash and her clothes. She had seen nothing untoward before she went to bed and she had no idea how the fire started. Other precognitions taken on 21 July by Tobermory Sheriff Officer Allan Cameron when the extent of the disaster became apparent suggested that the boys had indeed been swinging and enjoying themselves in the afternoon – and they had lit a fire in the grate to melt some lead. It was all a sad accident waiting to happen: so much dry wood stacked about the place, a stiff breeze from the south-west and no adult apart from Mrs Torrance to supervise bored young boys – or to tackle the blaze. Mr Cameron went to the see the site on the 21st and noted that all was as described by the witnesses.

That fire on 18 July 1854, had cost Mrs Torrance dearly, had destroyed Mr Clark's investment and six people were out of work. Overnight, a thriving factory serving a mighty industry had become part of lost Argyll. To lose half a dozen jobs in a city – and even to lose a small factory from the landscape – is hardly noticeable. In a rural area such as Ardnamurchan it was, and is, a disaster. The mid-19th century was a time when many jobs were being lost throughout Argyll because of changes in agriculture and the fluctuation of the fishing industry. In Ardnamurchan and Morvern, old and new landlords were evicting their tenants to make way for sheep. Cottages were left to crumble into the landscape while new industries which scarred the hillsides brought few jobs to the local people who no longer had land to cultivate. Lead mines brought strangers to these parishes from the Lowlands and from England, while boatloads of Scots were lost to Argyll as they made their way south to the mills run by Clarks or Coats or others less philanthropic whose grim factories offered little more than a death sentence to men, women and children from the West Highlands.

Investment in jobs for areas like Ardnamurchan and Morvern has been essential since the beginning of time, but even if the Salen bobbin mill had not gone up in smoke, there was no guarantee that Mrs Torrance, Mr Davidson and the boys would have had work for very much longer. As Mr Davidson, the 46-year-old manager of the mill explained to the Sheriff Officer, the mill and buildings were leased from Sir James Riddell of Ardnamurchan and that lease was due to expire the following Martinmas. Mr Clark had paid for the erection of the buildings and if Sir James were to evict him, he was to be paid £400 for the buildings. It was, however, Mr Clark who was planning to move: he had recently bought a steading in Tobermory on the island of Mull and he planned to make his bobbins there from the following autumn. In the meantime, he was negotiating a further year's lease from the Trust which ran Sir James's estate – after that, it was likely that the boys would be out of a job and probably the adults as well.

As it turned out, the Tobermory venture was almost as troubled as the Salen factory. In 1861, Duncan Macfarlane from Glasgow and David Murray from Gorbals, Glasgow, who were dealers in old metal and machinery, were accused of removing machinery from the Tobermory distillery at Ledaig which had been stored there by James Clark Jnr and Company of Glasgow 'with a view of converting it into a bobbin manufactuary'. The machinery was from the burnt-out mill at Salen on the mainland.

The mid-19th century found Ardnamurchan and Morvern very much as frontier territories. The Central Board figures and the Estate and Poor Law records show 'huge poverty in the Ardnamurchan peninsula' in 1850. Crime became violent: a policeman was assaulted in Salen; the windows and furniture in the Shiel Bridge Inn were smashed up and several people assaulted by Alexander Smith, a crofter's son from the island of Shona in the parish of Ardnamurchan. Dr Norman Macleod, the Presbyterian minister who became the voice of the evicted, said that the needs of the poor in his Morvern parish had risen from £11 a year when the population was 2,200 strong to £600 a year in 1863 while the population had halved. Nor did the loss of population stop when sheep farming peaked and became unprofitable. By the 1870s, deer forests were becoming the costly playgrounds of the rich at the expense of the poor tenants.

Yet Ardnamurchan had always been a place where people could scrape a living. Morvern and Strontian were founded on a bed of granite but along with Mull, Ardnamurchan was one of the two great tertiary volcanic sites – enormous terrestrial volcanoes now eroded down to their roots and offering up volcanic soil to be tilled. Mesolithic people roaming the area between 6500 and 3500 BC were perhaps repelled by the rocky coast and barren hinterland and preferred the islands, but even so they settled long enough on the island of Risga in Loch Sunart to leave behind a kitchen midden and they also left artefacts in the sheltered Kentra Bay, Drynan Bay and the more exposed Sanna Bay along the Ardnamurchan peninsula and at Acharn in Morvern. The Neolithic people who followed left little evidence of farming but much of their cultural habits behind them. Ardnamurchan had its settlements of 'Beaker' people – those settlers from 3000 BC onwards who made a special kind of pottery found throughout Argyll. Artists – or were they fishermen making bait holes? – from that period made their mark with cup markings on Carna, Oronsay and Risga in Loch Sunart; and standing stones, less prolific than in southern Argyll, remind us of this lost culture with its clever assimilation of geometry and astronomy.

By the middle of the second millennium before the Christian era, agricultural land was becoming less fertile in northern Argyll and perhaps that led to the need to protect what cultivation was possible. Scattered through Ardnamurchan, Morvern, Mull, Coll and Tiree it is possible to identify 42 forts with drystone walls but their remains are fragmentary and their architectural make-up impossible to evaluate. How many more have been lost completely? A quarter of these forts are on the mainland. Along with brochs and duns, forts were part of the protection system set up by people living in timber and wattle houses who were growing crops and rearing stock. Their houses and their brochs have disappeared: only four brochs have been identified in the *Argyll Inventory of Monuments, Volume III*[1] and none was on the peninsulas of Morvern or Ardnamurchan. Most of the defences came in the form of duns, mostly built on rocky crags and ridges. These Argyll ancestors were living a sophisticated lifestyle – sophisticated enough for their women to wear jewellery, to grind corn and for their men to wield socketed axes.

Many of the families who lived a communal life within these duns may have come from Ireland up the west coast. It was the route taken by Columba, the Irish priest with royal connections who brought Christianity to Argyll and who founded the monastery on Iona. He may have become a saint after his death in 597, but in life he was very much the itinerant priest. We remember him for anointing the first Christian king of these British islands at Dunadd in Mid-Argyll, but his daily work took him to Ardnamurchan to baptise a child and he was one of many priests from Ireland founding monasteries and extending the reach of religious orders. In Morvern, Finten is said to have founded *Kailli an inde* or Killundine. The Early Christian era gave Argyll some of its richest treasures: chapels and crosses and burial slabs. Some of the oldest monuments date back to the sixth century and Killundine has its share. The Middle Ages brought still more Christian building and craftsmanship. There were dozens of parishes in northern Argyll at this time but only four have retained any notable remains of their churches. Many have vanished completely, stone robbed for other building work. A number of these churches were dedicated to Columba, but some were dedicated to his nephew Ernan, son of Eoghan, and there were other saints who were commemorated: Comgan in Ardnamurchan, Saint Boadan, the patron of the parish of Ardchattan in Ardgour and Kingairloch.

There were always squabbles between neighbours, battles between rival families – St Columba himself left Ireland in a hurry after a royal battle that left a price on his head. But in the main, the sands of time washed over human traces. Dust to dust is not an unrealistic representation of the growth and disappearance of settlements in a climate where wind and wave are relentless. The Norse raiders, however, changed that organic process, wiping much from the Argyll landscape. They sacked Iona four times between 795 and 826, and of course took possession of all the western islands of Scotland and the Kintyre peninsula until 1256. Strangely, there is little positive evidence of this stay. Place-names became Norse rather than Gaelic. There were some burial sites. Yet while their aggression meant that much was lost to Argyll of its early heritage, little was gained by way of Norse remains. The Christian community continued to build its churches and chapels, bury its dead with increasingly elaborate stone decoration and develop schools of decorative stonemasons whose craft would flower between the leaving of the Norsemen and the coming of the Reformation in 1560.

Some of the fragments left to us from the churches and chapels of the late medieval period reveal a development of the intricacies initiated by the Celtic artists. Some have exceptional features, such as a freestone arch in the Lochaline church. Most of the larger churches and chapels of Mull and Northern Argyll have freestone dressings from the quarries in Carsaig on Mull or from Inninmore Bay in Morvern. Across the region there are 75 surviving free-standing crosses, effigies and grave-slabs of the West Highland type which date from the early 14th century to 1560, the largest groups being at Kirkapol, Tiree and Lochaline in Morvern. Although most are of the Iona school of carving, seen as the most skilled of the period, two at Lochaline are of the Oronsay school. Most are lost to us in the sense that they are damaged, either by wind and weather or by the iconoclasts of the Reformation. There were less violent attacks on crucifixes, altars and other religious imagery in the north of Argyll than in the south of the county, but it is gratifying to find a fine carved cross still upright – though not in its original site – in a village such as Lochaline, where there is also a late medieval effigy of Lachlan MacLean, Lord of Ardgour.

Dozens of pre-Reformation churches and chapels were lost to Ardnamurchan and Morvern, but there was no surge of new Reformation churches because of the intervention of the civil war. This bloody interruption with its intermittent imposition of an episcopal church meant there were few ministers. Some of those who did accept a calling in these parishes were Royalists or Jacobites. The earliest post-Reformation churches were built in the 18th century and Dr Samuel Johnson wrote in his *Journey to the Western Islands:* : 'The want of churches is not the only impediment to piety: there is likewise a want of ministers ... All the provision made by the present ecclesiastical constitution, for the inhabitants of about a hundred square miles, is a prayer and sermon in a little room, once in three weeks ... it is impossible to tell how many weeks or months may pass without any publick exercise of religion.'[2] The kind of rites of which Johnson highly disapproved and hoped would die out in the Highlands with the help of a good Presbyterian minister or two were being encouraged by the episcopalian clergyman John MacLachlan of Kilchoan, who was active in Ardnamurchan in the quarter century before Johnson's *Tour* was published – a man described as being 'at least half a Papist'. Colin Campbell of Acharn in Morvern was on the side of the Jacobites at Culloden and his brother Alexander, a convert to Roman Catholicism, left behind a Crucifix and Virgin by way of sandstone funerary ornaments at a time when such things were much more likely to be 'lost' if not overtly damaged. Little wonder that at the beginning of the 19th century the

Keil Old Parish Church (Cill Chaluim Chille), Arch in the
south wall of the north burial aisle. (RCAHMS.)

church authorities decided that seven unmanageable parishes throughout
northern Argyll should be assisted by the creation of seven *quoad sacra*
parishes with parliamentary churches built to the off-the-peg designs drawn up
by Thomas Telford. Acharacle was one of those parishes, while in Lochaline,
the architect P. MacGregor Chalmers, was employed to build a new parish
church in 1898, the third on that site and a guarantee that the already
diminished remains of one of the two medieval churches in Morven would
almost completely disappear. An archway of the medieval church leading to a
burial aisle was identified as dating from the 13th century, but even the
fragments of stone with dog-tooth carving which allowed Dr Thomas Ross to
identify it as such have now disappeared. Dedicated to St Columba, this church
was known as *Cill Chaluim Chille* in the early days and was supported in the
late Middle Ages by the neighbouring townships of Rhemore and Knock. Its
parsonage was in the patronage of the Lords of the Isles until those Lords were
stripped of that title and then the parsonage was decided by the Crown. Keil
Church is about 60 yards from the ruin and is the third church on this site. In
Ardnamurchan, still less survives of a chapel dedicated to the Blessed Virgin
Mary. A mound and a broken cross are the sole testament to its existence.

Mingary Castle – never a safe place to be. (RCAHMS.)

By the time Dr Johnson and his companion James Boswell were touring the Western Islands and Highlands in the second half of the 18th century, pre-Reformation churches were not the only buildings in a decrepit state. Castles, tower-houses and forts were also past their best and although he felt he saw one on every promontory and headland, Johnson found a defence system in decline. Little wonder. Just a century before, this area had been in the throes of the civil war which had seen no class distinction in the destruction meted out on all sides. Mostly built from stone and lime or with drystone masonry, castles had been built in this part of the world from the 13th century. Mingary in Ardnamurchan, a castle of enclosure on a natural promontory, lost its original courtyard but the lancet windows of the 13th century survived in the curtain wall along with the remains of wall-head defences. The castle was remodelled in the 16th and 17th centuries and the courtyard buildings were rebuilt in the 18th century. There was no need for insensitive planners here: as elsewhere throughout Argyll, a succession of owners and their enemies managed to wipe out the evidence of the past, leaving only the certainty that for centuries this was not a safe place to be.

In the 13th century, descendants of the legendary Somerled were rivals for

Ardnamurchan. It is uncertain whether it was always part of the Lordship of the Isles or held by Garmoran, but by the 14th century it was in the hands of the MacDonalds of Islay before being granted to Angus MacIan when the MacDonalds forfeited their possessions. MacIan's patron, James IV, was that much-travelled king who believed that his presence in the west could calm stormy waters stirred by some very autocratic lairds. He was also a king who built extensively – but he had no hand in developing Mingary. He simply stayed there on two of his disciplinary trips to the Western Isles and would have found a curtain wall of local rubble with freestone dressings from Lochaline and some from Carsaig on Mull. He would have entered across a drawbridge (which disappeared in the 1700s) and may have looked down on the courtyard from windows on the first floor. There was a well at the castle in James's day, long since disappeared.

James IV's presence kept the lid on much of the violence in the west and the example he set in building fine castles and palaces across Scotland may have encouraged others. His death, however, meant a reversion to the *status quo*. Sir Donald MacDonald of Lochalsh had aspirations to be Lord of the Isles; MacIan in Ardnamurchan opposed the idea. In 1515, MacDonald forces besieged Mingary and in 1517 didn't only take possession of the castle but destroyed it and laid the land waste. The structural damage was not permanent but did of course mean that the building evolved from its original state. The MacIans decided to throw in their lot with the MacDonalds, but some 50 years later that was no help when MacLean of Duart attacked Mingary using the guns of the Spanish galleon *Florencia* which had taken refuge in Tobermory harbour, along with some of her soldiers. The MacIans had to fight it out on their own and after the MacLean troops withdrew, the castle was once again strengthened by a reconstruction of the wall-head defences. By this time, however, simply being able to defend a property was not enough to keep it in the family. The Earl of Argyll had been given the superiority of the lands and castles of Ardnamurchan in 1519 after MacDonald was stripped of his titles and lands, and although the MacIans were in favour for the best part of a century, in 1612 the 7th Earl of Argyll gave Mingary to his brother-in-law. Perhaps the MacIans were well out of it. The feud between the Argyll earls and the MacDonalds, nicely disguised by the civil war, was to erupt time and again in the 17th century and Mingary suffered in 1644 when in the name of the Royalists, Alasdair Colkitto MacDonald attacked it as a precursor to his devastating blitz the length of Argyll. Three years later, General David Leslie retook the castle for the Covenanters and there seems to have been time to reconstruct the wall-head defences of the north-west curtain after fire and musket balls had wreaked havoc with the masonry. By 1651, the estate reverted to the Campbells of Argyll, but much was to happen before the end of the century when the 10th Earl gave Ardnamurchan and Mingary to Alexander Campbell, 6th of Lochnell, and his son Duncan. The 9th earl had lost his head and his family lands for plotting too soon to introduce the House of Orange of Britain. The bloodless revolution in 1688 which put William and Mary on the throne had happened nonetheless and the Campbells once more had property in their power to grant to cadet families.

A new century, a new ruler, a new period of peace and the way was open for a lifestyle not focused on defence strategies and reparation of artillery damage. New buildings were erected in the north of the castle courtyard and when Alexander Murray, son of Sir David Murray of Stanhope, bought the estate in 1723 it was with a view to improving agricultural methods and exploiting the minerals of Ardnamurchan and Sunart. He no doubt had few regrets that the castle he had taken on bore little resemblance to the original 13th-century fortress, however much 21st-century conservationists may regret that loss. Mingary was not a home, however, although Murray stayed in the castle from time to time and even repaired the roof in 1723. This was the century when windows were remodelled and the stairs were altered. But the upkeep of a castle and his mineral exploits took a heavy financial toll and Alexander Murray's estate was in the hands of the creditors when he died in 1743.

Not that the buccaneering days were over. The Young Pretender invaded the 18th-century peace in an attempt to put a Jacobite back on the throne and after his landing at Moidart a force of 59 government troops was set to hold Mingary castle, then in the hands of Donald Campbell of Auchindown, the Duke of Argyll's factor. Some of those troops were also sent south in March 1746 into Morvern where Jacobites were known. Culloden was history by the time James Riddell bought the estate in 1770 and his descendants lived in peace on the estate – but latterly not in the castle – until 1848. The castle had still been habitable until a decade earlier. Now it was to become an honourable hexagonal ruin lowering over the entrance to Loch Sunart and owned by Lord Howard of Glossop as part of his extensive properties in Moidart and Ardnamurchan.

Edward George Fitzalan-Howard was the second son of the Duke of Norfolk and an MP. As Vice Chamberlain to Queen Victoria he was ennobled. He ran his estate on the premise that people's condition would only be

Overleaf. Plan of Loch Sunart, 1733. (Courtesy of his Grace the Duke of Argyll.)

improved if their holdings were enlarged. He envisaged converting crofters into small farmers and followed an avenue common to many landlords in Argyll at the time, including the Duke of Argyll – parcelling crofts or runrig strips together and leasing them to one tenant rather than many. Argyll was a county where farming was frequently a communal subsistence practice. Little of the land in the Highlands was suitable for improvement farming – hadn't the very first inhabitants clung to the more fertile spots around the coast rather than venturing into the hinterland? – and the raising of black cattle had been the mainstay of the economy. The arrival in the 19th century of landlords such as Lord Howard, with their ideas of improvement, set the scene for the loss of a method of farming – but much more vital to Argyll and to Scotland, the loss of a people, a language and culture, and a continuity with the past.

Lord Howard died in 1883, the year that the Gladstone government set up a Royal Commission 'to enquire into the condition of the crofters and cottars in the Highlands and Islands of Scotland and all matters affecting the same or relating thereto'. The Napier Commission travelled throughout the Highlands and Islands taking evidence and identified the concerns of the crofters and the cottars, who paid their rent in labour as required. There were some shocking anecdotes of evictions in both Ardnamurchan and Morvern, where landlords had sought to clear their land first for sheep and then, when imports from Australia scuppered that industry, for red deer. Shooting parties were asked to pay for their sport and the area was turned into a scenic playground instead of a vast sheep-walk. The complaints heard by Lord Napier were that rents were high, holdings limited, land was lost to sporting pursuits, no compensation was paid for land improvements made by tenants, and that there was an overriding lack of security of tenure.

Lord Howard was to a degree posthumously exonerated from the worst offences committed by landlords in Sutherland and Northern Argyll, because he had been more sympathetic than many. The Howard submission to the Commission listed a number of tenants who paid no rent or very small rents. Ann McDonald, for instance, had a cottage with a cowhouse and some potato ground. She kept two cows and paid no rent. Roderick McDonald, whose household numbered six, kept a cow and grew potatoes and also paid no rent. Peggy McVarish, described as a pauper, paid no rent for her cottage. James McGillivray the blacksmith had a house and the smithy and paid £5 rent for them.

Other landlords were not so generous. The old clan chiefs had kept a feudal system alive which may have asked much of tenants, but those tenants were useful 'fencible' men who could be called on in times of war and were therefore supported in times of peace. The new landlords saw their lands as investments and labour-based economy was not as profitable as sheep farming. New roads created by General Wade in the wake of the '45 Uprising meant links with woollen mills in the south. Tenants were superfluous; a shepherd or two would suffice. Whole townships were dispossessed. The tenants migrated to the growing industrial belt of Scotland or to the mills of England, spinning the wool of the sheep who had replaced them on their homeland. Many, of course, went to Canada and America. Others tried their hand at fishing on the west coast or found jobs labouring in the local mines – jobs mainly taken by imported specialised labour from the south.

The Napier Commission heard evidence at Arisaig and at Salen in Mull. The voices of Ardnish, Mingary, Dalnabreac, Eilean Shona and Polnish were heard. They told of a type of farming unknown to the Commissioners where sheep, horses and cows were held in common, as Charles Cameron, a 65-year-old crofter from Acharacle in Ardnamurchan explained. This 'club' system didn't make them rich but it gave them life's basic needs. On top of that, so that they could pay the high rents of £18 a year, they ploughed or did other jobs for neighbouring crofters. Charles Cameron said he relied on money sent by his daughter in England to pay his rent. The new landlords not only did not understand the old concept of sharing the land (and of being its guardians rather than its owners); they did not understand the language either. In 1881, despite a decade-old Education Act which stated that English should be written and read by all school children, six out of ten people in Argyll were still native Gaelic speakers and the children spoke Gaelic at home. Communication readily broke down. How could the workers grasp that there was now no work to be had from their landlords as there had been in the old days? As Lord Howard of Glossop suggested, this reliance on the landlord for support could only lead to people being brought to 'the verge of starvation' when no work was forthcoming.

In the parish to the south on the other shore of Loch Sunart, a generation was also being lost to Morvern. Tragic stories of eviction were rife here, too, like that of 'Mary of Unimore' who later told the son of the local minister of the day she left her Morvern home. By then she was living in Glasgow, a country alien to this woman brought up in a village of 15 houses where most of the 75 inhabitants were of the same Cameron family. Her story was important because it was published in English and added to the weight of public opinion which led to Gladstone setting up the Napier Commission. Norman MacLeod, one of a line of much-loved ministers who championed the cause of the poor in Morvern, listened to Mary's account of her family's eviction by her landlady,

Miss Christina Stewart of Glenmorvern, who had her estate for just five years and according to Philip Gaskell in his book *Morvern Transformed*[3] was unlikely ever to have lived there. The estate had not been called Glenmorvern until she bought up 9,510 acres previously owned by the Duke of Argyll under the name of Fernish. There were five farms: Ardantiobairt, Barr, Fernish, Mungasdail and Unimore. When she took over in 1824, she immediately evicted the small-holders from Mungasdail and Unimore and some from Barr and Ardantiobairt. Mary of Unimore was one of the 135 unfortunates driven – literally – from their homes to make way for sheep. Mary blamed 'the Mac Cailein' (the Duke of Argyll) for selling the property in the first place. All that was left of a friendly neighbourhood where people were confident that they had a roof over their heads as long as they paid their rent was an English shepherd living in one of their cottages. They had no lease and did not want one. They had been used to getting eviction notices as the first step in a round of negotiations to raise the rent. The new owner didn't play that game. They'd even offered to pay more but Miss Stewart's agent wanted none of it and drove off their animals – a few sheep and goats, and in Mary's case the cow that provided milk for her children. She wasn't even allowed allowed to milk her goats, which stayed bleating not far from the cottage, as confused by events as she was. On the day of the eviction itself, the police came and the agents poured water on the hearths to put out the fires, just to add insult to injury. They were refugees and Mary's husband had to carry his old mother on his back in a creel while Mary carried one child at her breast and two toddlers walked at her side. They took a last look at home from *Knock-nan-Carn* (Hill of Cairns) and saw the houses were already being stripped of their contents – the modest furniture, pots and pans that had served Mary all her married life. The family then walked to Glasgow and with the help of Norman Macleod the minister got a job in a cotton mill.

In Morvern, about 150 families were evicted from the major estates between 1824 and 1868. Miss Stewart's 25 seem almost modest compared with the 48 families put off the Acharn estate in 1838 by Patrick Sellar, who cleared his whole property. Over the period, the Gordon family put off 34 families from their Drimnin estate and re-evicted three. Mrs Paterson evicted 28 families from Lochaline estate, but John Sinclair, her predecessor, had already sent at least 15 families packing between the 1840s and 60s. The farms cleared, apart from all the townships on the Acharn estate and those owned by Miss Stewart, were Cloundlaid-Uladail, Achleanan, Carraig, Auliston, Keil, Savary, Achabeg, Knock, Ahnaha, Achafors, Oronsay and Ardtornish. All ancient names stretching back in time – all settlements cultivated for millennia by communities answerable to landlords who may have seemed sometimes demanding; sometimes downright dangerous to know as they quarrelled with their neighbours or their king and enlisted tenants to fight their battles with them.

Ardtornish belonged to such a landlord. The castle, on a rocky outcrop close to the mouth of Lochaline overlooking the Sound of Mull, is within sight of Duart and Aros castles on Mull and is now only a ruin of basalt rubble walls, its interior filled with debris. Once it was one of the largest hall houses in Scotland, dating back to the 13th and 14th centuries. In the late 13th century, Morvern was in the hands of either the MacRuari Lords of Garmoran of to the Macdonald Lords of Islay. Certainly in the reign of Robert I and through the 14th and 15th centuries, the peninsula was held by the MacDonalds and Ardtornish castle was one of the principal residences of the Lords of the Isles. John, 1st Lord of the Isles died there in 1387, and in 1462 his great-grandson John negotiated the Treaty of Ardtornish there – an alliance between the Islay family and Edward IV of England wrought in council with Edward's commissioners. John may well have led his important guests up the mural staircase to the first-floor hall from the entrance in the castle's end wall. The hall was a vast 57 feet by 26 feet, impressive enough to make the commissioners understand they were talking with someone of power. John, however, forfeited that powerful lordship in 1493 and the Ardtornish lands remained in the hands of the Crown for over a century. It then came into the hands of the MacLeans, who already had interests in Morvern. Theirs was not a secure tenure of this impressive defence with its fine facings from both Inninmore Bay and Lochaline. The castle's builders probably quarried the basalt rubble from the east shore. It is hard to imagine the magnificence of the buff sandstone and white, fine-grained siliceous stone which the MacLeans struggled to hang on to for three centuries and more. James IV in litigious mood accused Ewen MacLean of Kingairloch of taking illegal possession of the lands of Ardtornish, but Roderick MacLean of Kingairloch was a tenant in 1541. Later that century and into the 17th century, the MacLeans of Ardtornish were bailies for the Morvern estates of the MacLeans of Duart from across the Sound. By the end of the 17th century, the Duart MacLeans had lost the Morvern lands to the Duke of Argyll and the castle was lost to posterity. The only surviving traces of original windows are sills on the south wall. There may have been wings to the building at some stage as there are seven smaller ruins beside the castle. One has been identified as a barn with a corn-drying kiln and another may have been a boathouse. When the building came into the ownership of the Smith family in the 19th century, the derelict walls were pointed in 1874 and then a plan was drawn up in January 1891 to restore the castle. This wasn't carried out but a window was put into the south wall. This may have been installed by the architects Ross and Macbeth of Inverness who designed Ardtornish Tower for Valentine Smith.

The earlier centuries were never stable. There was never a lost golden age and even when a more peaceful era was established under the Dukes of Argyll, the old feudal ways continued. The Duke's tacksmen sublet to tenants who paid their rents in produce, labour and to the early 18th century, military service. It was a frontier territory, a world away from Inveraray Castle. The 2nd Duke, however, was determined to carry out farming reforms in Morvern as he had elsewhere in Argyll. He offered 19-year leases instead of three and cut out the too often greedy man in the middle – the tacksman. Instead of kind, rents were to be paid in cash, although the high rents in Morvern meant these new 19-year leases would have to be given to new tenants. At first, rather than 'plantations' of favourable tenants such as those he had introduced to his Kintyre properties, the new tenants were from Morvern – and that meant a very big problem in 1745. These people were Jacobites and along with the tenants of MacLean of Drimnin, the area of the peninsula not owned by the Duke, they supported the Pretender who arrived just up the coast in Moidart. The government took revenge savagely, sending 'Butcher' Cumberland to destroy Morvern as a centre of disloyalty. The naval sloops *Terror* and *Princess Anne* arrived under the command of Captain Robert Duff, who ordered the destruction of every boat on the coast of Morvern and Loch Sunart and then, with the garrison from Mingary in Ardnamurchan he set out to burn the houses and possessions of all who had been involved in the Uprising. On 10 March 1746 they had torched houses from Drimnin McClean's town to Ardtornish, leaving Mungasdail untouched because the men there claimed not to have been involved. By 15 March, 400 houses, many with barns full of animals, had been destroyed and much of the Morvern woodland had been set alight too. Where it was burned between Drimnin and Lochaline, the full natural woodland never re-emerged and from that time gave a different landscape to that between Ardtornish and Inninmore which had escaped the fiery retribution.

Morvern was not dealt with as harshly as those areas where Cumberland's own men carried out reprisals but the Duke was justifiably horrified by the punishments, despite his involvement with the government. His reaction was not totally altruistic – his complaint was that his own property had been destroyed. Nonetheless, he was supportive enough of Morvern men to renew leases in 1750 and did not carry out his 'plantation' pattern of bringing in his Campbell relatives as tenants until 1754. By then Morvern was more or less his – he held the feus of a third of the land and was proprietor of the rest.

He and his descendants were keen to make it profitable and this policy was the beginning of the end for much of the population. There had been a growth in population between 1755 and 1795 and the 1801 census showed over 2,000 inhabitants compared with 1,200 in the middle of the 18th century. Lack of war may well have contributed to the better health of the working man and his family. But while they went about their business of growing the recently introduced potato and gathering kelp for this new industry of potash production which was making landlords a lot of money around the west coast and in the islands, the lairds had sheep on their minds. Not the little, native sheep of which Mary of Unimore and her neighbours kept a few for their fine fleeces, but the bigger animals from the south which could provide more wool, more meat and needed less handling. A shepherd could put these sheep out on the hill instead of the black cattle and the landlord could reap much bigger benefits than he got for having a lot of tenants farming in traditional ways.

Not only were the fine-fleeced sheep lost – so too were the smallholders, the folk like Mary, James and their children who in the long term would lose their homes. In Morvern, this began to happen in the 1770s, half a century after farms began to be combined and let out to small tenant farmers. Sinking under this tide of Cheviots and Black-faced Lintons, small tenant farmers were pleased that for a while, kelping became profitable in Morvern as it gave them some of the income they would traditionally have got from selling their cattle. Not that raising cattle was ever an easy option. Selling them on from remote areas like Ardnamurchan and Morvern meant using the old drove roads and the ferries. There were no direct overland routes to the markets in Falkirk and the south – or even to the nearer market at Kilmichael Glassary in Mid Argyll. Small ferries crossed Loch Sunart, Loch Linnhe, the Sound of Mull and Loch Aline. A main destination for the cattle was Kerrera, the little island off what is now the town of Oban, and then to the mainland for their arduous journeys on the drove roads to market. A ferry at the mouth of Loch Sunart, crossing from Glenborrodale on Ardnamurchan between the islands of Risga and Carna to Doirlinn on the Morvern peninsula, was the only regular ferry on the Loch in 1800. A track ran from Doirlinn to Drimnin on the Sound of Mull and then along the west shore of Loch Teacuis to Kinlochteacuis and Kinlochaline. It wasn't only cattle drovers who used the ferry of course. Funeral processions made their way from Ardnamurchan to the Cameron burial-ground in the ancient church at Mungasdail near Drimnin where a long fertile strip of coastal land had made this a favoured place to live – and to die – since early Celtic times. But while the dead came to rest at Mungasdail, the cattle were driven on to Rhemore to cross the Sound of Mull or to Lochaline, both ferry crossings with the destination of Kerrera in the 1790s. From there, the route south went across more ferries on Loch Awe and Loch Fyne. In time, additional ferries were introduced as the new landlords came in – some simply wanted their mail and more sophisticated provisions than Ardnamurchan and Morvern could offer. Others wanted more comfortable crossings for their guests. Others still wanted reliable crossings to bring in building materials and workmen for their developing industries and to take away the end product. A brief flirtation with kelp production around Savary and Salachen bays, on the Fiunary shore, and on the coast between the Killundine river and Auliston Point created a need for better transport; and the lead from the Ardnamurchan mines meant that boats had to transport industrial material. But to receive mail on either peninsula in the 1840s still meant its delivery via two islands and three ferries – from Oban to Kerrera, Kerrera to Mull and Mull back to the mainland. Argyll's commerce could only operate courtesy of these ferries, which meant landlords could make extra in rent from the ferrymen (sometimes these ferries were so important that the king held grant of the charter to run them; sometimes it was the local landlords). In the 18th century, as the lead mines increased operation in Ardnamurchan, a petition was made in 1749 to the Commission of Supply for Argyll by Alexander MacLachlan for a ferry from 'Ligisdale to Ellanvourich' (Liddesdale to Eilean a' Mhuirich, the little island which lies a mile west of Strontian on the north side of Loch Sunart). Another ferry on that stretch of the loch was rowed over from the Laudale Estate in Morvern to Camuschoirk, which today is on the main Strontian to Salen road. This was was also used by the lead miners and by Laudale estate workers. Further west was a ferry which ran from Glencripesdale Burn in Morvern to Camasinas on the Ardnamurchan shore between Salen and Glenborrodale. This one took mail from the Glencripesdale jetty every day at 4 o'clock during the week. In the early days, it was picked up at Camasinas by a pony and trap (in more modern times by a bus) and taken to Acharacle. There it met the steamer which had been introduced to Loch Shiel by the second Lord Howard of Glossop to benefit his Moidart estate. He put the *Lady of the Lake*, his personal steam launch, on a round trip of Loch Shiel in May 1898. It met the mail coach from Arisaig to Fort William. When this circuit proved successful, Lord Glossop ordered the *Clanranald*, a brand new steamer which began on the same run the next year. The traditional wooden ferries, rowed by local men with intimate knowledge of every inch of water, could run into trouble in bad weather. The *Clanranald* simply ran into trouble – too big for the shallow approach to Glenfinnan, she had to be replaced by *Clanranald II* in 1900. Because Lord Glossop and the North British Railway Company did not agree about the steamer's role on the loch, people from that part of Ardnamurchan continued to have the kind of roundabout journey that black cattle had had in the old days, travelling from Oban to Loch Sunart on a MacBrayne ferry. And despite the eventual extension of the railway to Fort William, this Loch Shiel mail route was needed until 1967 when the new Lochailort-Kinlochmoidart road was opened. When there was no mail, passengers who wanted to use to Glencripesdale to Camasinas ferry had to attract attention by a smoke signal from the rocks. Once the steamers began to run in the early 1800s, there were at last quicker options out of Ardnamurchan and Morvern. People could walk to Lochaline and take the MacBrayne's mail steamer to Oban as the bobbin-factory manager did that fatal day when the mill went up in smoke. Others would take the Loch Linnhe shore track to Corran ferry, which could take half a day to walk, or walk on up to Camusnagaul and take the ferry over to Fort William. Small ferries taking goods down the Sound of Mull continued long after the major steam-ferry companies had moved in on the major routes, until well after the end of the First World War, the *Mary* and the *Effie*, two 50-foot wooden sailing smacks, carried supplies through the Sound and into Loch Sunart, just as the puffers delivered coal up onto the beaches of remote villages and estates throughout Argyll until the 1920s and beyond. On the *Mary* and the *Effie*, there was no such thing as a quiet crossing. Passengers were dragooned into service to operate the boom and windlass and to unload goods onto horse-drawn carts. If goods had been ordered by people living around Loch Teacuis, a tug had to tow these venerable ladies into the loch. A steamer was also used to deliver goods on Loch Sunart, an exciting and panoramic detour for the *Brenda*'s Tobermory passengers. As the populations of Ardnamurchan and Morvern fell and roads improved, the ferries at Doirlinn, Liddesdale and Glencripesdale all became uneconomical and were lost to this part of Argyll, along with the ferrymen's jobs and in many cases the inn which was the ferry 'terminus'. Piers and jetties were lost to the Argyll landscape, too, as at Drimnin on the Sound of Mull, where two jetties have crumbled away, and Fiunary, where a pier fell into disuse. These were places where MacBrayne's cargo steamers picked up mail from ship-to-shore ferries, most of them no more than 20 feet long. In the old days, where the straits were suitable, these would have carried many cattle with many more swimming alongside. In the middle of the 20th century, the odd cow might be transported or even a tractor manipulated in a net from the bigger vessel's vehicle deck to the bobbing boat below. Smaller ferries still ran till the Second World War between Tobermory and Drimnin, Rhemore and Killundine – MacVicars of Tobermory were running a 50-foot smack called *Anna Bhan* on this route and Cameron of Kilchoan ran ship-to-shore boats from Drimnin and Tobermory to meet the mail ferry when the steamer couldn't get in to land. This same Cameron also ferried Ardnamurchan passengers back and forth from the *Plover*, the steamer which went to Tobermory. Sometimes he would take them all the way to Mull.

It was the lower Sound of Mull which had been most used in the old days for the great droves of the black cattle. They came over from Ardnacross on Mull to Rhemore at the turn of the 18th century and the change-house there must have been the scene of illicit drams and noisy get-togethers as the drovers rested for the next step of the journey. The lack of a pier at Rhemore must have made loading and unloading cattle from the small ferry boats all the more tricky. The drovers came to prefer a ferry from the mouth of Lochaline to a pier at Bailemeanach on Mull which started up in the first half of the 19th century. There was a cattle sale at Lochaline before the one at Salen on Mull. By the second half of the 19th century, the importance of the cattle had diminished immensely and only the smallest steamers could use Lochaline pier. But by then, a paddle steamer was calling once a year to transport between 2,000 and 3,000 sheep from Morvern.

The concept of a romantic history of these remote areas is misplaced even as far as the ferries are concerned. Rather than princes speeding their way in bonnie boats, cattle were their main cargoes. Some were introduced to avert the starvation of the local people. The Caolas to Lochaline ferry may have saved a seven-mile walk from Ardtornish Bay via Achranich to Lochaline village but its real *raison d'être* was to provide work for 31 families during the potato famine of the 1840s. There may well have been a pier in existence, but the new one, started in 1847, was part of a Poor Board scheme to support a population which had been evicted and was now starving in the hovels of Lochaline village. The Fishery Board finished the work the following year. A car ferry now runs between Lochaline and Fishnish on Mull, but the walk from Ardtornish to Lochaline on the private road built in the 1850s is as long as ever. The ferry took children from Ardtornish to school in Lochaline. Now there are few children and the ferry ceased as a public service. Although the ferry and the bell which summoned it are lost to the 21st-century visitor to Argyll, the pier is still there. Even the ferry where Prince Charles Edward Stewart landed

Opposite top. Bourblaige – detail of estate map by William Bold. (National Archives of Scotland.)

Opposite below. Bourblaige Township – one of the many deserted settlements in northern Argyll. (RCAHMS.)

and re-embarked in 1745 and 1746 at the head of the Sound of Arisaig has disappeared, although it remained in service until the 1960s. It was an unusual ferry in that it linked two jetties on the same shore of Moidart from Lochailort to Glenuig, a seven-mile stretch which connected Glenuig to the outside world until the coming of the Lochailort-Acharacle road. It was a dangerous route under towering mountains and in the 1930s it was appropriately manned by a former whaling skipper who took passengers, goods and mail to and from Glenuig three times a week, transporting groceries from the Fort William train every Thursday. Little wonder that this part of Ardnamurchan remained exclusively Gaelic-speaking until the middle of the 20th century. *Am Eala*, *Guide Me* and *Jacobite*, the latter a wooden vessel with a double diagonal hull and a Lister diesel engine from Bowling on the Clyde, served the route after the Second World War until 1968 when the new road closed the ferry. Those which have survived include the ancient route across the Corran Narrows where cattle were driven in medieval times between Ardgour and Onich – a ferry which was put out of action in 1745 by soldiers wreaking devastation in Morvern in the wake of the Uprising.

A new Parliamentary road was built in 1800 from Corran to the head of Loch Sunart and by the end of that century there was a rail link passing to Fort William, but rather than opening Ardnamurchan and Morvern up to the world the railway and new roads isolated them still further. For the estate owners of Morvern, this was no bad thing as they invited their celebrity guests to join them in shooting, walking, sailing or painting holidays. For the mine owners of Ardnamurchan, however, transport would always be the negative factor which denied them financial success. This peninsula had seen its evictions and had deserted townships to show for it – Bourblaige Township on Ben Hiant covers 14 acres on the bank of a burn which flows into Loch Sunart less than a mile west of Camas nan Geall. There are remains of around 36 houses, barns and byres and the ground carried traces of the lazybeds cultivated by the tenants here. A corn-drying kiln with a store-room and the site of a water mill on the side of the burn suggests a flourishing community. Their drystone houses were cruck-framed and hip-roofed but none had a stone-built fireplace or chimney. Some of these little houses, just 36 feet by 18 feet, had stone partition walls dividing the living quarters. Bourblaige was part of the Ardnamurchan estates which belonged to the Riddell family. When William Bold prepared an estate map for Sir James Riddell in 1806, the township was still there. The estate covered 553 acres, most of it moor and pasture. A report at the time suggested this was a good sheep farm but had too many tenants living on it. By 1829, most of those tenants had gone, leaving much of Bourblaige abandoned when it was

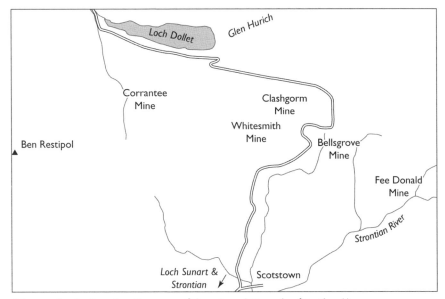

Morvern lead mines: location map of the mines. (Minerals of Scotland.)

joined with the neighbouring Tornamoany property to become one big grazing farm occupied by a single tenant. It may be thought that the quarrying and mining on the Ardnamurchan peninsula would have provided work for those evicted from their farming tenancies to make way for sheep. Most of the workforces, however, came from the south.

Lead-mining had been present in Ardnamurchan for centuries, but was commercialised by men like Sir Alexander Murray of Stanhope in the early part of the 18th century. An open-cast mine at Lurga in Gleann Dubh was first opened by Sir Alexander, who lived at Mingary, around 1733 when several 'biggings' (a 'biggin' in Scots is something 'piled up') were constructed in the glen with a road from them to a storehouse in Liddesdale. Production went on for a decade but in 1749 the workshop was flooded and the smithy, storehouse and workers' cabins were demolished. The Swiss geologist Rudolph Raspé visited the site four decades later during the mineral survey of the Highlands and Islands he carried out for the Duke of Argyll. He told the Duke that the site was very promising and advised him to resume work there. His advice was followed in 1801 but production was in fact small and the mine was closed by the middle of the 19th century. Much more extensive were the old lead mines near Strontian where there are remains of workings from the 18th and 19th centuries on a south-facing hill between 600 and 1,000 feet up around three miles north north-east of Strontian. A main vein of ore was exploited over a mile or so in three separate sections: Whitesmith, Middlehope and Bellsgrove

Remains of Corrantee lead mines. (Minerals of Scotland.)

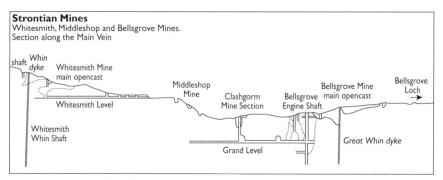

Strontian Mines – plan of the main lead vein at Whitesmith, Middlehope and Bellgrove. (Minerals of Scotland.)

(Bell's groove) mines. Other veins were exploited at that period: Corrantee on the west slope of Meall Iain, a mile or so west of these main workings; and at Fee Donald east north-east in the valley of a tributary of the Strontian River. These were being worked when William Bold drew up the estate map of Ardnamurchan and Sunart in 1806-7. The pit heads survived with the drains and some buildings from the mid-19th century.

Sir Alexander Murray chose Corrantee as a base for the first miners to come to the Strontian area in 1725. This wasn't the most worked mine, however,

Corrantee lead mine remains. (Minerals of Scotland.)

and it is thought that the earliest mining was done in an open-cast groove in the Allt Tarsuinn valley (NM804658). The machinery from those days disappeared but the pit-head wheel for driving an ore crusher seemed to survive well into the 20th century. The Whitesmith mine was called 'a horrid and frightful gulph' in the late 1700s but in 1728 it had been described by John Whitesmith to Sir Alexander Murray as being 'one of the richest grooves that I ever see'.[4] Mining was started there in the middle of a drought when the Middlehope pumping engine was not able to work. There was a shaft over 650 feet deep at the beginning of the 19th century. The Fee Donald mine was exploited in 1727 by two groups of miners but the visible spoil heaps probably date, according to the Commission for Ancient and Historic Monuments Scotland,[5] to the period between 1852 and 1871 when a lease was operated on behalf of the Feedonald Mining Company by G. Fowke. No traces remain of the smelt mills, store-houses, quays and workers' houses built then by the Duke of Norfolk's company and the York Buildings Company at Strontian village. Nor is there any sign of the smelt mill built there in 1806. That was the year the Middlehope mine was opened and it ran to the Bellsgrove engine shaft (NM837657). This was a less productive seam but there was also an open-cast work called the Armstrong vein worked at this time. The former had been heavily worked in the 1720s and then in the 1750s the lead was taken from this seam for the roof

Corrantee mine remains. (Minerals of Scotland.)

of the new Inveraray Castle being built by the Duke of Argyll.

Sir Alexander Murray was very interested in developing both land and mines when he bought Ardnamurchan and Sunart in 1723 and went to live at Mingary castle. The next year he granted the rights to mine to a company whose senior partner was the Duke of Norfolk – a forbear of Lord Howard of Glossop who was born in 1818, second son of the 13th Duke of Norfolk. Shares were held by Sir Alexander Murray himself, Sir Archibald Grant of Monymusk and General George Wade of military road fame. Living on the spot, Murray was the one who brought the workers from the north of England, built huts for them at Corrantee and appointed a manager, William Neilson, to run things. This Neilson was a hard man who made 'bargains' for how much ore was lifted rather than paying wages: in other words, the men were on piece-work.

If that wasn't hard enough on men working in appalling conditions, the subsequent manager – Edmund Burt, who wrote *Letters from a Gentleman* and was under the wing of General Wade – showed he was even less of a gentleman by reducing the workforce in 1729 to save money. Little wonder that some were reduced to stealing tools from the smithy and bringing the Whitesmith's Grove operations to a standstill. Burt, manager and director of the Sunart lead mines 'in the name of his grace the Duke of Norfolk and the other proprietors, brought charges against Donald McEan Vic Gown, alias McDonald, the smith in Mingary, and John McWilliam, alias Cameron, from Garvalt in Sunart'. The two men appeared in court at Inveraray before Mr Archibald Campbell of Stonefield on 20 February 1730. The men were accused of meeting together to plot the theft the previous autumn and on Sunday, 26 October 1729, of breaking open the smiddie in the lead groves and stealing 'many iron toolls such as hammers, gavelocks, dreels, jumpers and other instruments of a considerable value belonging to the said lead works'. As a result of the theft, Mr Campbell heard, 'the myners and labourers belonging to the said groves were cast idle and could not work to the great hurt and prejudice not only of the proprietors of the said work but also of the poor labourers' – although we may take with a pinch of salt the great concern for the workers. It seemed that Cameron had done the deed and then delivered the tools to McDonald. McDonald was said to have received seven iron hammers, two iron gavelocks and nine or ten wimbles, dreels or jumpers and in return gave Cameron a guinea. He was then, according to the Justiciary Records of Argyll and the Isles,[6] seen walking across the hills with this great quantity of ironmongery in the early hours of the following morning. Accosted, he claimed he was going to attend to his work as the only smith in the area and that was why he was out so early. John McWilliam or Cameron had been employed in the mines but was a somewhat unreliable character who moved about between his neighbours and rarely slept at home with his wife and family at Garvalt. He was described in court as 'a vagrant person, *sub mala fama*' – of bad character. There was much discussion in court as to whether a person convicted for the first time of theft should receive the death penalty. Not surprisingly, with that possibility looming over both men, they produced character references from their neighbours and work-mates. These were, of course, scrutinised by the procurator fiscal and dismissed as being provided by people who simply gave their 'mark' – illiteracy preventing them from giving a signature – and who were 'strangers' to the area. The defence insisted these people were no strangers, having worked at the mines for four or five years. McDonald was presented as 'a simple, credulous, ignorant man apt to be ensnared...' while Cameron's legal representative suggested McDonald simply tried to 'roll over the guilt' on him and pointed out that 'the month of October is the only time in the year smiths have least ado for then the harvest is over and the labouring not at all begunn', so his reasons for his 4 a.m. outing did not hold water.

The 'myners' gave evidence that they had handed over their tools to John Smith, the smith at the lead mines, for safe keeping at the end of the working week, had seen him lock up and been present when the broken door and windows were discovered on the Monday morning. It is difficult to judge the size and shape of the tools and equipment, but added together, hammers, wedges, picks, drills and iron bars, two of which 'weighed upwards of a hundred pound weight', would not have been easily transported. Footprints were seen leading to 'Corrintie' where McDonald lived; some Irish workmen had seen prickers and scrapers on the road and Cameron swore he'd never seen McDonald until he saw him a prisoner at Strontian. In his efforts to prove his innocence when he was discovered at 4 a.m. on the road with a load of ironmongery, McDonald had left his plaid as surety with the men who apprehended him to go and find a witness. It was all in vain: while the case against McWilliam, alias Cameron, was found not proven, 'McDonald, the smith in Mingary' was found guilty of receiving the tools and was sentenced to be scourged through the streets of Inveraray by the hand of the common executioner on Friday, 17 April between 10 am and noon. His 40 stripes were to be given at various places in the town: five at Neil McCallum's house in the Townhead, ten at the mercat cross, five at Provost Brown's house, five at Finlay McNicol's house, five at Mr Alexander Campbell's house, five at Donald McNachtan's house and five at Provost Duncanson's house. He was then to be returned to the jail until he could 'find caution for his good behaviour in time coming'. On 18 April 1730, Donald McDonald of Kinlochmoydart pledged himself as cautioner for the smith's good behaviour and he presumably returned to Mingary. But the bit of business he had done with the tools had not helped the mines and in July, 1730, the Duke of Norfolk's company assigned the lease to the York Buildings Company on disastrous financial terms for a company which was already operating on shaky ground. The new tenants worked the mines for three years, laying out cash for new shafts, furnaces and buildings and for workers' houses at 'New York' – one of a number of villages in Argyll given that appellation by the company at industrial sites where they were involved. This one was about a mile north of Strontian. There were around 500 workers employed but the ore smelted did not compensate for the £40,000 invested. In 1734, the company got out of Strontian in poor financial straits. Sir Alexander Murray transferred his rights and liabilities to his brother Charles, who once more let out the mines in 1751 to a new partnership – Andrew Telfer, head-hunted from the lead mines of Wanlockhead in Lanarkshire, and Edward Lothian. Again, new shafts were sunk, a new smelt mill built and a water-driven pumping engine was installed. The mines produced 60 tons of lead to roof Inveraray Castle in 1753, but drought and frost meant there was no water to drive the pumps and local workers were accused of inefficiency. After Oliphant's dam burst, the partnership collapsed in the 1760s.

The history of the mines did not stop there, however. James Riddell bought Ardnamurchan and Sunart estates in 1767 and he continued to have the mines worked. In 1791, Thomas Hope discovered strontia (strontium monoxide) in the local mineral strontianite, but it was the lead which gave new life to the mines in the early 1800s when, after a period of inactivity, the Napoleonic wars demanded arms manufacture. Scotstown Farm and 20 acres of ground in Strontian village were leased by the contemporary mining company in 1806. The end of the wars brought a slump for lead and although the estate owner subsidised operations to provide local employment the total output in 1839 was just 39 tons. Low wages meant skilled labourers wouldn't come to 'remote' Strontian in 1846 for new management and despite a bumper year in 1853 when 240 tons were extracted, the workings gradually dwindled away until Bellsgrove, Fee Donald and Corrantee were abandoned in 1871. In 1901 and the 1950s, attempts were made to reopen the mines, but strontium monoxide was much more profitable and the lead mines became a lost commercial cause.

The remoteness of Sunart, Ardnamurchan and Morvern meant that until a modern infrastructure was in place, heavy industry had its limitations. The steamship allowed heavier cargoes and faster transportation, but many quarries in northern Argyll served mainly local needs. In Morvern, there were old quarries at Inninmore Bay, south of Loch Aline, where millstones and tombstones were cut from the coarse-grained white to yellow sandstone in the 18th and early 19th centuries; and beyond Quarry Burn where buff-coloured fine-grained sandstone is found in thick outcrops along the shore. A jetty made from boulders was built here (its remains are visible) to transport this attractive stone to building sites up and down the coast and the quarries were probably being worked in the 13th century to provide facings for the many medieval chapels and defensive buildings. Operations here finished around the middle of the 19th century, at about the time the lead mining finished at Lurga, leaving abandoned industrial buildings. Sir Alexander Murray had also had an involvement in the Morven mining rights and he had bought Kinlochaline Castle – once a tower-house on a rocky ridge west of where the River Aline flows into the loch. Built in the 15th century, remodelled in the 15th and 17th centuries (it was taken by Alasdair MacDonald in the civil war) and squabbled over at the end of the 17th century by Campbells and MacLeans, this was a three-storey defence built from limestone and faced with triassic sandstone, both quarried locally. When Sir Alexander Murray bought it and the neighbouring farm in 1730 it was roofless and he commissioned Alexander Noble and some Lowland masons to repair the walls, door and windows so that the roof could be replaced. He had bought it as a headquarters for the company to which he sublet his Morvern mining rights and intended the building to be used for storage and accommodation – something of a comedown for this fine defence of earlier centuries. The miners, however, said it was far too inconvenient and the repairs would have cost £200, so the castle was abandoned and instead a store was built at Liddesdale, which, like the castle, in time became derelict. Squatters went into the castle in the 1880s but were evicted when Valentine Smith, by then owner of the Ardtornish Estate, made the place watertight and did some rather unsympathetic restoration work, lowering the gables and flattening the roof.

Men like Sir Alexander Murray had their role to play on the mining front, but it was agriculture which had traditionally sustained the majority of the inhabitants of Northern Argyll, and when agriculture changed and no longer needed so many to work the land, it brought at least as much hardship as any mine or quarry closure ever did. The fifth Duke of Argyll had tried to support the Morvern tenants in the last two decades of the 18th century by going against the modernising trend and cutting down on the size of farms, but there was an inevitability about the encroachment of the massive sheep-farm. It has been argued that taking the people from the land was to their benefit. The houses of the poor with their earth floors, draughty thatches, central peat hearths and accommodation shared with the farm animals did little to help nurture underfed, uneducated families. Mortality rates were high and wasn't it kinder to pack them off to the city to a waiting job in the mills? But as Mary of Unimore's minister and many others noted, those mills were dangerous and disease-ridden, the pay pitiful and the city slum dwellings harbingers of death. It was a question of city poverty or rural poverty. There were almost 50 known paupers in the parish in the 1790s but there were also over 60 tradesmen – weavers, tailors, brogue makers, drystone dykers, joiners, blacksmiths, coopers and carpenters – supporting the population of farmers, who produced enough grain to supply three mills at Acharn, Mungasdail and Savary, and busy ferries transported people to Ardnamurchan, to Lorn and to Mull. A poorly-paid schoolmaster was employed to teach about 500 children in the parish (a tenth of whom turned up), which was overseen by Norman MacLeod, the Skye-born minister whose sympathetic support of the people diverted them from their adherence to the Jacobite cause. There were at that period around a dozen tacksmen with leases on combined properties giving them between 1,500 and 10,000 acres, and even then, several employed managers and lived elsewhere. Smaller tacksmen held between 500 and 2,000 acres and farmed themselves.

There were few elegant houses then and most have been lost in the move towards modernisation and improvement. Ardtornish House was a solid mansion built between 1755 and 1770 by Donald Campbell of Aires, the Duke of Argyll's factor in Morvern. The house was built by Lowland masons near the ruined Ardtornish Castle at the bottom of Ardtornish Point and when Angus Gregorson or Macgregor became tacksman of Ardtornish – by now 10,000 acres and including Tearnait and Eignaig farms – he was a wealthy man whose natural place was in the best house in Morvern. Gregorson had become rich as a tacksman in Mull. Now he became richer still, paying the highest total rent of the Argyll tacksmen at £186 a year and able to buy the estates of Durran, Loch Awe, and Acharn in Morvern in the 1790s and early 1800s. His son John succeeded to this fortune in 1813 and lived in Ardtornish House's 20 rooms, employing a tutor for his children. In 1819, the sixth Duke of Argyll's trustees sold off the rest of the Morvern properties, including Ardtornish, and so John Gregorson borrowed £9,000 to buy the property his father had rented.

These were the years when sheep and wool prices peaked and Gregorson perhaps became over-confident. He bought and sold a number of Argyll estates in the coming years but eventually had to put all the property in trust while he still owned them. Finally, in 1844, he left Morvern, having sold Ardtornish for £11,000 to Patrick Sellar, a professional sheep-farmer whose other properties were in Moray and Sutherland. During the time the Grigorsons held the

Ardtornish Castle ruins. (RCAHMS.)

property, the Tearnait farm became a sheep-walk supporting just two shepherds, a widow and their families. Ardtornish itself had only 39 people living on it, excluding the Gregorson family. Sellar, who rarely came to Morvern, pursued the same cruel policy of eviction that he had followed in Sutherland. Philip Gaskell suggests he was the most widely hated man in the Highlands.[7] Ardtornish was not his first investment in Morvern: he had bought the Acharn estate north of Lochaline for £11,250 in 1838. It comprised seven farms and 6,816 acres and he evicted 44 families on them to make way for a flock of sheep driven down from Sutherland. He followed this up with the purchase of Clounlaid and Uladail – 4,794 acres for £7,500 and the remaining Kinlochaline fishing rights which he had not acquired in his first venture. Clounlaid's 100 families had already left when the census was taken in 1841 and he cleared the Gregorson's tenants when he bought Ardtornish. He now had 21,575 acres in Morvern, bought for £29,850. It included the mansion house at Ardtornish and after renting five more grazings on which he put over 8,000 sheep during the 1850s.

The Sellar family now started coming to Morvern in the summer, living in the Ardtornish House. If Patrick Sellar was responsible for a large percentage of the population losses and the disappearance of vernacular houses in Morvern, his family was responsible for introducing the highland-holiday concept to the area. Strangers to Morvern with an alien culture, they brought their friends to walk, shoot and fish, entertaining guests such as Tennyson and Palgrave at Ardtornish. Sellar died in 1851, after quarrelling with Octavius Smith, his new English neighbour who had bought Achranich estate to live on for half the year. His children became friendly with Smith, and in 1860 sold the Morvern estate to him for £39,500 – a £10,000 profit.

But while such fantastical prices were changing hands in high places, the remaining tenants in Morvern were having an even tougher time. The threat of eviction, a failure of the corn harvest and the potato famine in successive decades meant a dire need for the creation of the Highland Relief Board. In 1847 and 1848, Morvern received oat and wheat-meal consignments. In the second year it was decided people would have to work for this charitable distribution of food, and among the projects started then was the pier for Lochaline opposite the Caolas ferry which gave work to 39 families. The pier survived to the 20th century but fell into disuse. At Bonnavoulin, a new road was started by 46 families receiving famine relief on the Drimnin Estate. Only three miles were finished at that time between Bonnavoulin and Killundine, but eventually a full road was created. The wall surrounding the Portabhata settlement in Drimnin was also built then and paid for in relief supplies by Lady Gordon.

This had been a site of combined farms for centuries. There had been shielings nearby for summer grazing and lazy beds were cultivated there. Now there was just one farm and a gamekeeper. A few small tenants were allowed to keep holdings at Knock, Achabeg and Fernish, but more and more of those thrown off their land were living on the periphery of the big estates in shanty villages where they tried to cultivate allotments. Lochaline was the largest of these villages. It was founded in 1830 and by 1851 there were over 300 people living there, mostly seven to a room. There was little work and much poverty and disease, as there was in smaller 'villages' which had been thrown up after the evictions.

Yet even the champion of the people, John MacLeod the minister, son of Norman from Skye, said he understood that landlords had to be allowed to develop their land for maximum profit. While his parishioners lived in squalor, he was living in an improved manse at Fiunary. Not that it could be compared with the luxury of the new landowners who were by now using their estates either as giant sheep-walks or as playgrounds. Octavius Smith and his family used inherited money and money made in distilling – he owned the largest distillery in England – to buy into what he saw as the 'glamour of the West Highlands' at Achranich in Morvern. Morvern had not been seen as a place of beauty before this, but Octavius and his eight children sold this viewpoint to their friends and business associates who visited there and later at Ardtornish. When he bought Achranich there were only 67 people living on the estate – less than half the number resident in the early part of the century. Subsistence agriculture was lost to the estate, and although there were some tradesmen, there was no mansion house and no shooting or fishing. The farmhouse was a plain two-storey house with 14 rooms and was not replaced by anything bigger until the 1880s. The farmhouse was the family's 'country cottage' which became a second home, displacing the seven farm workers who normally lived there. By the mid 1850s, shooting guests were coming at the rate of five or six a year, killing around 150 birds a season. Shepherds were paid extra to look after the game. Deer began to be shot in the 1860s but fishing was always a passion. It was over fishing rights that he quarrelled with Patrick Sellar but came to an agreement under which Smith gave £400 to Sellar for half his fishing rights. Smith also began building houses on his estate for workers and a house for himself. Achranich New House, which was to become Ardtornish Tower, took ten years to build. It had 35 rooms and was designed in an Italianate-Gothic style with a romanesque clock tower. Built in a cruciform style it had steeply pitched gables, heavy dormer-braces and patterned stone work. The delay in completing the house was partly due to repairs being made to Ardtornish

House. This 1860s work may have been designed by Alexander Ross of Inverness, who later designed the second Ardtornish Tower for Octavius's son Valentine in the early part of the 20th century. Although much money was being spent, it was at least providing jobs, and Octavius was seen as a benevolent landowner in Morvern, even receiving some praise from the Napier Commission in 1883.

His purchase of the Ardtornish estate to complement his Achranich property gave Octavius sole fishing rights on the River Aline, the coastline from Ardtornish Bay to Eignaig and fishing in Loch Arienas. He paid 27 shillings an acre for Achranich in 1845 but by 1859 sheep were big business and he had to pay 40 shillings an acre for Ardtornish. His property included Achranich, Acharn and Ardtornish and he renamed it the Ardtornish estate. These 30,000 acres were the biggest estate ever farmed in Morvern and 80 per cent of its income came from wool and sheep sales. Smith built new steadings, installed 200 miles of sheep drains, improved the estate roads and organised county roads. He also built six new shepherds' cottages.

Ardtornish House was demolished in 1907 and Achranich farmhouse came down to make way for the Samuel Barham-designed manager's house built in 1880. The first Ardtornish Tower built in 1856-66, was demolished in 1884 when it was found to be infested by dry rot, leaving its re-roofed clock tower standing. The far grander Ardtornish Tower II with its 75 rooms designed by Alexander Ross of Inverness, built in 1884-91 under the supervision of Valentine Smith's local master of works, Samuel Barham, remains at the heart of the Ardtornish estate self-catering holiday complex where it is possible to choose between the 'big house' looking down Lochaline to Mull and those six estate cottages built for the shepherds between 1857 and 1866. At the end of the 19th and beginning of the 20th centuries, after Valentine Smith had bought up Lochaline estate and created a 39,000-acre empire, deer and English grouse were introduced to the estate. Pheasants – not native to Morvern – were raised in hatcheries and the celebrities flocked to enjoy the lifestyle. Smith and his heir, his sister and her husband Craig Sellar, reversed the employment trend and there were jobs for over 100 people in the estate's heyday. Beaters were the part-time by-product of this new use of the land. Nonetheless, Smith, like so many lairds of the day, was running his estate at a deficit of £4,000 a year.

Today, many Northern Argyll properties provide hideaways (the singer Madonna is one of the modern wealthy who has considered property in Morvern), or have been converted into hotels. Castle Drimnin was the seat of the lairds of Drimnin, who owed fealty to the MacLeans of Coll in the 16th and early 17th century. The castle may date to the later 1600s when the MacLeans of Drimnin became a family of standing. Just a century later, they abandoned the castle to move into a more modern residence – Drimnin House. This, with Auliston, Portabhata and Poll Luachrain, was sold on to MacLean of Boreray in 1817 and then to Sir Charles Gordon from Banffshire, secretary of the Highland and Agricultural Society of Scotland. He enlarged Drimnin House in 1838, and at the same time shocked the local minister by demolishing the ruins of the castle to build a private Catholic church designed by James Anderson of Edinburgh at a cost of £520. It was Gordon's Roman Catholicism in a Protestant area which was the problem – not the loss of the castle ruins. The laird's house was destroyed by fire in 1849, four years after Sir Charles's death. It began with a fire in the kitchen chimney and little was left but rubble. A new Gothic-style mansion house was built in 1861 but the Catholic church is now derelict. The Gordons were responsible for evicting around 200 people between 1824 and Lady Gordon's death in 1881. In 1851, Auliston was home to around 115 people in 22 houses. All were evicted in 1855 to accommodate sheep, leaving a deserted and crumbling settlement.

Lochaline House, also known as Fiunary House, was built near the manse where the succession of MacLeod ministers live and championed the cause of the evicted. It was situated on land bought from the Duke of Argyll's estate in 1821 by John Sinclair of Lochaline, who had made his fortune as a merchant in Tobermory, the village created by the Duke and the British Society for Extended Fisheries in 1788-9.

Sinclair had a fleet of trading vessels and he also married money. His first property venture in Morvern was to buy a fertile stretch of coastal land from Savary to Loch Aline which included the farms of Achnaha, Achabeg, Keil and Knock. He bought it in 1813 from MacDonald of Glenaladale and used it as a summer home for his family. When he bought up Fiunary and Savary in 1821, Sinclair owned all the coast from Salachan Burn to Loch Aline, and he called his new 7,650 acres Lochaline Estate. He built a new house near the old manse, first calling it Lochaline House and then Fiunary House. During his tenure there, Sinclair was responsible for the eviction of at least 15 families. The house was altered by its next owner, Magdalene Campbell Paterson, who bought the place after Sinclair's death in 1863 for £43,000 – and evicted a further 28 families from the estate, amounting to around 150 people. We know Fiunary House had views of Ben More on Mull, and that in the 1870s, Mrs Paterson changed the plain Sinclair house with its central block and two wings into a grand affair with an Italianate façade – all that remained of the building when it was deliberately burned down in 1910 because it was no longer needed.

The estate was bought in the 1880s by Valentine Smith and added to the Ardtornish estate. The house was never lived in after 1888 and when Valentine's heir took over, he avoided paying rates by sending it up in smoke. There were those who would have put an effigy of the late Mrs Paterson on the pyre: the Napier Commission hearing evidence after her death from her nephew William Hardie, who managed the Lochaline Estate trust, condemned the evictions. Lord Napier said: 'The people were removed for the benefit of the sheep farm, and you may say for the benefit of the estate.' And however benevolent the Smiths may have been, the house was also removed for the benefit of the estate.

Killundine House was another Morvern mansion to fall because of its high rateable value. In the mid-19th century it was owned by the MacLeans of Killundine, and the property covered 4,422 acres across Killundine, Lagan and Salachan. Remains of a summer shieling near *Gleann nan Iomairean* settlement give an idea of the bustling population of the 18th century. There is no evidence of early remains on the site of Killundine House, which was built in 1871 and demolished in the 1950s. There were people living at Killundine in 1755 when it was part of the Argyll estate. When it was sold off by the Duke in 1821 it had a succession of owners, but Lt-Col Charles Cheape, who bought the house in 1859, was the one who enlarged it in 1871, creating a Victorian façade. After the Cheape family sold the estate in 1895, there were several more owners but it was the Department of Agriculture which, having bought the estate before the Second World War, destroyed the once-elegant interior and removed the roof to avoid paying rates. The shell was demolished completely in 1965 when a private owner took on the estate. By that time, people had given way to trees – trees being the 20th century sheep.

There have been 'modern' castles built to satisfy the Victorian sense of Gothic grandeur, such as Shiel Bridge Castle at Acharacle, erected in 1898 for diamond merchant E.C.D. Rudd by Sydney Mitchell and Wilson.[8] According to Michael Davis of Argyll and Bute Libraries, this was designed in conventional Scottish Baronial style. The house had a number of owners and eventually was sold to a Glasgow fishing syndicate which demolished *Tigh na Drochaid* – House of the Bridge – in the 1950s, a bad time for big houses.

Killundine Castle, known as *Caisteal nan Con* or the 'Castle of the Dogs', was perhaps a hunting lodge for Aros Castle across the Sound of Mull. Built in the 15th or 16th century, it has just a gable left standing. Glensanda Castle, in Ardgour parish, was a 15th-century tower-house which still retains high walls. The Morvern Mining Company's storehouse at Liddesdale, converted into a house for the tacksman Lieut-Col Colin Campbell in the 1750s, is now a two-storey ruin. The remains of shielings and over 50 abandoned settlements have mostly disappeared into the Forestry Commission plantations, which have to an extent subsumed some of the oldest woodlands. The big pier at Fiunary is disused and jetties at Drimnin Mains have crumbled away.

Some ruins, such as the settlement at Auliston, tell of heartbreak and distress. Some tell of bloodshed. But just as the old castles and duns fell into disrepair and were cannibalised or converted for new generations, so the estates of 19th-century Morvern and Ardnamurchan have become the industries of the 21st century, bringing tourists to the areas to see for themselves the remnants of that lost Argyll.

CHAPTER 2

THE ISLANDS:
FEUDS, FAIRS, FISH AND FERRIES

When Martin Martin published his observations on the Western Isles in 1703, there was much which had already been 'lost' in the islands of Argyll. On Mull, he described 'an old Caſtle at Aros in the middle of the iſland, now in ruines'[9] and while he refers to only two churches, there had once been as many as 14 on the island. At the time of the Reformation in 1560, ancient parishes were joined together as the parish of Mull. On an island 40 miles long with a primitive infrastructure, this would not do and two parishes were created: one north of Aros to be called Kilninian and the rest of the island to be known as the parish of Ross. As the good Dr Johnson noted on his own tour of the Western Isles in 1773, large Presbyterian parishes and a lack of ministers meant that the spiritual needs of the people were not fully nurtured: had the 'new' church been able to bring itself to use all the old buildings and to persuade ministers to 'exile' themselves to the islands, the landscape (and much more) might have been very different today. As it was, many of the ancient churches and chapels melted away into the rocky terrain from which they had been created, joining the lost remnants of previous societies which had come and gone on the island.

The Beaker people were living on Mull around 3000 BC, making their distinctive pottery, and fragmentary remains suggest that there was a thriving community. Later island populations had to become more defensive and the largest of the 42 forts mentioned in the *Argyll Inventory of Monuments*,

Opposite top. Dun nan Gall, one of two brochs on Mull built by expert masons. (Graeme Waters collection.)

Opposite below. Dun Aisgean, designed to have timber doors. (Graeme Waters collection.)

Inch Kenneth Chapel – a ruin in Dr Samuel Johnson's day. (RCAHMS.)

Volume III, for Mull, Tiree, Coll and Northern Argyll[10] has its remains on a promontory at Sloc a' Mhuilt on Mull covering 2.47 acres. Brochs, unusual in this part of Scotland, were built by professional masons contracted by immigrants and duns built in the first three centuries of the Christian era show an admirable degree of expertise.

Much of our knowledge of the people who lived in Argyll in the earliest Christian times comes from the ruins of chapels and monasteries and from the writings of Adomnan, whose biography of St Columba written in 690 is set against a backdrop of contemporary lives. This was a people which took its religion seriously. Just as their pagan forebears had erected massive monuments and created burial cairns, so these people put up boundary pillars, carved crosses and gravestones. Pillar stones and small slabs from the 6th century have been found at Killundine and Calgary on Mull, and at Carsaig on the island's south coast, St Mary's chapel dates to those early times. In the Nun's Cave and Scour Cave, early crosses were carved. From the sixth to the ninth centuries, the Celtic church made its presence known on Mull but, like the chapels which had become ruinous by the 18th century, much of the cultural evidence has disappeared. Stone-robbing means that only Kilvickeon and Cill an Ailein have any real remains in Mull's many medieval parishes. Kilvickeon, built at the same time as the chapel on Inch Kenneth in the 13th century, retained a double lancet east window as testament to its once fine appearance, while the large Cill an Ailein, situated on a wild shore as most of the contemporary communal hermitages were, crumbled to rubble. Pennygown, probably the earliest surviving church, dating from the late 12th century, gives an idea of the kind of buildings in which Mull's people, rather than its religious community, worshipped then. Many of Mull's chapels and churches were dedicated to Columba, to his nephew or to other Celtic saints. Ernan, son of Eoghan was named on Mull and the island of Ulva and Saint Findoca may have had a dedication on Mull as well as on Coll.

The early monastical settlements were lost to the Norsemen, those fire-wielding invaders from the north who torched so many of the monks' little cells, burned their crops and drove off their cattle. The only real remains from pre-medieval times are the circular enclosures at Cillchriosd and Kilbrenan on Mull. The name Annaid, which means 'old church' , is given to places in Mull and Tiree but only the name remains. The Norse raiders, who sacked Iona four times between 795 and 826, wiped the landscape of these islands almost clean, leaving little evidence of their own presence outside the place-names and some burial sites.

The pathetic burnt-out cells and chapels gave way instead to medieval churches, but the Reformation and the civil war made their grievous impact too. Chapels at Laggan on Mull and Cairnburgh Castle in the Treshnish Isles on the way to Coll and Tiree date to the late medieval period but there are only fragments of other Mull buildings from that date – the decorated window-head at Killean chapel, the octagonal font at Laggan and the mass-clock at Kilninian. Mull provided the freestone dressings for many of the chapels and churches not only on the island itself but throughout northern Argyll. It came from quarries at Carsaig or Inninmore Bay. Had Martin Martin listed churches past and present on Mull in the early 1700s, he could have included Pennygown Chapel, the Old Parish Church at Kilvickeon, Cill an Ailein Chapel (swallowed by 20th-century forestry plantation), Inch Kenneth Chapel, Killean Old Parish church (a large building by the standards of the day), and the tiny chapel of Crackaig.

The chapel at Inch Kenneth had been dedicated to St Cainnech of Aghaboe in the 13th century. Now a ruin above the beach, it was built from rubble and greenish sandstone quarried locally with yellow sandstone dressings from Carsaig. It had a chancel lit by single light windows and a pair of lancets in the east wall. In 1815, the chapel's gables were intact but one began to lean outwards and was propped by clasping buttresses. It had begun life as a parish church in the 1200s but by the 16th century it belonged to the Augustinian nuns on Iona who had considerable lands in the south of Mull. The last prioress gave the convent lands to Hector MacLean of Duart in 1574, 14 years after the Reformation. The church was probably no longer used for worship after that, although it was used for burials.

The MacLeans of Duart held the earliest castle built on Mull. It began as a simple rectangle like Castle Sween in Knapdale. It had a courtyard some 65 feet square, a curtain wall and lean-to domestic accommodation. Part of an original square tower survives at one corner, but reconstruction in the 14th, 16th, 17th and then 20th centuries means most of the early structural features have been lost. A massive tower-house was added to one side of the courtyard in the 14th century, while the courtyard buildings seen today date from the 16th and 17th centuries. It was taken over by the Campbells in 1674 and in 1748 it was roofless and derelict. When it was re-acquired by the MacLeans in 1911, it was renovated by Glasgow architect Sir John Burnet. Is this a castle which can be said to have been lost – or preserved? Like much of Argyll's landscape, Duart has evolved. Built for defence, it was used for defence and suffered the consequences in a frequently bloody history. Buildings of this kind are organic in their development, like the families who build them and the land which supports them.

The MacLeans of Duart were key players in the Western Isles from the 1400s. They were Royalists in the civil war and supported Montrose. In 1645, the Campbells invaded Mull and Sir Donald Campbell of Ardnamurchan wrote to his son-in-law, who was then the captain of Dunstaffnage Castle, asking him for cannon and other military supplies. The castle held out until 1647 when General Leslie garrisoned it. From 1653 it remained in the hands of Cromwellian forces who had plans to strengthen it, but these plans were never carried out. The civil war was hard on the MacLeans and in 1670, the Earl of Argyll took all their lands. These remained in dispute for years and eventually went to the 10th Earl of Argyll. In the next century, one when it had been hoped peace would bring some kind of prosperity, the Jacobite Uprising again put Duart Castle in the firing line. Government troops garrisoned it in 1745, and in 1748 the barracks were said to be in such a ruinous state that it would take £1,500 to repair them. By the time the 6th Duke of Argyll was selling off much of the Argyll Estate in the first quarter of the 19th century, Duart was included in the Toronsay section of the former MacLean estates which went under the hammer. A Colonel Campbell of Possil bought the property, and then A.C. Guthrie in 1875. It was something of a triumph for the MacLeans when Sir Fitzroy of that Ilk, 10th Baronet of Duart, took possession of the restored building in August 1915. Today, one of its roles is as a lynch pin in Mull's tourism industry. The architecture purists may not like it and deem it lost. Many would disagree.

Part of the MacLean lands, gifted by the Augustinian nuns, included the slopes of Ben More, at 3,171 feet the island's highest mountain. When Skye-born scholar Martin Martin visited Mull, those slopes and the other hills and glens of the island were said to offer good pasture for black cattle, sheep and goats. There were deer, ptarmigan, blackcock and grouse in abundance and foxes which caused problems for farmers with chickens. Martin described the horses and cattle as small in size but said the flesh of the black cattle was 'very delicious and fine'. Mull's economy then, as for much of Argyll, was based on the raising and selling of black cattle. The beasts had, of course, to be shipped from the island, either to local markets in Morvern, more distant ones in Mid-Argyll, or to the major trysts at Falkirk. Some went from Fishnish to Loch Aline. Others were walked along ancient drove roads to Grass Point in the south-east and shipped to Kerrera and then to the mainland, heading south to Loch Awe and Loch Fyne across many ferries.

In the days of the nuns, the cattle would mainly have been for home consumption. There developed, however, a trade not only from Mull but through Mull, with most of the cattle from Coll and Tiree being landed at the other end of the island from that owned by the Augustinian sisters. Croig was at the mouth of Loch a' Chumhainn on its own little bay. The cattle were unloaded there and driven down through Dervaig, through Glen Aros to Salen and then Grass Point (or Auchnacraig as it was then known) – the diagonal length of Mull from north-west to south-east. This was obviously a very important drove road, but it was lost when at the beginning of the 19th century it became easier to land the cattle at Bunessan and Kintra on the Ross of Mull. Perhaps it was then that Druim Tighe Mhic Ghille Chatain began to diminish in importance as the site of one of Mull's principal markets and fairs. Drimtavickillichattan was still in the almanacs of Scottish fairs in the early 1800s and fairs were held there in mid May and mid October for cattle while in mid August the horse-dealers held their events. At the end of the 18th century it was considered to be the biggest horse fair in the West Highlands and the week-long event drew pedlars from the south of Scotland and from Ireland. Although the lairds began to stay away from it, the ordinary folk had a field day, sleeping and eating in temporary huts or tents. All that was left by the mid 20th century of the huge fairground that had been a focal point for the business and social life of Mull in the 18th century were the scant remains of 50 or so stone foundations of those temporary huts, which would have been covered by blankets in the way of other Highland fairgrounds as shelter for families and friends.

Wherever the cattle had come from to reach the centuries-old Druim Tighe fair, none of the journeys would have been easy. The ferries from Coll and Tiree were across a stretch of sea that could be very unkind, and there were frequent wild seas between Auchnacraig and Kerrera. In more ancient times, it wasn't only the seas which could threaten a crossing's safety. These ferries were owned by the lairds of Dunolly, their headquarters being at the castle of that name north of what is today the town of Oban. Sir John MacDougall, the laird in 1622, was taken to task for levying heavy tolls on the shipping of cattle from Mull and his punishment was a heavy one: the MacDougall lands and the ferry were forfeited for the rest of that century. For the first 50 years of the 18th century, ferries from Mull were running to Ardmore in the south of Kerrera and Slaterach in the north. A more sheltered landing place was made at *Barr-nam-Boc* (Barnabuck) Bay in the centre of the island and it was an obligation of their tenancies that the people of Kerrera worked three days a year on the Barnabuck ferry quay. It wasn't a cheap crossing from Auchnacraig to Kerrera for the drovers: the tariff in 1756 demanded that from July to January they paid ten Scotch shillings a head for black cattle and from January to July it was eight shillings. There were huge numbers of the cattle to be ferried and the mooring at Barnabuck was made even safer when the 23rd laird of Dunolly applied for £14 to blast the rocks there in 1760. Money was paid to local contractors – Hector MacLean, a quarrier, and Donald Sinclair, a smith – but the Commissioners of Supply for Argyll were not convinced that it was done when they met in 1760. Some thirty years later, the Commissioners were planning for a ferry which would bypass Kerrera, but as long as cattle were being transported, it remained a viable route. The usefulness of cattle, of course, was their ability to swim, allowing them to be landed at places that the sheep which replaced them on Mull in the early 1800s could not negotiate. From 1817, the sheep travelled directly from Auchnacraig to Dunolly Farm, but the cattle continued to be transported from Coll, Tiree, Morvern and Mull to Kerrera at Ardmore, from where they were driven to the north of the island to swim to Rhu Cruidh, the shortest crossing, right up until the 20th century. The laird of Ardantrive (a corruption of the Gaelic *Ard-an-t'snaimh*, the point of swimming) was not happy about this arrangement as his crops were trampled by the cattle. The laird of Dunolly had a 22-foot ferry boat built for £24 at the Port Kerrera boat yard, which was founded in the early 19th century. It was to be rowed by four men and it was intended to stop the swimming. According to Walter Weyndling, author and former ferry inspector,[11] these cattle boats were tarred inside and out and the bilges were protected by brushwood bedding and the gunwales had rings to which the cattle were fastened during crossings. The capacity was four cows, eight stirks or 50 sheep, but Weyndling said this capacity was often exceeded.

By the middle of the 19th century, steamboats were well established on routes around the islands, but although Lord Breadalbane had floated the idea of towing cattle-boats by steam, it was decided instead that boats carrying cattle would go via Kerrera while passenger ferries would make direct journeys to the mainland. When the cattle market was built at Oban, there was yet another incentive to cut out Kerrera and the Mull cattle sailed straight to the market. Kerrera continued to be a staging post for mail ferries delivering to Mull, Iona, Coll and Tiree, in part because the postmaster general was not convinced that steamboats could deliver. There was a post office subsidy for new sails on the old ferries; both sail and rowing boats got a post office subsidy in 1856 to maintain two ferries at Auchnacraig and Barnabuck. Quite understandably, the people of Mull wanted their mail delivered six days a week in keeping with mainland Scotland and a sailing smack was built for the route which ran until the 1880s.

Sir Colin Campbell, the Argyll Estates factor, made no exaggerated claims when he described the cattle traffic and the need for better ferries and landing places. In 1786, there were 400 cattle a year coming from the rich grazings on Coll and 500 a year from Tiree. *The New Statistical Account* of 1780 said that some 20 open or half-decked boats travelled between Coll and Tiree or Tiree and Mull where they landed at Kintra on the Ross of Mull. Twenty years later there were plans to extend the road along Loch Scridain from Kintra along the old drove road that went through Glen More to the Grass Point. Those drovers from Coll who wanted to catch the Salen fair still found it easier to land up in the north at Croig and the men from Tiree brought theirs in at Ulva and drove their cattle across the narrow isthmus to Salen. Our friend John Sinclair, the Tobermory merchant who went on to be a Morvern laird, made some of his fortune by investing in 1801 in a ferryboat running between Coll and Mull. His partners included a ferryman, the Duke of Argyll, his chamberlain of Tiree, Malcolm Maclaurin, and a Scaranish inn-keeper. It carried potatoes, passengers and, of course, cattle. When the steamers began to make major inroads into the islands these boats became ship-to-shore ferries as they had done around Morvern and Ardnamurchan. Official rowed ferries ceased in the 1950s, but in the 1960s such boats still brought almost entire island populations to Tobermory for Mull week: frequently a safe inward journey but a little more perilous on the way home after a few days of celebration. In the 1970s, the

Perspective sketch of the intended Town, 1790. (National Archives of Scotland collection.)

major change brought about by vehicular ferries was a direct crossing from Oban to Craignure in the south-east of the island, losing forever the magical entrance by steamer into Tobermory Bay.

But then, Tobermory had not been there since time immemorial, just as Oban was a new location. It was not an organic settlement but one created for a specific purpose. That purpose failed and the proposed industry was lost, but the attractive design of the little town meant that it survived and flourished. In 1787, the British Fisheries Society was in the process of establishing bases throughout the Highlands for the herring industry, and Tobermory was chosen for its fine natural harbour on the north-east coast of Mull. This was the harbour chosen in 1588 by a captain of the Armada when the Spanish fleet tried to escape the English navy by sailing north from the Channel and round the north of Scotland rather than taking the direct route home. Many were lost and one which took shelter in this safe harbour blew up, taking – so tradition has it

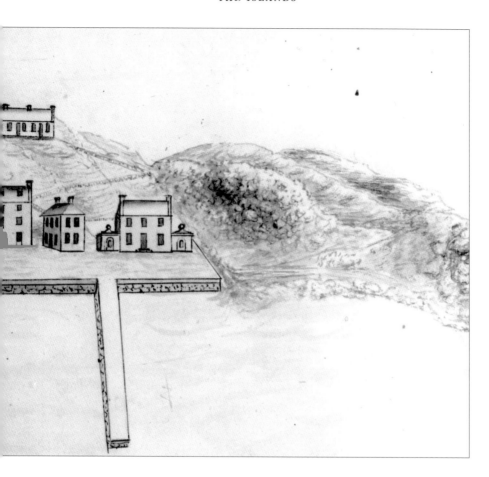

– its treasury of gold doubloons with it to the bottom of the sea. The Sound of Mull was, of course, a busy sea route throughout millennia and was the scene of fierce fighting during the civil war of the 17th century when Cromwell sent ships to quell those clans which supported the royalist cause. One wreck investigated by an archaeological diving unit from St Andrews University off Mingary on the Ardnamurchan shore, yielded up five cannon cast between 1640 and 1670. The gold fished up from the Spanish ship in Tobermory harbour has never reached the fabulous fortunes tradition suggests lie with the fishes. Fish, however, were intended to provide the fortunes for those who invested in the British Fisheries Society scheme of the late 18th century, and Thomas Telford was the adviser on the Tobermory project from 1790. The village was built on two levels to compensate for the restricted space. Public buildings and merchants' houses were separated from a rectilinear layout of smaller houses on a terrace above the bay. The architect Robert Mylne provided plans for the

49

inn as a gift to the county. When the site had been surveyed in June 1787 only the old chargehouse or ferry inn existed at Port Mor at the north end of the bay. A sub-committee of the BFS, which included the 5th Duke of Argyll as president and Lord Breadalbane as vice-president, came to visit the site and called it British Harbour. John Campbell of Knock sold the society 500 acres from his Mishnish estate and the Duke of Argyll kindly sold the society 1,500 acres of his own land south of the Tobermory River. This was intended to be developed as agricultural land by the settlers, because even the enthusiasm of the society could not guarantee constant good catches of herring.

The following year, James Maxwell, who was the chamberlain of Mull and Morvern for the Argyll Estates, was appointed the society's agent for Tobermory and he was responsible for the street plans. Two-storey slated houses were built for the merchants and the new inn and there was a footpath to the upper town where the houses were much more simple, intended as they were for the workers and fishermen. Not surprisingly, streets were named Argyll Terrace and Breadalbane Street. Although Thomas Telford was the man of the moment in Scottish construction, some of his designs, including that for the custom house, were turned down and Mr Maxwell's less elaborate plans were used instead. By 1797, settlers had arrived and tradesmen moved into their new homes on the north-west side of the south part of the main street. There were 49 families in all, ten of them tradesmen. Both Telford and Maxwell recommended that a new pier should be built, but this wasn't done until 1814.

The planning and building were well carried out, but the herring were, as always, unpredictable. Throughout history, fishermen throughout Argyll had experienced either feast or famine. Now it was famine. The Duke of Argyll tried to set up fishing villages at Creich and Bunessan, too, and around 1800, Alexander MacLean of Coll created another 'planned village' at Dervaig. This was almost completely lost and most of the houses were rebuilt. The Duke's solo venture was a failure, but Mull did gain the village of Bunessan, of which some of the early 19th-century houses survive although the church is vastly altered. But while the fishing industry as planned by the BFS was lost to Mull, a very attractive town was gained in the shape of Tobermory – so attractive that tourism has been boosted by children of the early 21st century persuading their parents to take them to the picture-book location of their favourite television programme.

Not that the planned village has survived as planned. It has, of course, grown, and in the growing, it has lost some of its earliest features. The storehouse of the 1787 plans was replaced by a Free Church in 1878, which in its turn changed its use. The collector's lodging later became the Temperance Institute and Maxwell's two-storey custom house became the 20th-century post office. Some merchants' houses were demolished in 1900 to create a site for a United Free Church and others were rebuilt in the late 19th century. Numbers 45, 49-51, 55 and 59, retained their original features much longer than the rest, with their three windows in the second storey. Number 37 had had a hipped gable on the street and Robert Mylne's inn became shops. But whereas other BFS villages at Ullapool and on Skye remained underdeveloped, Tobermory became a bustling port and lynchpin of a very different industry – that of tourism. One industry's loss was very much another's gain – but even Tobermory, 'traditional' as it may appear, has not been preserved in aspic. When Martin Martin visited Mull, there was simply a good harbour with a well – 'Tonbir Mory' as he spelt it, despite his Gaelic upbringing, or *Tober Mhoire*, Mary's Well – the waters of which were said to be medicinal. There was no village, but a settlement where some claimed they had relatives who remembered the Spanish galleon *Florencia* blowing up – which must allow not only for long memories but longevity. Where the well actually was has been disputed: some say it was on the site of the medieval chapel dedicated to the Virgin; others that it was to the east of the chapel. But with a healthy invasion from tourists and the sailing fraternity, it can be forgiven if legend and fact do not entirely agree over the lost origins of the little town's name.

By the time Martin Martin visited Mull, a lot of the carved relics of the past had already disappeared. Many of Mull's Celtic crosses had been destroyed by the iconoclasts of the Reformation, leaving an intact but displaced carved stone cross on Inch Kenneth and fragmented crosses at Pennygown. It is certain that many carved grave slabs would have been made to honour Mull's dead in the late middle ages – the Iona school of carving across the narrow sound off the south-west of the island makes quantities of such work inevitable. Yet only one late medieval effigy has survived at Kilninian. In the wake of the Reformation it took until 1760 for new churches to be even considered on Mull. The disruption of the civil war throughout the 17th century allowed no time for constructive work of any kind and the people of Mull were not all entirely swayed by the new religion. When the Franciscan missionaries came from Ireland to Argyll from around 1620, carrying out their work in caves and on hillsides, they made converts in the Ross of Mull – devout people who continued to worship in secret and who left their own graffiti in the caves at Carsaig in the 1630s. Replacing the 'inadequate' places of worship which a committee of the General Assembly of the Church of Scotland found a century and more later, were Kilchoan and Kilninian churches. The Telford off-the-peg church design was used on Ulva but Kilchoan got a new T-plan design by William Burn in 1827. The Ulva and Kilchoan pulpits survive. A much altered church built in 1804 by local contractor James Morrison survives at Bunessan, one of two built for the united parish of Kilfinichen and Kilvickeon. Both interior and exterior have been altered, introducing a porch, buttresses on the north side and hanging eaves, instead of the original plain harled building with a gable-ended roof and Gothic windows.

Not all stone carving ceased, of course, after 1560. It simply omitted depictions of saintly figures, Christ on the cross, and the Blessed Virgin Mary – an irony as Mull's chief town was to be built at a site dedicated to Mary and called after her. A cross at Pennycross was carved to commemorate two members of the Beaton family (Martin Martin reported a Dr Beaton blown to safety in the explosion which blew the rest of the *Florencia* to smithereens; a man who was probably physician to the MacLeans of Duart) and an effigy of a smith at Kilninian dating from the late 16th, early 17th century. A man in armour lies at Inch Kenneth and effigies of a man and woman from the 17th century are at Pennygown. Perhaps the influence of the Campbell tacksmen who were 'planted' on Mull by the Argyll Estates at this time encouraged these flamboyant testimonies to the deceased. They had stones carved to commemorate their deaths at Cill an Allein and Kilvickeon but many others may well have been stone-robbed.

In urban areas, it is the town planners who are most to be feared by those who wish to preserve the historic, the traditional, the beautiful and the unusual. In rural Argyll, the threat has come from weather, from invaders, from modernising landlords and from the man who needed a stone to fix his wall, put a lintel over his door, or who took his plough over the land and shifted any obstacles in its way, whatever their origin. The earliest and biggest castle on Mull, Duart, was repaired and modernised. Dun Ara was perhaps the smallest – a continuous curtain wall built round a rock and a scattered township clustered at its base – while Aros was one of the largest known Scottish hall houses from the 13th and 14th centuries. Very incomplete remains show that Aros was around 70 feet by 26 feet and its first-floor apartments had windows with pointed archheads. Sophisticated for its time, it had latrines in a corner turret and like the similar hall house at Ardtornish on the mainland had dry-stone and turf outbuildings. At Aros, these were built in a court surrounded by a curtain wall made from stone and lime. It had a defending ditch on the land side. Moy Castle was built later and defended the west-coast Lochbuie properties of the MacLeans. It had been built in the 15th century as a tower-house by Lachlan MacLean and it was far more the family home than the defensive castle – although it did have a pit prison for MacLean captives. The castle was remodelled in the 16th and 17th centuries, when chimneyed fireplaces were installed and many 15th-century features lost, and this is the building in which Johnson and Boswell were entertained as they travelled through Mull. Yet another ruined defence in this area that once bristled with fortifications is Dun Ban, a large medieval building that was the stronghold of the MacQuarries of Ulva.

But just as elsewhere, there had to come a time when the feuding stopped

The turret of the ruined Moy Castle. (RCAHMS.)

– or at least became less violent – and the leading families of Mull could enhance their lives by moving into much more domestic premises. Some did not survive, many were altered. In the way of the Highlands and Islands, new homes either evolved from the old ones or the old ones were demoted to outhouse status and continued to loom in the background of the latest building. Old Erray House, less than a mile north of Tobermory, literally took a back seat to a later mansion. The older house had two main storeys built from harled rubbled masonry with sandstone dressings and was gable-ended. The original two rows of small chamfer-arrised windows on the symmetrical frontage were blocked up and the interior was gutted. A plan was drawn up by George Langlands of Tobermory in 1786 which shows single-storey wings flanking the main block of the house, and it seemed to have a central staircase off a lobby with a single room on either side. James Boswell was not impressed. When Dr Hector MacLean received Boswell and Johnson there in 1773, Boswell noted that it was 'a strange confused house'. It was already around 60 years old but the chilly kitchen seemed unfinished and they were led through it to a timber staircase and 'along a passage to a large bedroom'. Perhaps few of the lairds' houses of the day would have impressed the intrepid travellers: there had been a continued economic and social depression throughout Argyll and the old creel or wattled buildings had certainly not been swept away to build in more modern styles with more modern materials.

Erray was typical of the two-storeyed lairds' houses of the period: whether it was the lead company storehouse at Liddesdale in Morvern which was converted into a tacksman's house in 1754 or the house at Lochbuie on Mull built in 1752, plain and functional was the order of the day. When Lochbuie House was rebuilt for Murdoch MacLean in 1790, some sense of the style already being indulged in the south was beginning to appear. This was similar to the house Hector MacLean had built at Breachacha on Coll in 1750 and Hugh MacLean's Ardgour House which went up in 1765. Both were square and had three storeys – although Ardgour House was renovated after a fire in 1825 and lost its original appearance. The house at Lochbuie had an advanced central pedimented feature embellished with urn finials. Torloisk House, built on Mull for Lachlan MacLean in 1780, repeated this elegance but Victorian remodelling altered it out of recognition. On the island of Ulva, the mansion house built in 1790 had just two storeys and a three-bay façade with urn-decorated pediments on each façade. This was altered by 1815 with the addition by MacDonald of Staffa of hipped end-bays, because by then the nearby island of Staffa was becoming a major attraction to visitors and Ulva House had its share of guests, including Sir Walter Scott. There was even a cottage built as a shelter for those early tourists who were cut off by stormy seas, much as Johnson and Boswell were delayed during their tour. Further changes were made as the property changed hands. The house had Adam chimney-pieces in both the dining room and drawing room, which was, according to Michael Davis,[12] either round or oval. Extra bays were added to the house making access difficult and the Clark family, which owned the mansion for a century until 1935, added a door from the first-floor drawing room. Edith, Lady Congleton, bought the island in 1948, but sadly, Ulva House burned down in 1954.

It was the influx of new landlords which brought new building in a more flamboyant style. There may no longer have been a need for castellated defences, but these families wanted to create their own version of Highland history. Mull had its fair share of Gothic splendour and the best architects of the day were commissioned to create castles more impressive than anything which had stood its ground against Roundhead or Royalist, Campbell or MacLean. The earliest was Calgary House, a symmetrical castellated Gothic house built for Allan McAskill some time around 1817. Toronsay Castle was designed by David Bryce in 1856, Glengorm Castle by Peddie and Kinnear in 1858, and Gruline House by the same firm in 1861. In 1825, Aros House had been designed by William Burn, then an architect to watch, for Hugh MacLean of Coll and was then called Drumfin. The plans were not followed and the result was a sprawling Tudor-style building. A crenellated tower was added in the 1870s by J.M. Wardrop for the Allan family, who gave the house its second name, Aros. It was eventually demolished in 1960 but the Forestry Commission, which had bought the estate, opened the land to the public as a forest park in 1969.

The island of Mull is the biggest of the Argyll islands. It has its own satellite islands, including Ulva, Inch Kenneth, Eorsa, Erraid – and of course, Iona. When Johnson and Boswell visited Mull, Dr Johnson recorded: 'Mr Boswell's curiosity strongly impelled him to survey Iona, or Icolmkil, which was to the early ages the great school of theology ... I, though less eager, did not oppose him.' They had been staying at old Erray House in the north of Mull and the journey to the south-west was daunting. It took several hours on horseback through what the doctor called a 'black and barren' tract. It was October, but there had also been a very severe winter in 1771 from which the Western Isles had still not recovered. Cattle had been lost; harvests failed. Passing a ruined chapel on their way made the expedition still more gloomy. Dr Johnson could only wonder why these naked hills could not be clothed in trees to 'give nature a more cheerful face'. Perhaps he would have been an admirer of the 20th-century work of the Forestry Commission which clothed the hills, subsumed settlements and still did not make an adequate living for local people when the time came for harvesting. The intrepid travellers were under the protection of the laird of Coll (or Col as Johnson had it) with whom they had stayed, and therefore were confident of their safety. However, the man with whom 'Col' had planned to lodge them for the night turned out to be terminally ill in bed and so they headed instead to the island of Ulva. The ferry-boat was gone and there was no house in sight, but as they waited and wondered what to do, Captain McLure, the master of the *Bonnetta*, an Irish ship out of Londonderry which was at anchor in the Sound of Ulva, picked them up and took them across to stay with Lauchlan MacQuarry, who was the proprietor of Ulva and Staffa. The unexpected visit allowed them to visit the ruins of the medieval church there, and then to go to Inch Kenneth, the mile-long island south of Ulva at the mouth of Loch na Keal. Sir Allan MacLean and his two daughters were the only people on the island and for once, Dr Johnson was impressed by the 'polished manners, and elegant conversation' they provided. Johnson describes walking to the mansion where there was a cottage for Sir Allan and two more for the 'domesticks'. Boswell and Johnson's room was well floored, well lit, and the food was 'delicate'. This cottage (derelict when Sir Walter Scott visited in 1810) became the site of the farm and a new mansion (perhaps more as Johnson imagined mansions should be) was built by Lt. Col. Robert MacDonald. The house changed hands and appearance many times in subsequent years, and having been burned down it was rebuilt with a flat roof and an extra storey by a 20th-century proprietor. What the original looked like it would be hard to hazard a guess – as it was for Johnson and Boswell when Sir Allan MacLean tried to point out the foundations of what he claimed had been an ancient seminary. The pair were not even convinced the ruins were there, as the 21st-century traveller might not be convinced of the original Inch Kenneth mansion, despite its rich and varied history. The more solid ruins of the roofless chapel with its bas relief of the Virgin Mary on one side of its altar and its little bell impressed Johnson more, as did the graveyard around the chapel where he saw stones dedicated to 'chiefs and ladies'. Boswell took a spade and in the floor of the ruined chapel buried some human bones he had found exposed there. They were not the first exposed skeletal remains the pair had found as they investigated such ancient sites. The following day, when they went to visit Sandiland, the island off Inch Kenneth, Johnson was more inclined to concede that when there had been a college on Inch Kenneth, there may well have been a hermitage on this four-acre island. If the ruins were hard to discern in 1773, little wonder that so much more is lost to the traveller of the 21st century.

Sir Allan was persuaded to take Dr Johnson and his companion to 'Icolmkil' – the island of Iona where St Columba had founded his monastery in the 6th century after travelling throughout Argyll determined not to settle until he could no longer see his native Ireland and feel its pull. They took their leave of their kind guardian, the laird of Col – only to hear before the publication of Johnson's journal that he had drowned in the waters between Inch Kenneth and Ulva. Having experienced rough waters and soon to experience more, this may have saddened Johnson but could not have surprised him. To get to Iona, they sailed all day, eventually passing Nun's Island where stone was quarried for the Iona buildings. As they approached Iona itself, they could see what Boswell called 'the cathedral' – and more welcoming, a light in the village of Icolmkil. They were welcomed because they were with Sir Allan, a MacLean, as the Iona residents were. Iona had been a MacLean stronghold in the past, but by the late 1700s it was part of the estates of the Duke of Argyll. They slept the night in a barn, yet Dr Johnson could still say of the island: 'That man is little to be envied ... whose piety would not grow warmer among the ruins of Iona.'

Much has been written of the ruins of Iona (which of course are medieval and not from the period of Columba, whose monastery was built from impermanent materials destroyed by marauding Norsemen) and much that was ruined at the time of Johnson's and Boswell's visit has now been restored through the willing hands of many thousands of volunteers. Then, Boswell was told as they walked from the convent to the abbey that the old broken causeway had been a street with houses on either side. Four chapels and a monastery were said to surround the abbey and the convent. They were disappointed that the stones said to mark the burial place of the kings of Scotland, Ireland and Denmark, as well as a king of France, were nothing more than 'gravestones flat on the earth' and with no inscriptions. Boswell wanted the marble of Westminster Abbey and Johnson was a little taken aback that cows were housed in the chapel of the nunnery. The Vikings had laid the island waste almost a millennium before their visit. The Reformation had damaged some of the monuments still further. If four – or as Johnson remembered it, five – chapels were still visible, another three were not. The Crosses of St Matthew and St John were to be seen and traces of monastic fishponds and the aqueduct which fed them were, the intrepid travellers said, 'yet discernible'.

The renovations on the island make the descriptions of Johnson and Boswell, Pennant and Martin fascinating reading. Have we lost or found the spirituality of Iona? Have we created a Disneyfication of Columba's hallowed island or rebuilt Britain's cradle of Christianity? As so much of Iona's history has been described by so many, it is perhaps more fitting here to turn instead to losses on the island other than the ecclesiastical. Many vernacular houses have disappeared which, like the 18th-century farm that had been the bishop's house, had boasted chimneys but no fireplaces. Even in the two-storey former bishop's house, the fire was on the floor in the middle of the room in the late 1700s.

Agriculture was the main occupation of the island and the smell of new-mown hay still adds to the special atmosphere of Iona. But people also earned their living by quarrying – an industry now lost to the island and to Mull. On Mull, granite from the Ross was quarried extensively in the 19th century. Pink granite for Skerryvore and Ardnamurchan lighthouses was quarried from Camas Tuath (North Bay), from a quarry specially opened in April 1839 for this purpose. This was not an easy place from which to extract stone. It was 100 feet or so above the high water mark and wagons were lowered down a steep incline from the quarry floor to a wharf on the shore. Rough blocks of the stone were shipped out to Tiree for Skerryvore. A railway track once ran at the bottom of this steep slope. There was a forge at the jetty and some two-storey quarriers' houses, flatted for about 40 people, were finished in August 1839. The ghost of this industry remains, as does the evidence of much longer sandstone quarrying in Carsaig Bay. Old Quames was where they hewed sandstone from the Jurassic age to face the castles and tower-houses of medieval times and, much later, lairds' mansions. Beautiful sandstone, it ranged in colour from pale green to buff and had a fine grain to it. Rhubh 'a' Chromain was the main centre of the excavation and it went by sea to its many destinations – but no sign remains of the jetty that was used. The Nun's Cave, more than 150 feet north of Rhubh 'a' Chromain, with its crosses carved on the walls, became a shelter for the quarrymen working in this exposed spot. The sandstone at Carsaig was quarried from around the 12th century for buildings on Iona, Mull and Lorn. In 1795, after Johnson and Boswell's visit, freestone was also discovered and was used for the new wave of mansion building. Nearby, the modest Carsaig House was built in the 1850s. Today Carsaig House is a country house hotel surrounded by woodlands and sheltered by the hills. The quarry did not continue operations much after the building of Carsaig House, although it did

Opposite top. Rubha na Carraig Geire marble quarry on Iona. (RCAHMS.)

Opposite below. Inivea abandoned township on the island of Mull. (Graeme Waters collection.)

Cruach Sleibhe, the hillside where the tenants of Inivea lived out their lives. (RCAHMS.)

have a brief burst of activity when it was reopened in 1875 to provide stone for the restoration work on Iona Abbey.

Iona itself, of course, was in medieval times the home of the most famous school of stone-carving in Scotland, emulated and admired throughout the west and its exponents commissioned to do work far and wide. The stone from which they created such beautiful swirling images and relief figures was not the stone found on the island itself, however. An anonymous reference to quarrying in the island in 1693 said: 'In this lland is marble enouch whereof the late Earle of Argyle caused polish a piece at London abundantly beautiful.' There are remains to be seen of the marble quarry Rubha na Carraig Geire on the south coast of the island which was operated up to the start of the 20th century. There had been a short-lived operation there, opened by the Iona Marble Quarry in the 1790s after the Swiss surveyor Rudolf Raspé carried out his survey for the 5th Duke of Argyll. The Duke formed a company with the industrialist William Caddell, with Raspé as adviser. The distinctive green marble was beautiful – the table of the high altar of the medieval abbey church had been made from it – but the Duke found it too difficult to transport and his company abandoned work at the quarry. Almost the whole bed of the marble had been removed by 1819 but there was enough left for another spell of excavation when the quarry reopened in 1907. It is from that period that the industrial remains date: a rock-cut reservoir, some machinery, a roughly built quay and a gunpowder store were visible in the mid 20th century. A round angled drystone building known as *Tobhta nan sassunaich*, or house of the Lowlander, sat at the head of the gully. Even here, evolution rather than out-and-out loss was always the order of the day. After the Duke's company abandoned the quarry because of its transport difficulties, the storehouse was converted into a schoolroom in 1794, as the push for universal education began in earnest in the Western Isles.

The need for schools has swelled and fallen away over the centuries in Mull and its satellite islands as populations have come and gone. The islands did not escape the sheep-walks or the shooting parties and the clearances which went along with them. Inivea township on Mull was quite a large settlement on Calgary Bay, built some 250 feet above sea level on the lower slopes of Cruach Sleibhe. About two dozen buildings were clustered in twos and threes with the barns at right angles to the wind to allow a through draught. The houses were made from blocks of local basalt set in clay mortar bonded with pinnings. The external corners were rounded with stones hammer-dressed to a curve and some of the buildings had curved corners inside the houses as well. They were mainly two-roomed cottages about 30 by 20 feet and they had hip-ended roofs with their rafters resting directly on the tops of the walls. None of the internal walls survived to the 20th century, but it was easy to see that some had lintelled windows overlooking the bay. The houses had kailyards and the cultivation was done on a terrace above the houses using the old runrig methods. It has been suggested that one of the ruins may have been a corn-drying kiln. The settlement was lived in during the 18th and early 19th century but Pont's map from the late 16th century shows a farm or township at Inue, which was at that time part of the MacLean of Duart estates. In 1670, rent at 'Imvic' was recorded as £80 Scots a year. In 1739, under the new ownership of the Campbells of Argyll, the 2nd Duke gave one of his new nineteen-year leases to four sitting tenants at £93. 6s. 8d. a year. Forty years later, the place wasn't even mentioned in the census and seems to have been swallowed up by the neighbouring Frachadil farm. It was lost to Langland's map of 1801. In 1817, the land was bought by Captain Allan McAskill of Mornish and the local memory is that it was he who evicted the township's tenants, but other evidence suggests that by then there were few left to make way for the improvements planned by the new laird.

On Ulva, a similar deserted township is to be found at Ormaig, with a ruined cruck-framed corn mill about 700 yards away on the banks of a burn.

The mill, water-driven and very modern when it was recorded in 1807 in Carr's *Caledonia Sketches*, was built from lime-mortared rubble masonry and stood about 32 ft by 18 ft. Inside it had four bays created by cruck couples set in the walls. There were splayed windows in the south-west and south-east walls and the grinding machinery stood in the north-east bay. The mill stones were carried on a framework of timber beams set into putlock-holes (holes for a cross piece of scaffolding) in both the side and gable walls. This framework carried a floor supported by a buttress in the north-east gable wall which in the loft above was lit by a window. The gear cupboard had a slit in the south-east wall to admit light. The mill had two stones of micraschist some 60 inches in diameter. There was a dam on the stream to create a pond north of the mill and a few yards to the south it seems likely that a ruined two-storey building would have been the miller's house. When these ruins were examined by the Commissioners for Ancient and Historic Monuments in the mid 20th century, no kiln was found. Corn-grinding mills can indicate the importance and prosperity of an area. Tenants were thirled to particular mills (they were obliged to take their grain to that mill as part of their tenancy agreement) and the laird granted its operation to the miller of his choice. Modern though this mill may have been at the beginning of the 19th century, its presence would no longer have been necessary as sheep replaced grain and people – and even Ormaig itself – disappeared. Iona was not immune from clearances, but at least in the 19th century, people were not burnt out as they had been when the Vikings torched the island time after time. Staoineig was a settlement in the south of the island and there is evidence from pre-Improvement days. There had been some good pasture there and the valley of *Port na Curaich* was farmed on the runrig system. In medieval times the area was part of the property of Iona convent. By the middle of the 1700s it was part of the lands held in tack by John MacLean before Donald Campbell, the bailie of Tiree, became the proprietor. A turf dyke known locally as *Garadh Dubh St Aoineig* (the black dyke of St Aoineig) delineated its boundaries and parts of it can still be seen, in some places reaching almost four feet high. No remains of houses are left, but there is evidence of summer shielings. The fate of the Staoineig tenants is silently recorded by clearance cairns.

Many of the islands around Iona were linked with Columba's monastery and the nunnery from the 6th century. Some were outposts where hermits lived, sustaining themselves on the land – and of course, it had always been the fertile ground and good grazing which had attracted people to this western fringe of Britain from the very earliest times. Small though some of the islands are, they were still able to sustain cattle and to grow grain. Tiree, bigger than many, was said to have been one of these outposts by those who translated the name as Tir-I, land belonging to Iona. The island is fringed by white sands, is flat and treeless, but was nonetheless able to produce barley in quantity. In that ancient debate about the meaning of the island's name, one suggestion was Tir-ith, old Irish for 'land of corn'. Another suggestion was Tir-reidh, or 'flat land'. Whatever its name, it is an island with a history: some of it living, some of it lost – blown away like the sand swirling in the fierce winds which sweep across it from the Atlantic. It is a place of the unexpected. The Reef in the centre of the island has a sandy base and a layer of rich black soil which the *First Statistical Account* of 1792 recorded as a 'beautiful carpet variegated with flowers'. In that same account, the Reverend McColl, the parish minister, wrote that there were three small licensed stills on the island and four public houses at the ferries and harbours of Tiree and its neighbour to the north, Coll. Some 70 years later there were two licensed inns on Tiree and one on Coll and some 'low tippling houses' to which, of course, the workmen building the Skerryvore lighthouse were attracted like moths to a flame.

Coll and Tiree, just 50 miles to the west of Mull, are very different to Argyll's inner isles and have more of an appearance of the Outer Hebrides. Neither is higher than 455 feet and must therefore have been welcoming to the

Dun Mor broch at Vaul on Tiree – the entrance and interior from the north-west. (RCAHMS.)

Late Neolithic Beaker people who were the first known settlers on both islands. Both islands were fortified and two brochs were built on Tiree: Dun Mor a' Chaolais and Dun Mor at Vaul, both within 650 feet of the sea. Built in the middle of the first century, Dun Mor was inhabited by farmers and potters, and Vaul pottery has become an archaeological byword for the level of sophistication found at the site. They also worked in iron, cast in bronze and spun their clothes. And then suddenly – they were gone. By the third century of the Christian era, the Vaul settlement was abandoned abruptly, having been lived in for perhaps as long as a thousand years.

Their successors seemed to welcome the Irish missionaries who attempted to bring Christianity to this western fringe and the remains of five chapels from the early Christian times have been found on Tiree. Only one of them still shows evidence of its position: St Patrick's Chapel, Ceann a' Mhara, was probably a place where monks lived and worshipped on a site taken over from earlier settlers. Built on Balephuil Bay at the south end of the island, it was polygonal and made from limestone and local rubble. The richness of the crosses and carvings dating from the 6th century in these islands suggests that much more has been lost. At Hynish, Kirkapol and Soroby, however, there are pillar stones and carved slabs from the earliest times, and at Cill Mhairi, Soroby, there is a cruciform slab dating from about the 11th century which seems heavily influenced by the elaborate decoration found on earlier Pictish slabs and Irish high crosses. The medieval church at Soroby has disappeared, as have the chapel and burial ground at Balephetrish, which is marked on the OS map as Cill Fhinnein (the Chapel of St Finnen or Findbarr) to the east of Balephetrish Farm west of Vaul. The chapel and burial ground at Caolas on Tiree, said to have been built on the site of a croft at Crois a' Chaolais (NM081487) are scarcely able to be identified; nor are there any remains left of the chapel and burial ground at Breachacha on the Ardnish of Coll. There had been ruins on the site until a tenant removed them for building in 1846. At Kilbride on Coll, the enclosure of a burial ground was identified but neither the chapel suggested by the name nor any evidence of burials have been found. On Tiree, however, medieval churches have fared marginally better. A parish church was first recorded at Kirkapol in 1375, and along with the church at Soroby was dedicated to St Columba. A chapel there has no recorded history although both church and chapel were within yards of the 'modern' church at the head of Gott Bay. Kirkapol was one of the few sites in the Western Isles outside of Iona where a medieval church and chapel sat together, suggesting monastic activity in the early Christian period. It is here that the largest groups of free-standing crosses, effigies and grave slabs from the early 14th century to

Kirkapol Chapel, Tiree. A reconstructed cross was taken from the medieval chapel to Inveraray for safe keeping. (RCAHMS.)

the time of the Reformation in 1560 are found. A reconstructed cross from Kirkapol was taken to Inveraray Castle; from its inscription it appears to have been commissioned by Finguine, the Abbot of Iona, around 1357 to 1408. Most of the Tiree stones, including those at Soroby, are from the Iona school. The medieval church may have been used until the 18th century but it was abandoned, leaving the ruins of its walls. Kirkapol was one of the two medieval parishes of Tiree until in 1618 it was joined to Soroby and Coll to become the parish of Coll and Tiree – leaving it at risk of becoming one of those unmanageable and neglected parishes described by Dr Johnson. With the post-Reformation lack of ministers, it is doubtful that Kilkenneth Chapel on Tiree or Killunaig Church on Coll would have been much frequented.

Kilmoluag on Tiree suggests yet another chapel – but there are as many names which reflect Viking settlements as there are those which maintain the old Earse language brought by the Irish monks and transmuted into Gaelic. There was no easy transition from those early days of the monks to the more organised, more power-structured medieval times. The Vikings came and they did not come peaceably. The Vaul broch became the grave of a Viking who met a violent death and other corpses from that time of land-hungry young men

Breachacha Castle, Coll. A painting by Poole. (National Gallery of Scotland.)

from the north have been found in the Tiree dunes. Even when the Vikings had gone, there was no peace, as the local families began to feud over strategic areas. It became a time to build serious defences and at Breachacha on Coll a tower-house on the style of Kisimul Castle in the Bay at Barra was erected in the 15th century of Carsaig stone from Mull. There was no water supply and it took most of its protection from the site's natural defences. By the time Boswell and Johnson visited Coll, a house had been built nearby and the laird was using the vestibule of the castle as a prison. Coll had been part of the MacDougall lordship of Lorn in the 13th century. Early in the 14th century, Robert I defeated the MacDougalls and gave their lands to others. Coll went to Angus Og of Islay. Some reshuffling then went on between John of Islay and John of Lorn which put Coll back in the hands of the MacDougalls in 1354 – but with the MacDonalds retaining their superiority. The island later went to John Garbh, son of Alexander Bronnach of Duart and the founder of the Coll MacLeans. It was probably he who built the tower-house in the first half of the 15th century and it became the focus of feuding between the MacLeans of Coll and the MacLeans of Duart. In 1578, the Duart family under Lachlan MacLean took Breachacha and garrisoned it. The earliest castle was then lost under a massive reconstruction programme carried out between 1588 and 1593, when the curtain wall was raised in an effort to keep the Duart MacLeans out. It was to no effect: when Hector MacLean, 6th of Coll, died in 1593, the Duart invasion was renewed, and having taken the renovated castle, the Duarts determined to demolish it and put paid to the Coll defences altogether. The Coll MacLeans did not get the castle back for another three years, and more re-strengthening was done. The civil war in the following century had highlighted a dispute between the Earl of Argyll and the Coll MacLeans. This was settled in 1679, and by the 18th century, the way was clear for Hector MacLean, 13th of Coll, to build himself a house rather than spend money on fortifications. The 1750 mansion was where Dr Johnson and his companion were entertained by 'Young Coll' in 1773. The MacLeans were then proprietors of the centre of the island, while the Duke of Argyll's estate sandwiched them north and south. Young Coll was trying to improve his land and had planted an orchard, which Johnson felt might succeed if it was sheltered by a wall. He had also introduced turnips to the island to feed his cattle throughout the winter – a revolutionary idea at the time. Johnson said the idea had at first been seen as 'the idle project of a young head, heated with English fancies', but the turnips had grown and the hungry sheep and cattle had eaten them and the scheme was slowly being accepted by the islanders.

At the time of the Uprising in 1745, there were around 140 'fencible men' on the island – men between the ages of 16 and 60 who could be called upon to fight. When Johnson visited, the population of the island was around 800 – but only two houses were large enough for their tenants to pay window tax, which was paid on houses with six or more windows. One of them belonged to Coll himself, the other was rented by Mr MacSweyn, the tenant of the farm of 'Grissipol '- a man whose wife could speak only Gaelic but whose hospitality impressed Johnson greatly. That her spoons were horn and not silver was forgiven. Johnson saw a land little cultivated, while Martin Martin discovered that the inhabitants lived on the oats they grew and made their barley into whisky. Johnson certainly found Coll a poor island, where multiple tenancies of farms scarcely fed the whole population and where frequent tragedies at sea must have made the fishing industry seem less than inviting. Tiree, less rocky than its neighbour, was seen by Johnson to be more fertile and even more populous than Coll (Martin Martin said there were more boys than girls on Coll and more girls than boys on Tiree and that 'Nature intended both thefe Ifles or Continent to be matched'). A shop on Coll and two on Mull impressed Johnson, who had by now travelled throughout the islands and seen little of this sort of 'civilisation', but it was a DIY society where every cottage made its own candles, with wicks manufactured from linen shreds, extracted its own oil for

Grishipol House, Coll. Dr Samuel Johnson and James Boswell visited here during their 1793 tour. (RCAHMS.)

lamps, tanned skins and made brogues. The gardens grew potatoes and kail and there were several stills on the island. These cottage industries were lost to the islands when the next century saw the invention of the steam engine: boats imported goods from outside and exported people to the mainland.

Such modernity certainly made the castle on Coll redundant. Not only the castle fell into disrepair, however. Grishipol House, the mid 18th-century laird's house where the MacSweynes lived and entertained Johnson and Boswell royally, despite their horn spoons and whisky served from seashells, became a roofless ruin standing on the south-west shore of Grishipol Bay. Boswell described it as an excellent slated house of two storeys. It had been built by Hugh MacLean and completed around 1754. There was a garret with doocots on either side of its window. The house was harled with local mortar and there was a finish of Carsaig sandstone on the skewputs. The widely spaced windows on either side of the central entrance had squared arrises. The original door was later partially blocked.

Although Breachacha was from a later era, Coll's defences had dated back to medieval times with a fort at Dun Anlaimh on Loch na Cinneachan. Exposed as it was to danger it is surprising that one of the earliest domestic, unfortified houses in Northern Argyll should be on Coll at Breachacha, built with screen walls linking the main block to pavilions. But while conditions for landlords changed for the better in the post-civil-war period and they were able to spend less on fortification and more on domestic and agricultural improvements, life was no better for the poor of the islands than for those on the mainland. Dr Johnson said that not many of the Coll people had been persuaded by what he called 'the American argument' and emigrated to what was being suggested was a kinder land, but on Coll and Tiree the changes in farming meant changes for those who worked on the land. These were islands where the elements could not be ignored. Today, the location of Tiree may be hazy in the minds of many, but it is associated with weather forecasts and its frequent claim to being the place with the longest hours of sunshine in the UK. The flip side is that rain-bearing clouds are carried on to mainland Argyll by gale-force winds.

From early times, vernacular houses here were built to withstand such winds. On Tiree, they had double walls with earth-filled spaces and two doors so that the one facing the blast could be kept shut during gales. However, for many, that was the limit of the snugness of their homes. Instead of wooden doors, many blocked the entrance with thick bundles of heather or straw tightly bound together. There were no chimneys and the smoke from the central hearth found its way through a gap in the roof thatch. The principal rafters rested on the inner wall-head and on angle-corbels. The roof apex was formed by an intersection of rafters. Although these houses are lost to us, we have an idea of their appearance in the remaining 19th-century versions which in essence looked the same but were mortared and had chimneys and fireplaces. The later cottages also had wire netting and stones to keep the thatch secure.

Sorisdale – one of Coll's traditional villages pictured in 1908. (RCAHMS.)

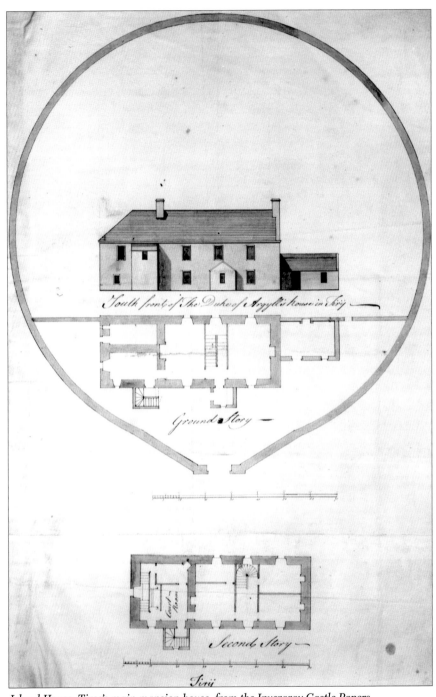

South front of the Duke of Argyll's house in Tiry

Ground Story

Second Story

Tiry

Island House, Tiree's main mansion house, from the Inveraray Castle Papers.
(Reproduced by permission of his Grace the Duke of Argyll.)

But Tiree townships became deserted as the population fell and on both Coll and Tiree, the old summer shielings where cattle were summered fell into disrepair. The remains of a corn-drying kiln were found at the deserted township of Mannel, a reminder of the importance of the Tiree crops. A shieling on the slopes of Ben Hynish on Tiree and another at the north-east tip of Coll at Sorrisdale show even in their ruins the same need for solid building, even for summer shelters.

But agriculture was not the only industry for these islanders. Just as the earliest settlers had worked with iron, bronze and clay as well as raising domestic animals and growing crops, so later populations diversified.

Limestone and marble were quarried at Balephetrish on Tiree and the limestone was probably used to build Island House and the parish church. Turnbull's map of 1768 pinpoints a limestone outcrop here and marble was first recorded in 1764 by Dr John Walker. Both quarries were abandoned before 1800, yet Rudolph Erich Raspé, surveying for the Duke of Argyll in 1789, suggested that this was a good source of marble. The 5th Duke set up an operation in 1791 with Raspé as adviser – a position he held in so many of the Duke's mineral operations which came to so little success, posing the question as to whether Raspé was as good a mineralogist as his employer imagined or whether the Duke simply was a bad businessman. Certainly, the Tiree marble, much admired when blocks were taken to Edinburgh and Inveraray, gave the Duke financial and transport headaches and the place was closed after three years. Bad local workmanship was blamed, as it was so often in such cases. The suggestion was that it was managed by 'workmen apparently ignorant of the use of the feather wedge or other modes of raising unstratified rocks'. The industry, which had been worked as one venture with the marble quarry on Iona, was lost and the marble continued to lie in blocks in the Balephetrish quarry.

Technology, however, was to bring yet another industry to Tiree, and while it came to a natural end it left a legacy which has now become one of the island's main resources at Hynish.

When Alan Stevenson, son of Robert, built his lighthouses at Skerryvore in 1844 and at Ardnamurchan in 1849, the local quarries on Tiree were found to be unsuitable and so pink granite was used from the Old Quarry at Camas Tuath on Mull. It was opened in 1839 for the purpose and for the Skerryvore light, the tallest in British waters, the marble was transported from Camas Tuath in rough blocks to a workyard at Hynish Harbour and Lighthouse Establishment. Hynish, on the southern tip of Tiree, has a small harbour which in 1836 was seen as the most convenient place to set up a workyard where the

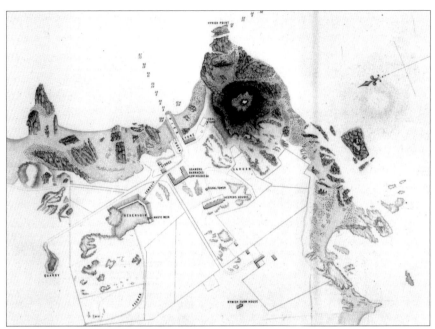

Plan of the establishment at Hynish Harbour, Tiree, for building Skerryvore lighthouse.
Copied from the 'Account of the Skerryvore Lighthouse' by A. Stevenson, 1848. (RCAHMS.)

materials could be prepared for the new lighthouse. When it was found that the
Hynish quarries' granite-gneiss rock wasn't suitable for Skerryvore, the Camas
Tuath marble was shipped into the harbour. The stones from Mull were then
dressed in the Hynish workyard and laid radially on a circular platform before
the next stage of their journey out to Skerryvore where they were finally
assembled. A semaphore tower was built at Hynish to communicate with the
new lighthouse and in 1843 the pier was extended to around 250 feet to provide
a dock for the lighthouse service vessel. Alan Stevenson's own plan of the
Hynish operation, with its seamen's barracks and lighthouse workers' houses,
was published in 1848. When sand blocked the entrance to the dock, an
artificial scouring system was devised and the remains of the reservoir, sluice
mechanism and conduit survived. Although this was obviously going to be a
temporary industry for the island and it was possible that the whole operation
would have been left to rot away, in fact it is now a superb museum and an
excellent outdoor centre. No more gunpowder is needed and no quarrying
takes place but visitors can learn not only about the history of Skerryvore and
the role Hynish played in it, but can also explore the island from quarters used
by the workers and the lighthouse men. Skerryvore itself remains a monument
to Stevenson's engineering skills and the workmanship of the people of Mull

and Tiree, but its interior was lost in a fire in March 1954 and it had to be re-equipped. The original lantern framework of the lighthouse, which stands some 11 nautical miles out from Tiree, survived the blaze. The Skerryvore reef was a dangerous hazard to shipping and an 1814 Act of Parliament authorised the building of the lighthouse. Things did not move quickly however, and after the work had begun in the late 1830s, the first light did not beam out to seamen until February 1844. It was designed and built at a total cost of £90,268 12s. 1d. by Stevenson, who succeeded his father as engineer to the Board of Commissioners in 1843.

An industry of which much less evidence is apparent is the kelp-burning which took place at different times throughout history, no doubt for very different reasons. Remains of small huts on Tiree suggest it was a domestic industry in prehistoric times. Later there were drystone open-ended rectangular kilns as the industry became more important as an 'export' in the late 18th and early 19th centuries. It was back-breaking work which brought little return for the tenants assigned to collect the seaweed from the shore, burn it in the kilns for anything up to eight hours and then pound it into the ash for which their landlords received a cash return. From the end of the 17th century, this ash was used in the making of soda and potash for the glass, soap and linen-bleaching industries. Before the kelp was discovered to be a source of these chemicals, they came from Spain. During the Napoleonic Wars, Spain became off-limits for trade and this new source from the Hebrides and the Orkneys became particularly valuable. In 1790-1, the price of kelp rose from £6 to £10 a ton. At the height of demand, it was worth the modern equivalent of £7.5 millions a year to the Hebrides alone. But it took 20 tons of wet seaweed to produce one ton of ash and when a source of potash was found in Germany, the labour-intensive industry off the west of Scotland dwindled to nothing and the mechanics of the industry were lost.

Like the mainland, the islands are evolving: out of the losses there have so often been gains. Few would wish for people to live in the kind of earthen-floored houses where hens roosted in the kitchen and smoke, trying to escape through a hole in the roof, blackened babies' faces. Few would wish to condemn islanders to travel with cattle in an open 30-foot smack across fierce seas to reach Mull or the mainland. Few would wish to live in a world where there was a need for the grim and menacing fortifications which once studded the coast of Argyll and its islands.

Overleaf. Cairnburgh Castle, Treshnish Islands. A plan by Robert Johnson. Original drawing in the National Library of Scotland. (RCAHMS.)

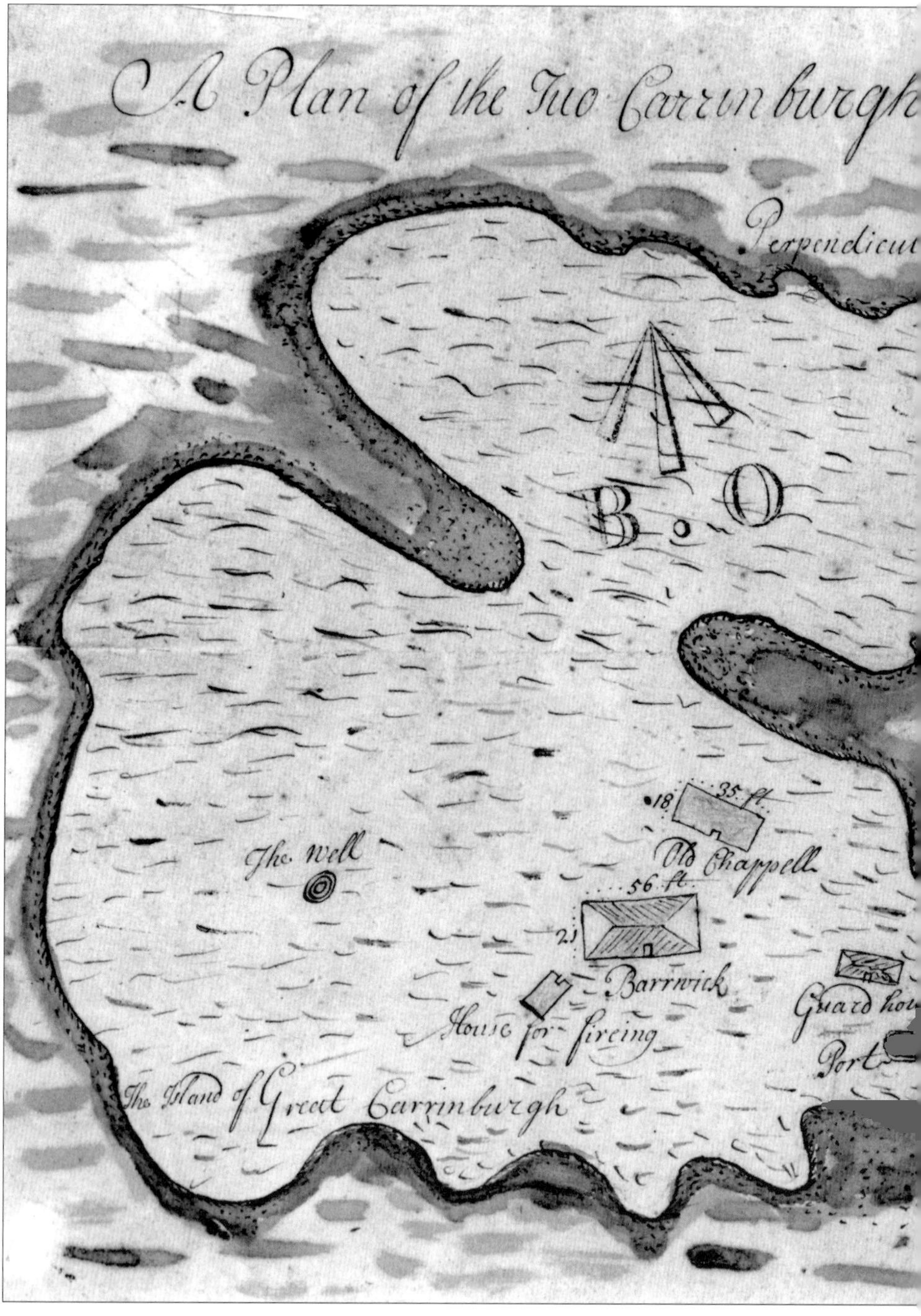

A Plan of the Two Carrinburgh

Perpendicut

B. O

Perpendicut

•18   35 ft.

Old Chappell

·····56 ft.

2í

The well

Barrwick

House for fireing

Guard hou

Port

The Island of Great Carrinburgh

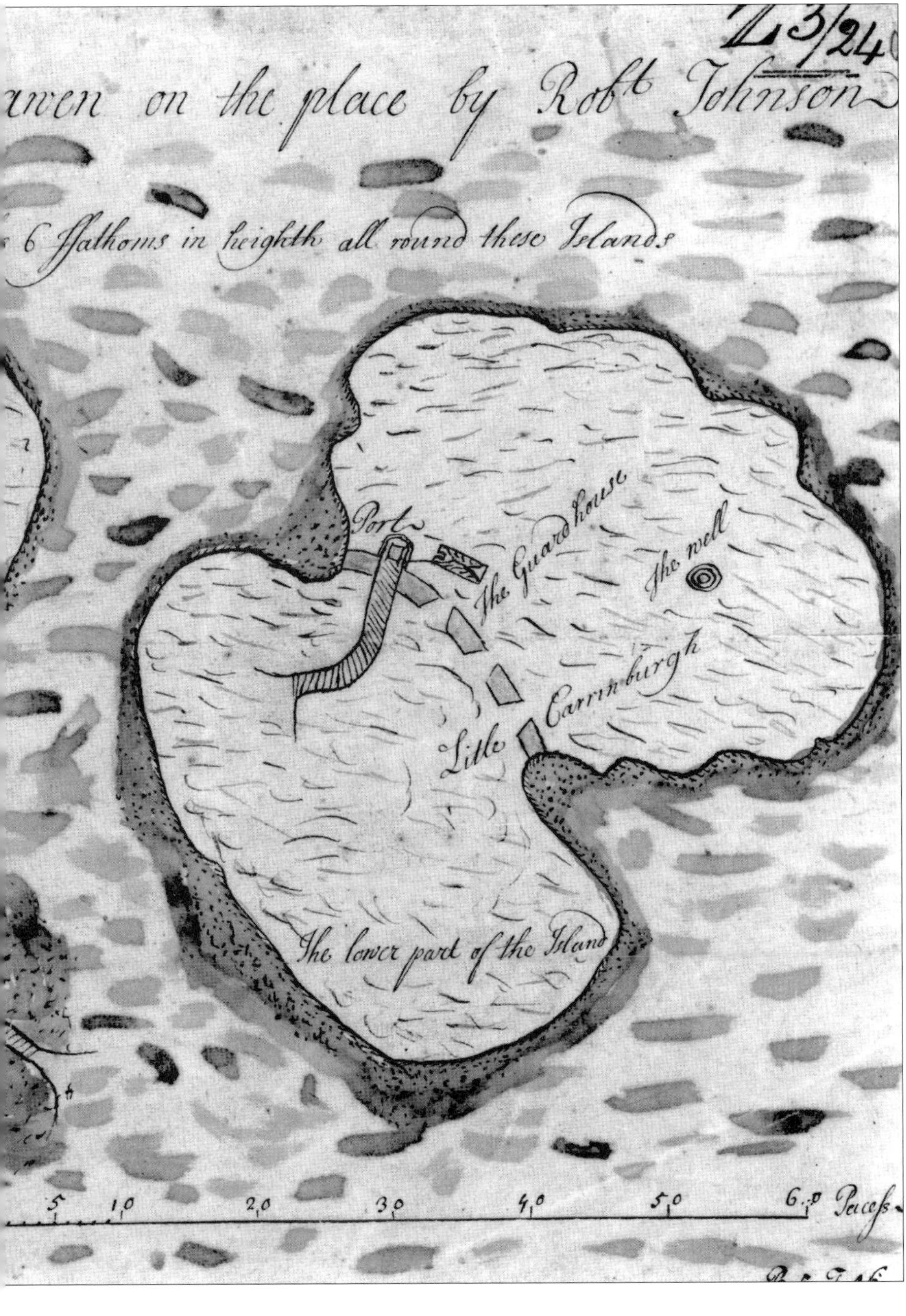

...wen on the place by Robt Johnson

...6 ffathoms in heighth all round these Islands

Port

The Guardhouse

The well

Litle Carrinburgh

The lower part of the Island

Z 3/24

5 10 20 30 40 50 60 Paces

There were feuds between the Duke of Argyll's ferry company set up in 1801 and MacLean of Coll who ran an economy-fare packet boat – but both found there wasn't enough traffic between Coll, Tiree and Mull to merit a large boat. There were no trees on Tiree but there was a boat-builder at Scarinish who made esteemed skiffs from imported larch on oak with cabins made on the south of Hynish Bay at Mannel. The 120-year-old *Heather Bell* came from this boat-builder, but while the passing of such distinctively shaped craft is to be regretted, the coming of the steamers to Coll and Tiree gave people a new freedom, and there was still a need for rowing ferries taking passengers and goods from ship to shore until a new pier was built in 1960. Vehicular ferries introduced in the 1970s changed things yet again, and while discussion continues about the probity of one ferry company having a monopoly in the islands which can dictate prices and timetables, the safety and comfort of CalMac's ferries compared with the boats of yesteryear cannot be discounted.

From another age with a different set of values, we can mourn the order which went out from the Synod of Argyll in 1560 as the fledgling reformed church set about putting the world to rights by declaring that 360 crosses should be thrown into the sea. Should we also mourn the crumbling of fortifications such as 'Castel Loch Hyrbol' as Castle Loch an Eilean at Heylipoll on Tiree was marked on Blaeu's map or the lowering Cairn na Burgh Mor and Beg defences at the northernmost end of the Treshnish islands?

Historically and architecturally they are – were – fascinating, of course. But most who live in castles today find them too big, too cold and too costly. And the fighting is over. In 1678-9, MacLean's garrison held Castle Loch an Eilean – an island fortification in the style of the ancient crannogs – against the 9th Earl of Argyll. It had a drawbridge, later replaced by an embanked causeway which converted the island into a peninsula. In 1700, it was described as 'ruinous' and perhaps it says much for the development of humankind that its stone was used for building material during the building of Island House in 1748. Cairnburgh Castle was of huge strategic importance as far back as medieval times and probably before that. 'Kiarnaborg' was first recorded in 1249 as one of four castles held by Ewan, Lord of Lorn, from King Hakon of Norway. Less than two decades later, the Vikings had left Scotland after the Battle of Largs and the Treaty of Perth and it was taken into the possession of Robert I who gave it to Angus Og of Islay. Angus's son and successor, John of Islay, lost it when he fell foul of David II, but got it back in 1343 under a charter which gave him the keep of the royal castles of Cairnburgh, Iselburgh and Dun Chonnuill in the Garvellach Isles to the north of Jura. The squabbling and in-fighting continued into the next decade when the MacDougalls renounced these three castles on the premise that Cairnburgh would never go to a MacKinnon. In 1390, Donald of Islay, Lord of the Isles, granted the Constabulary of the castles of Cairnburgh and Iselburgh, certain of the Treshnish Islands and lands in Gometra and Mull to Lachlan MacLean of Duart. When John of Fordun made his list of castles in the Western Isles in the 15th century, he said of 'Carneborg' that it was an 'exceedingly strong castle'. It is suggested that Iselburgh was in fact Cairn na Burgh Beg (the cairn of the little castle). Cairn na Burgh Mor means 'the cairn of the big castle'. Cairns in this context are massive rocks rising majestically from the sea, topped by threatening fortifications. These were forfeited in 1504 by the MacLeans of Duart after a rebellion which brought the might of the Scottish navy from Dumbarton to quell it. MacLean took the castle back in 1513 but eventually had it returned legitimately. Royal rents in Kintyre paid for the expense of the custody of the castle and grain for the household came from Tiree. By the end of the century, the MacLeans of Duart granted its custody to the MacLeans of Treshnish. In the civil war it was captured by General Leslie and then held for him by Hector MacLean of Torloisk, who with the MacLeans of Duart were royalists. It must have been a frightening and lonely prospect for the 30 men who were stationed there. It is doubtful that they would have taken time to search for the Iona manuscripts which legend suggests were hidden there for safe-keeping from the Vikings. Towards the end of the 17th century, the 9th Earl of Argyll went after the MacLeans. Having captured Coll and Tiree he demanded that Hector MacLean of Treshnish surrender. Bad weather and MacLean bravery meant the castle stayed with the MacLeans until the 10th earl took it in 1692, four years after William and Mary were installed on the throne. The first Jacobite Uprising saw Cairnburgh in the front line again, but in 1745, it escaped attack. Made from Carsaig sandstone and local rubble, the buildings which still survive date from those ferocious years in the 16th and 17th centuries. Natural defences formed much of the outer walls. The smaller of the twin castles was defended by a breastwork overlooking the approach but the rest was left to the hazardous cliffs.

Modern defences are equally disruptive to ordinary lives but more mobile. The Polaris missiles on the Holy Loch in the mid 20th century left little but 'midden heaps', the altered use of buildings and much social change. The nuclear installations stretching from Rosneath up into Gareloch and Loch Long have scarred the landscape but could leave almost without trace. Past fortifications of Argyll, whatever their state of repair, help create the modern landscape but their purpose should never be forgotten.

CHAPTER 3

LORN:

CATHEDRALS, CASTLES,
BURIALS AND BEECHING

His name was Dr Richard Beeching and he was appointed chairman of the newly formed British Railways Board in June 1961 by a Tory Minister of Transport. His remit was to produce a report on the state of the railways in the UK and to identify uneconomic lines. He was paid extremely well for the time – £24,000 a year – but the far-reaching effects of his four years in post were to cost some Scottish communities much more than a hefty salary. Dr Beeching's report was released in 1963 and in essence recommended cuts to Britain's 17,000 miles of railway track. Although he left the job in 1964 and a Labour government replaced the Tories, the 1965 'Beeching Plan' lopped more than 8,000 miles from the network, closed 2,000 stations and denied 70,000 people their jobs. It was, in fact, the Labour Government which carried out most of the cuts which *The Reshaping of British Railways* report called for. In 1966, Argyll felt the swish of Dr Beeching's axe, but did not benefit from the Transport Act introduced by Labour Transport Minister Barbara Castle in 1968, which introduced a 'social railway' with subsidies. The links which less than a century before had opened up Argyll were severed. Goods had to find alternative routes. Freight was pushed onto inadequate roads – economic disaster in any area of the UK where Beeching's plans had been implemented. But the train in parts of Argyll was used to take children to school, to do the shopping, to visit family in hospital, to get the doctor to patients. A way of life, brief though it may have been, was lost to people living on either side of the corridors created by the Glasgow to Fort William line, the Callander to Oban railway and the link between Oban and Ballachulish. It may well have been true that around half of Britain's stations produced 95 per cent of British

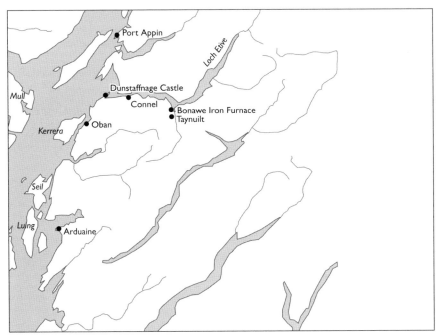

Oban and surrounding area

Railways' revenue, but the cruel amputation was performed in Argyll without thought for the social conditions which Mrs Castle tried too late to address.

The lines had offered industries, hampered for centuries by the difficulties of transport in remote areas, a way of getting their wares to market. The railway had become essential for the heavy industries which existed in this part of Argyll; indeed, the slate quarries at Ballachulish were the original reason for the Ballachulish branch of the Callander–Oban railway. The line ran from Connel Ferry to Ballachulish and turned a 'remote' area into a busy crossroads. Today, roads follow the route of the track, but when the railway was built, roads were little more than paths.

The slate quarries had been in existence since at least 1693, when the Stewarts of Ballachulish opened them as a business venture. Although that company went bankrupt in 1862, the quarries remained open. Three decades later, the West Highland Railway (Ballachulish Extension) Act was passed. It wasn't an easy line to construct, but then again, the main line from Callander to Oban had presented its own range of problems. That had all started with a new locomotive shed at Stirling, built in 1850 for Scottish Central Railway. This was in time used for freight locomotives and the Callander and Oban Railway. These companies were, of course, privately owned and were part of the exciting spirit of industrial revolution which had gripped Britain from the early

Achnacloich – shut down by the Beeching Axe. Another aspect of the Appen way of life that has been lost. (Ewan Crawford collection.)

part of the 19th century. Some projects, such as the Glasgow and North Western Railway, were over-ambitious and companies had their fingers badly burned. By the 1860s, however, investors saw the railways as a safe bet once more, and as Oban had grown from very small beginnings into a hub of west-coast steamer services, Oban businessmen pushed for a rail link. The route to Callander was 71 miles long and chosen because it was the cheapest option. Callander was the terminus of the Caledonian Railway from Dunblane and therefore would connect Oban to all the main cities overland. Not everyone was convinced that this was a good idea and there was an investment shortfall. A stop-gap plan was to build a temporary terminus at Tyndrum and coaches and horses linked passengers to Oban. This part of the line was laid by Blythe and Westland, the Edinburgh engineers, whose first innovation was a series of bowstring girder iron bridges from Callander to Strathyre. By the 1870s, the cash became available to complete the line, and engineer John Strain was hired to lay track to allow the first steam train to whistle its way into Oban in 1880. This was a difficult stretch, with the Pass of Brander forcing Caledonian Railway to design new small-wheeled locomotives for the task. Stones frequently fell on the single-track line here and a system was devised to warn drivers. It had taken 16 years from the Royal assent to the arrival of a train in Oban's new station, but it was welcomed with unprecedented enthusiasm. People from the Highlands and Islands came to see Oban station as a landmark of homecoming and departure. It was a place of assignation, of romance, of heartbreak and of joy.

In 1903, the promised branch line to Ballachulish was opened, seven years after the Act granting permission for its operation. It ran from Connel Ferry and was constructed by the contractors Robert MacAlpine and Company. It called for the creation of two large bridges: the one at Connel Ferry was the second-largest cantilever bridge in the world and spanned the Falls of Lora where the sea meets Loch Etive and creates a change in depth in a narrow channel. It was designed by Formans and McCall in association with H.M. Brunel and E. Crutwell, famous names indeed, if only for their links with the London Tower Bridge design. The Arrol Bridge and Roofing Company of Glasgow built it at a cost of £42,837. The station at Connel Ferry had five platforms: three through platforms and two bay platforms at either end. The trains came down from Oban, reversed, then crossed the bridge for the journey to Ballachulish, crossing the Creagan Bridge on the way. This one also came from the stable which designed and built Connel Bridge and it cost an estimated £11,642. 7s. 9d. The line, which had a concrete base, was single-track with passing places in the stations. Connel Ferry bridge had it own history. Initially, local people who wanted to cross the loch used a charabanc which had been converted to run on rails. When automobile traffic increased, the trains carried cars, with loading ramps at either end. After the closure of the railway in 1966, the bridge was converted into a road bridge with traffic lights. A small station at North Connel with a timber platform and timber shed disappeared when the road layout was altered. The line ran through Benderloch, where there was a two-platform station which partially disappeared under landscaping, and a car park. The Connel Bridge company gave a bell to the local church, St Modan's, which suggests that 'sweeteners' are no modern phenomenon. A goods station was built at Barcaldine to the north of Benderloch with a wooden passenger halt; then the line went across the

Connel Bridge – began its life as a rail link taking freight from Ballachulish.
(Michael Hopkin collection.)

Above. Benderloch, 1907. Black's Stores and the track through Appin. (Michael Hopkin collection.)

Left. Duror Station and the station-master who knew every passenger. (Les Howett/Ewan Crawford collection.)

Creagan viaduct, near the Creagan station. A new road bridge meant the end of this particular landmark. Creagan station itself had an island platform but station and platform have been subsumed within a holiday site. The Appin station, with the now renovated Stalker Castle as a backdrop, had two platforms. Then came Duror, where Mr John Chalmers was stationmaster in the 1920s. This station has become a house and Kentallen station became a hotel and restaurant called the Hollytree – not a name plucked at random, but chosen because a holly tree was planted every quarter of a mile when the line was being built. In the days of the train, a ferry ran from a pier there to Fort William, and there was a station at Ballachulish Ferry (itself lost when the road bridge was built in the late 20th century) before the station at Ballachulish itself. The ferry station had a single platform and a shelter, but the building has long gone. Ballachulish station had two platforms and the goods line ran from north of the station to the slate quarries which themselves had a network of narrow-gauge lines. It disappeared under a housing development: the goods shed became a garage and the old station building was turned into a GP's clinic.

In its heyday, this line carried students to high school in Oban, milk and livestock to Corson's Mart in Oban, and on the return journey, brought medicines for what was then known as 'the wee hospital' on the side of Loch Linnhe, now Craig Linnhe guest house. The guard used to throw the parcel of

Top. Loch Awe hotel and the complex rail lines which are no longer needed.
(Michael Hopkin collection.)

Above. Taynuilt Station – the attractive timber building was destroyed by fire.
(Michael Hopkin collection.)

medicines from the train to save the nurses having to go four miles into Ballachulish to collect them at the station. The slate and the aluminium from the Kinlochleven British Aluminium Factory went on freight trains and the community thrived with the help of the artery for 63 years, until the Beeching closure on 26 March 1966.

On the main Callander-Oban line, an extension line ran from Tyndrum to the lead mines. Tyndrum Lower Station is still open, although one platform has been demolished; Falls of Cruachan is only used in summer for visitors to the hydro-electric scheme; only one platform remains in use at Loch Awe; the Awe Crossing loop has closed and the signal box house has been demolished. Taynuilt's timber station building was destroyed in a fire, Achnacloich station closed, Connel Ferry itself is reduced to a single platform, while Oban station, once a glittering glass-canopied Victorian masterpiece, was demolished in 1988. The ferries for the islands leave from the harbour here and a modern shopping mall obscures the former entrance. Oban Station's glory days have been deleted but the memories linger on.

Despite the lack of a beautiful station, Oban is still an essential stop for 21st-century tourists, just as it was for the Victorians. But when the first steamboats arrived, transporting people from Glasgow via the Crinan Canal north to Fort William and on to Inverness, the most direct route of the day, Oban was as old as time and as young as the new fangled *Comet* itself. It had sheltered the Mesolithic incomers in its caves and in the Bronze Age, timber

Gutting herring in Oban at the height of the fishing industry's presence in the town. (Michael Hopkin collection.)

round houses were built. A major archaeological project sponsored by Historic Scotland, Highlands and Islands Enterprise, Tesco plc and William Low plc, and directed by Clive Bonsall and Mark Macklin of Aberystwyth University has discovered 21 new caves and rock shelters and almost 300 archaeological sites. This project was hampered by housing and commercial developments and road building, but that is the very nature of Argyll. It welcomes newcomers, allows them to flourish, lets them fade away as new blood gushes into its veins. It does not need archaeologists to confirm that the site of today's seaport and tourist centre must always have been attractive to man. Its harbour is sheltered and a natural place from which to fish the surrounding waters. But its steep backdrop meant that approach and exit would always be most easily achieved from the sea. It was protected by the island of Kerrera but because it was easier in pre-steam days to land cattle from the islands on Kerrera and then ferry them to the south of Oban on the mainland, Oban remained a tiny fishing settlement and a place where seafarers would call in to trade but not to stay. The fishing industry was one which was vital to the existence and then the growth of the town. When visitors started arriving by steamer, the sights and smells which greeted them spoke of herring. Like the fishing ports of Loch Fyne, Oban's quayside was awash with herring guts, and the men, women and children who wielded the sharp knives to clean the catches couldn't move for barrels. The dark-sailed fleet went out on the tide to chase the silver darlings and came back to warm themselves with whisky from the town's distillery.

Kerrera Ferry – a route for passengers and for black cattle from the islands to the mainland. (Michael Hopkin collection.)

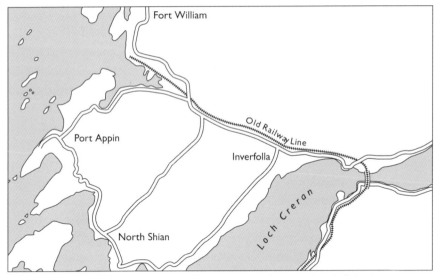

Lost ferries and railways have changed lives in Appin. (Appin Historical Society Collection.)

The drovers from the islands would also take heat from the product of the Oban distillery, now the property of foreigners, but unlike the late Victorian railway station and the fish gutters still part of the Oban scene. The men and cattle came in open boats from Tiree, Coll and Mull and a complex network of droving and swimming based on the Kerrera axis has been described earlier. Alcohol obviously played its role down the centuries because there were three inns on the tiny island of Kerrera in the days when 2,000 cattle were ferried in from the bigger islands. Passengers frequently had to stay on the island several days because of the weather and it was a rough and ready place with neither drove roads nor slipways for the boats until the middle of the 1800s when the cattle traffic had already diminished greatly. It wasn't until 1832 that a road between the two Kerrera ferries, north and south, was opened.

Oban's own ferry routes, which today take cars, goods and passengers to Mull, Coll and Tiree, the Uists, Barra and Colonsay, were very different in the days when it was scarcely on the map. The important place then was Lismore, where monks had developed a religious order in early Christian times and where a medieval cathedral was built. Viewed today as something of a backwater approached either by road through Appin or by water up Loch Linnhe, this island was once the geopolitical centre of Northern Argyll. An island ferry from Oban in modern times has not proved viable. In earlier centuries it would have been an essential route. Then as now, however, the shortest ferry was from Port Appin and perhaps because of its long history as the home of a church of a different persuasion, in 1643 the Minutes of the Synod of Argyll recorded that kirk services at Appin were disrupted because the ferryman refused to take the minister there from Lismore. This minute perhaps gives the older perspective: today, Port Appin is a busy little village bustling even out of season with visitors; then, it was a convenience for the hub of activity, Lismore. Yet even in 1752, there was a demand by John Campbell of Fiart on Lismore to the Commissioners of Supply for Argyll to establish a regular ferry and for quays to be made in specific harbours. Progress was slow but by 1832, two boats and two men were operating out of Lismore. Then the steamers became established and a steamboat pier was built. In 1874, Donald MacFarlane had the contract from the Airds Estate to rent the ferry and ferry house at Port Appin. He paid £5 a year rent for the two and was responsible for a quarter of the repairs to the boat. As one of the ferries was a large cattle-boat, he may have found even that expensive to meet, and there was also a small passenger ferry to maintain and run. He offset his costs by helping the pier master at the steamboat pier and was paid £8 a year. He was able to charge 6d. a passenger, 9d. a horse, 6s. for a four-wheeled carriage and 3s. for a boatload of furniture. As in most agreements over ferry rights, the heritor and his family travelled free and Donald had to give shelter to his passengers in his house if the weather was bad and they couldn't travel. This short ferry journey survives, but many more around Appin and Loch Linnhe have been lost, as have those ferries used by the drovers (and passing armies) further south in Lorn. On Loch Creran, a couple of miles south of Port Appin, a ferry operated between North and South Shian, saving 15 miles on the Oban to Fort William journey. The crossing at Creagan, where the railway and then road bridges were later built, saved just half that distance. According to Walter Weyndling[13] neither of these ferries was seen as reliable, and in the 1700s the Argyll Road trustees sought to create another crossing. Certainly, when Dorothy Wordsworth made the Shian crossing in 1803 she was afraid she'd lose her horse, but things improved in later years and sufficient people were using the ferry, then operating with two men and two boats, to merit an inn being built on each side of the loch. When Lord Cockburn travelled from Ballachulish to Oban in 1848, the journey took seven and a half hours by coach and ferry. In his *Circuit Journeys*,[14] the Court of Session judge described his 9 September expedition as 'a drive of singular magnificence'. Unfortunately, the weather meant that much of that magnificence was lost in thick fog, rain and high wind but the judge and his party – son George, George's wife, daughter Joanna and friend Marion Thomson – were impressed nonetheless. They covered 26 miles, excluding the two ferries. Lord Cockburn said that the Shian crossing was over

Ballachulish railway junction on Loch Leven, 1908. The slate quarries made this a busy freight line. (Michael Hopkin collection.)

a mile and the one at Connel about quarter of a mile. Fresh horses from Oban had been waiting for them on the south side of Shian. They travelled in a heavy carriage which the horses refused to pull uphill with their passengers aboard, so the party were wet the whole day. He wrote candidly: 'Like an idiot, I let us be put into the same open boat with the carriage at Shean [*sic*], though the sea was as rough as a violent headwind could make it in a space one and a quarter mile wide, and we only had two oars, each with two rowers.' The crossing had therefore taken over an hour, the carriage had swung about, the 'Celts' who had charge of the party 'jabbered and roared' [presumably in Gaelic] and it was, all in all, a frightening experience. 'Mrs George was in dreadful agitation. Marion resolutely composed, though in great alarm.' Lord Cockburn wished he had waited for a separate small boat for the party and let the coach be taken over on its own, but as he remarked: 'They are disgraceful ferries, having too few boats and none of them good; no landing places; no planks, or gangways, or cranes; no men, excepting such as can be withdrawn for the occasion from their proper land occupations.' The muddle, the mix of passengers, animals and carriages, the lack of rowing skills and the 'loud, discordant, half-naked, and very hairy Celts' did not impress Lord Cockburn, so his remarks about the magnificence of the scenery are doubly impressive. He put this confusion down to the lack of traffic on the route and the 'insolvency of the lairds' whose responsibility it was to run such ferries.

Conditions changed very little in the period between the building of the main Callander-Oban railway line and before the Ballachulish railway line was built, passengers for Appin left the train at Connel and still travelled by coach to South Shian for the ferry. During this time, between 1880 and 1903 when the branch line was built, mail for Appin travelled on the Oban to Ballachulish and Fort William steamer. It was put onto a small boat at Port Appin and taken to Appin. This was an improvement on the previous system: from the 1840s when the penny post was introduced, mail was carried on foot by a postman who went from Taynuilt to Bonawe Ferry, Barcaldine, Creagan Ferry and on to Appin. It is to be hoped someone gave him a dram – or at least a cup of tea – on the way. As more people began to write letters, the mailbags got heavier, and when the railway arrived in Oban, the mail was taken by train to Appin. With the closure of the Ballachulish branch line, which had improved communication so much for the people of Appin, the mail was put onto a bus. That system was replaced by an arrangement for Appin post office staff to collect the mail from Oban.

The Creagan ferry was lost when the railway bridge was built in 1902 and the Shian ferry became the province of travelling people and tourists. In the early 20th century it still wasn't in the best of condition despite the fact that the fares went up to a shilling at the outbreak of the First World War: it had rotten planks and a propensity to take in water. To cross on the Shian ferry, passengers had to write ahead to North Shian – although this was when a postcard sent in the morning would arrive in the afternoon, so perhaps it wasn't too inconvenient. The rowing boats took 12 minutes to cross in good weather, rather than the hour and more which Lord Cockburn experienced in that September storm. When motor-boats took over during the Second World War, the journey time was cut to five minutes. Passengers and farm stock still travelled together in an 18-foot beam motorboat, but even this fell out of favour as motor traffic increased and the roads improved after the war. The last ferry ran in 1948.

A tourist haven today, this was not always a land of peace and tranquillity as the menacing castles around these waters testify. Argyll was won through the strength of the 3rd-century Irish invaders under the leadership of Erc, who then gifted Lorn, Cowal and Kintyre to his descendants. These Celts came to a land which had already been inhabited by people whose chambered burial cairns – like those at Port Sonachan on Loch Awe, Dalineum on Loch Nell and on Lismore itself – would be stone-robbed, stripped of their Beaker vessels and vandalised for their flints and Neolithic tools. No doubt each generation of incomers, from the early Beaker people through the Vikings to the land-enclosing lairds of recent centuries, has been as guilty as the next. The monks who followed in the wake of the Irish invaders cleared land to farm. The loss of prehistoric treasures was not always wilful – and sometimes a flint or an axe head will come to light millennia after they were first lost. 'Misplaced' has often been found to be a better word.

There are so many sites – some no more than a pile of stone-robbed rubble, some townships, some villages – where names are prefixed by 'kil', showing the presence of Early Christian religious men and women and their places of worship. Lorn had two monastic sites – one at Cladh a' Bhearnaig on Kerrera which shows evidence of being Irish in origin because of its divided enclosed area; one on a promontory site at Kilmaha on the north-west shore of Loch Awe, where there are remains of a number of buildings, rock carvings and two carved stones dating from the Early Christian period. The Kilmaha rock carvings date to the 7th or 8th century AD, but on the island of Lismore in Loch Linnhe there is evidence that as early as the 6th century, there was a church dedicated to St Maluag or Lugaidh, an Irish religious who founded an order on the island just a little later than Columba was founding his own order on Iona. Nothing from that time remains except perhaps the circular enclosure which is thought to have marked out the confines of that early monastery. What has survived are ruins of the nave and choir of a later medieval church – and the choir was restored to become the parish church. The island of Lismore is a hospitable ten miles long and a mile and a half wide. The Gaelic name (*lios mor*) means 'great garden', and that is what it presented itself as to Maluag and his followers.

The area of Appin takes its name from the Lismore cathedral. The Gaelic *Apuin* meant Abbey Lands and these were the lands of the St Maluag abbey on Lismore. Lismore in prehistoric times, just one of many islands in Lorn and Lochaber, and Port Appin, Portnacroish and Cuil Bay have raised beaches which remind us that the sea level then was some 45 feet higher than it is today. Climate change in the millennium before the Christian era meant an exodus of population from this area, but as the rain decreased and the climate got warmer, the Picts moved back in to build their brochs, fish and grow crops. At Tirfuir ('cold land') on Lismore, a broch dating to the first few centuries of the Christian era was still occupied when Maluag came to the island around AD 563. *Lios* can also mean a fortified place, according to *Dwelly's Gaelic Dictionary*, so perhaps the two meanings come together here on the island. Whatever the meaning, the first holy ground in this area was consecrated by Varalmus, one of Maluag's followers. Maluag travelled extensively in Scotland, but Lismore claims the saint as its own, and while the buildings of his day have crumbled, his pastoral staff survives on the island in the care of the Livingstone family, its hereditary guardians. St Kieran of Clonmacmois – known as the

The island of Lismore was once the centre of ecclesiastical power in Argyll – Tirfuir (or 'Tirafoor') Castle was one of its defences. (Michael Hopkin collection.)

apostle of Kintyre – also worked from Lismore, and the remains of his island chapel are at Kilcheran. These islands in sheltered Loch Linnhe were a hotspot for sainthood in the 6th century, and to the west of Lismore on the tiny island of Bernera there are the remains of yet another chapel where Saint Columba is said to have preached in the shade of a yew tree. As the monastery on Lismore grew, the name of Apuin or Appin came to include the wider area stretching north and east on the mainland. The tranquillity of the holy place seems not to have been disturbed until the arrival of the Norsemen. Territory was disputed and Castle Coeffin was built on Lismore by the invaders.

Even before the Vikings had left the west of Scotland after the Battle of Largs, the Cathedral Chapter of Lismore had been constituted in 1249 and it is possible that the cathedral church had already been founded around 1189. Although there are no remains from earlier than the 14th century, building went on over the next two centuries using local limestone and whinstone rubble with dressings from the quarries at Ardtornish. It was never to be an ornate cathedral. It had no aisles and only one chapel on the north side of the presbytery. Its doors were of a unique design for the age and the area. The bases of the nave walls, about 124 feet long, were strengthened with slabs of slate and in the choir a huge stone gallery was erected in late medieval times over the ornamental partition separating the choir from the nave and replacing an original timber screen. The choir walls were around four feet thick and a semicircular-headed doorway had greenish sandstone dressings which may have come from Barnacarry or Ardentallen. When it had been decided that Lismore would be the site of a new cathedral, Argyll was part of the massive

Dunkeld diocese. In 1249, the money was not coming in for the building and not everyone wanted it on this remote island. The building did go up, however, but by 1411 it was already in disrepair because there had been plagues, famine and wars and no-one had enough money for its upkeep. Distant though he was, the Pope heard of these problems and gave financial support to get it back to its original state. A century later, in 1512, James IV, the builder king, was writing to Pope Julius II saying the cathedral was in ruins – no doubt after one of his visits to Castle Stalker. He had his motives: he wanted to transfer the bishopric to Kintyre and build a cathedral at Saddell on the site of the Cistercian monastery which was by then simply a lay organisation trying to survive in another crumbling building. Saddell was more accessible from Dumbarton, more financially viable than Lismore because the revenues of the abbey had been annexed to the bishopric of Argyll, and it was politically strategic in terms of personnel. As a decorative stone gallery over the choir screen went up about this time, it seems that the king's letter was not entirely honest in terms of his description of the state of the Lismore building. Whether the Pope ever received the letter asking for Saddell to become the heart of the diocese, Lismore remained the cathedral church – a dangerous title in the face of the Reformation when the iconoclasts meant business. In whatever state James IV found the building, after 1560 it certainly did become a ruin and a tower which had been added to the west of the building decayed. In the coming century, the civil war interrupted the training of Presbyterian ministers; this area had Episcopal leanings and was therefore at odds with mainstream Scottish thought, and by 1679 the cathedral was roofless. The neighbouring parish of Appin and Duror had its own church and the whole area's economy was in ruin anyway, so it wasn't until 1749 that the building was given the attention it so badly needed. In that year, much change was wrought. Dressed sandstone was taken from the then ruined nave and used to build the Presbyterian manse and its barn the following year. In time, the cathedral choir was converted into the parish church, and after some bad restoration work in 1900, the mid-20th century saw modern plaster taken from the stone screen's archway and other medieval features in the choir exposed once more. Not all the efforts of the past have been lost to time and 'modernisation' and the 1950s excavations at least show the extent of the original cathedral.

Other chapels, like Killean, have indeed crumbled to dust, however. Cill-an-Suidhe on Lismore, built in medieval times, leaves nothing more than a circular ditched enclosure. Clachan on Lismore may have been an Early Christian burial place. Around half a dozen sites in Lorn have the name *Anaid*, usually associated with an ancient chapel or cemetery, but yield no evidence of

Killean, site of a Celtic chapel on the island of Lismore. (Michael Hopkin collection.)

their past. The graveyards of many of the parish churches and chapels from late medieval times in Lorn were in use long after the buildings themselves collapsed. Despite the Reformation, a hundred late medieval crosses and funerary monuments were recorded by the Commission for Ancient and Historic Monuments as surviving in Lorn, mostly carved by the Loch Awe School. Not in the same league as the Iona carvers, the Loch Awe craftsmen travelled the area taking commissions and after 1500 they turned to more domestic monumental sculpture, no doubt shrewdly to meet the demands of a market which no longer wanted elaborate religious carving.

Does cold weather make populations more aggressive? In medieval times, the west coast climate took another turn for the worse – but there were perhaps more political than climatic reasons why local clan chiefs became more territorial and started building their forts and castles. With the departure of the Vikings, war lords were out to stake their territory while the royal household wanted to make sure this vulnerable western fringe remained in Scottish hands. Lorn has more fortifications from this period than are to be found in the rest of Argyll. Many survive, though often in greatly altered form from their 12th- or 13th-century appearance. Innis Chonnel went up ahead of many of the rest in the 13th century. Little survives from that era but the roofless remains of the 15th-century remodelling of the castle show courtyard buildings and a first-floor hall. The episcopal castle of Achadun was built before 1300. The remains are from that date and indicate a large square courtyard with stone buildings. One of the entrances had a drawbridge. Among many others was Maiden's

The imposing castle Gylen on the island of Kerrera was occupied for only a few decades. (Michael Hopkin collection.)

Castle at Glensanda on Shuna, off Luing; Castle Coeffin (a ruined 13th-century tall house restricted in size by its site) and Achaduin on Lismore; Dunollie (built by the powerful MacDougall Lords of Lorn overlooking the north entrance to Oban bay where Dalriadan rulers had earlier constructed a fort and one of Lorn's major tower-houses – four storeys high and threatening); Gylen on Kerrera, an L-shaped tower which was a late 16th-century residence of the MacDougalls; Dunstaffnage; the Black Castle at Benderloch; and Castle Stalker in Appin. There were also artificially constructed islets with timber defences dating from the 14th and 15th centuries, like those at Loch Nell, Loch Tulla, Loch Tromlee, Loch n' Sreinge and Loch a' Phearsain – the latter, south of Oban near Melfort, was enclosed by a drystone wall and occupied right up until the late 17th century.

Some are only partly in ruins, like the 13th-century castle at Dunstaffnage, once home of the Scottish coronation stone. This was originally an impressive enclosed quadrangle with three cylindrical angle towers and a curtain wall punctuated by fish-tailed arrow slits. Built by MacDougalls in the 13th century, it was confiscated by Robert the Bruce in 1309, who put it in the hands of the Campbells. A continuous walkway around the parapet disappeared in the rebuilding of the castle in the 15th and 16th centuries and other alterations were made as it was snatched back and forth in various skirmishes. It was in

Campbell hands when it was gifted to the nation in 1958. Four miles north of Oban, this was an important defence at the entrance to Loch Etive and the Lynn of Lorn. Abandoned as a private residence in 1810, only the gatehouse remains inhabited – but it has become as much of a landmark image for the Oban area as Castle Stalker has become for Appin. Stalker was built in the 15th century by the Stewarts, then Lords of Lorn, to replace a former MacDougall fort. The castle hosted James IV when he was showing his presence in the Highlands as an authoritarian strategy, but in later centuries the Stewarts and Campbells batted it back and forth as each family went in out of favour with the monarchy. Pro-Jacobite in the 18th century, the Stewart followers were invited to surrender at Castle Stalker after Culloden. It was a time of suppression for Appin – its regiment was in Prince Charles Edward's front line at Culloden and had shown bravery at Prestonpans, Clifton and Falkirk. There were 300 fencible men in that regiment – around the figure for the whole population in the 21st century – of whom 94 died and 64 were seriously injured. Of the survivors, according to Appin Historical Society, many became travellers.[15] Those who returned to surrender at Castle Stalker were treated well by the 4th Duke of Argyll, acting for the Government – a very different story from that further north in Morvern and Ardnamurchan – but from that time the castle fell into disrepair. In the mid 20th century, the Allward family bought and renovated the castle, but while this iconic building was eventually saved for the Appin landscape, because of the Stewarts' allegiances, much of Appin's population was lost. Poverty drove people south or to the New World.

Dunstaffnage Castle on Loch Etive was once of the most importance defences in Argyll. (Michael Hopkin collection.)

The Napier Commission's report on the conditions in the Highlands led to crofting legislation in the 1880s which gave land rights to tenants. Poor laws also helped ease the situation but lost settlements such as the one above Taraphocain Farmhouse in Glen Creran, where there are also the remains of a grain-drying kiln, show the extent to which Appin suffered. This corner of Argyll, known to the outside world for little more than the romance of allegiance to Charles Edward Stewart and the tragedy of the infamous 'Appin murder' (Colin Campbell of Glenure, factor of the Stewarts' confiscated lands, was slain, prompting cruel government reprisals) had been a busy place of subsistence farming, mining and charcoal burning. It could sustain weavers and shoemakers. At Invercreran there was a lead mine and miners' cottages sat below Glasdrum farm. On the shores of Upper Loch Creran, there are the remains of charcoal burners' huts and the platforms where they worked to produce charcoal for the Bonawe smelting furnace. In the 18th century, the woods there were coppiced to produce the fuel for the furnace, a good earner for the local landlords. A lime kiln was also in production on this part of the loch. The old route from Loch Etive to Appin followed Glen Ure and across Glen Creran. It was a well-trodden route with an inn, long since gone, on the hillside in Glen Creran. Much of Appin hinterland has now become Glen Creran and Glen Duror Forests, the 20th-century Forestry Commission blanketing the past.

Many of the houses of the powerful of the past have become the pleasure palaces of the present, their exteriors to a great extent preserved, their interiors often lost in a maze of bars and en suite bathrooms. Druimneil offers accommodation in the 'big house', self catering in the coach-house. The early 18th-century Appin House, built by Robert Stewart, 8th of Appin, is a country house hotel – but a very different version of its former self. Originally a two-storey building, it was enlarged to three storeys – probably, according to Michael Davis,[16] by Hugh Seton of Touch, in the late 18th century. A one-storey south-east wing was added abround 1883 and the mansion, with its small classic windows, was embellished with pinnacles, balustraded parapets and an entrance porch. In 1965, the main block and offices were demolished, leaving the 1831 south-east wing which was extended by a single-storey modern building. Tourism has helped some of these architectural treasures to survive. Some have been changed out of all recognition: Fasnacloich House, famous for its gardens, was pulled down and rebuilt, while others have gone the way of the vernacular houses – lost to time.

In times of poverty, man the world over seeks solace – and in Argyll that often came from whisky. Barley was grown in the fields of Appin and was milled at small water mills, such as the one at Kinlochaich farmhouse. The system of thirling operated, with tenants of the Stewarts of Appin required to take their grain to specified mills as part of their tenancy agreements. But the stills in the hills where the whisky was made were in the main illegal, secret affairs. Whether it was an illicit distillation which was served in the inns along the road from Loch Creran through the Strath of Appin to Duror is not known – the ruins of the inns are lost, let alone the origins of their beverages. A locally brewed beer would also have been served in these inns and at the ferry inns – as it was in households in days when neither tea nor coffee were part of the domestic scene of the poor. In 1737, there was an inn and brewstead at Portnacroish run by Duncan MacColl, whose son fought with the Appin Regiment in 1745. In 1860, the brewer there was John Buchanan. Today, the inn is a private house. Brewing, like distilling, wasn't always done in places where alcohol was officially sold. Donald Stewart, another rebel, brewed in a hovel at Tycharnan on the slopes of Loch Laich, but there are few remnants of the building two-and-a-half centuries later. Nor is there much evidence of the brewstead at the Rhugarbh ferry inn where a boat crossed to Barcaldine. Lachlan Paterson of Mid Lorn brewed there from 1770 to 1799, but now the ferry is gone, and of the two ruined houses which remain, it isn't known which was his brewstead.

If the fishers, farmers and ferrymen enjoyed their whisky (and Lord Cockburn's journals indicate that the hirsute Gaelic-speaking part-time ferrymen he encountered on his Loch Creran adventure certainly did) then how much harder drinkers were the tough slate workers of Ballachulish? The North Lorn village on Loch Leven was once and is now a quiet Highland village. But in 1693 this 'village of the narrows' (*baile a'chaolais*) was marked out for change when a gang of slate quarriers on their way from the slate islands south of Oban to Dunkeld noticed a seam of slate as they passed through the west end of the village. Not men to miss a chance, they told the local heritor, Stewart of Ballachulish, who employed them and some local men to quarry the seam. The community which grew there in the coming three centuries was founded on slate. The quarry grew to four levels above its floor and despite bankruptcy in 1862, by 1875 it was at its peak, employing 587 men and manufacturing and shipping out 26 million slates a year. The tiny township of 1,693 had grown into a village with a population of 2,500 and the people who lived and worked there were proud to know that Ballachulish slate roofed cathedrals, lighthouses and buildings of note at home and abroad. After the First World War, the industry declined but the quarry continued until 1965. Its closure meant lost jobs and a diminished community, but the scar left by the quarry is

Ballachulish ferry – typical of the many ferries crossing Argyll's sea lochs.
(Michael Hopkin collection.)

now healing and in time will blend in with the surrounding beautiful landscape as imperceptibly as the ancient quarries which produced stone for fine mansions like Ballachulish House, which survives as part of the tourist industry that replaces quarrying.

For those who demand that industries should be confined to brown field sites and the landscape maintained as nature intended (covered in sitka spruce?) Lorn has a disturbing history. Across the Benderloch peninsula from Appin are the Bonawe quarries and on the other side of Loch Etive there were the Bonawe Furnace and lead mines at Taynuilt. To the south of Oban are the slate islands, and there was a gunpowder works at Melfort on one of the coast's most beautiful lochs. The 21st-century photographer may find fascinating compositions in the landscape of Lorn – but the picturesque ruins are testament either to feuds and wars, to poverty, or to industries which in their time were ugly and exploitative but fed a population unable to survive by land and sea alone.

The castles were in themselves a sustaining industry for those who lived feudally under a MacDougall, a MacDonald, a Campbell or a Stewart laird. The lairds always needed food and clothing and shoes, as did their horses. Their crops and cattle needed to be cared for. Their buildings were in constant need of repair, engaged as they so frequently were in some form of conflict. The master builder who was responsible for Barcaldine Castle may also have built Dunderave in Mid Argyll, but the labourers who erected the building with its extruded staircase linking the main block and wing would have been drawn from the men who already worked for Sir Duncan Campbell of Glenorchy, a man who built a number of castles and consolidated his Barcaldine dynasty by throwing the MacGregors out of Glenorchy and marrying his son Colin off to a daughter of Lord Lorn.

Local labour would have been used to build the religious establishments, too. The Valliscaulian monks who erected Ardchattan Priory on the north shore of Loch Etive between 1230 and 1250 would not have laboured alone, however harsh their Carthusian rules may have been. It was founded by Duncan MacDougall for 20 monks who made their living from relics and tithes from endowments. In the middle of the 14th century, the priory was remodelled and refectory and choir extensions were added, again probably using local labour, although the lay brothers probably worked the arable land at the foot of the Benderloch hills and tended their fish-ponds themselves. Medieval carved stones, today maintained by Historic Scotland along with the priory ruins, are possibly all that remain from the earliest days of the priory when it was an important place in a political sense: this was the scene in 1308 of the last Scottish Parliament held in Gaelic. In 1510, Prior Duncan MacArthur revived the religious ceremonies for the community and there was religious activity there until 1730, although the monastic order ceased in 1545, some 15 years before the Reformation. Building work using facing stone from the Carsaig quarries on Mull and Inninmore in Morvern continued in the 16th and 17th centuries, when it was already a dwelling house belonging to the Campbells. When the monastic endowments were taken from Ardchattan in 1602, the buildings themselves came into the Campbell family. They were burned down in 1654 and the reconstruction replaced the original oak timbers with pine. When a parish church was built in 1731-2, the monastic church fell into disuse and the stone was used for building materials. The dwelling house was enlarged and remodelled from the 19th century, using the old priory refectory as its hub and extending over the nave and cloister area of the old building. It is from that time that the now famous Ardchattan Priory garden dates, which can be visited along with the ruins of the priory.

Today the priory seems a reclusive sort of place. But this spot on the north shore of Loch Etive, a main waterfare in the days when the priory was built, has in the last millennium seen not only the unfolding of some major historical events (tenants on the Dunstaffnage Estate were burned out by Montrose's army in 1655, wiping out byres, barns, a kiln, a mill and dwelling houses with cruck-framed roofs and straight gables) but the development of some of Argyll's major industries. The Bonawe quarries, to the east of the priory, are still in operation. On the south bank at Taynuilt lay the Bonawe Furnace, and Connel Ferry was the site of a woollen mill. The woollen mill was demolished in 1902 but there are interesting restored remains of the foundry, making it a fine museum of the early industrial revolution.

Argyll – perhaps because of its many pensinsulas facing out to a prevailing wind – has much evidence of 'bloomerys'. These were ancient and fairly primitive iron-smelting furnaces which used the wind to get up sufficient heat to deal with the local ore. There was no large-scale smelting, however, until the beginning of the 18th century when English and Irish companies with established industries in their own countries started looking to Scotland for further sites. The first site established by an Irish company was at Glen Kinglass on Upper Etive, set up around 1722. Timber rights were negotiated with Sir Duncan Campbell of Lochnell. Two more smelting centres were set up in Inverness-shire in the late 1720s, then Bonawe was established in 1753 and Goatfield (now Furnace) on Loch Fyne was built in 1754. These latter were owned by English companies from Furness in Lancashire, and while some local Argyll bog iron was used it was from Furness that most of the iron ore was transported north. Local landlords had a field day as they made deals for their timber with the furnace bosses and platforms were set up where tenants were employed to make the charcoal. Timber in the west of Scotland became a very valuable commodity, although the 600 local charcoal burners who produced the fuel for the smelter received no substantial pay rises. There are tracks west from Taynuilt into the Barguillan hills where the men took the horses to fell timber for charcoal production. The works in Inverness-shire did not last long, but there are still the remains of the Irish company's 30-foot-square furnace and turf-walled sheds at Glen Kinglass, which operated until 1738. The Bonawe and Goatfield projects continued their activities till the 19th century, with the Taynuilt works having a boom making cannon balls during the Napoleonic Wars. On Cnoc Aingeal a monument to Lord Nelson was erected by Lorn furnace workers in 1805 to mark this profitable increase in production. Today the industry is lost, but the buildings remain as a very different kind of monument to those who worked there. The operation was part of a family business founded at the end of the 17th century by Richard Ford from Cheshire, who managed an iron company in Cumbria and then formed a series of partnerships to mine iron ore. In 1747 he built the Newland Furnace and when Richard set up the iron ore furnace at Bonawe his company was known as the Newland Company. It leased about 54 square miles of land in the area and charcoal and ore sheds, the workers' and manager's houses, and various stores went up around the furnace. Some ore was shipped from

Ach-na-Cloich ferry – a more modern way to make a difficult crossing, but even it could not survive with the advent of a road network. (Michael Hopkin collection.)

Cumbria to augment local mining, according to Anthony Ainslie, a descendant of the 18th-century partners. Mr Ainslie says that the ample supplies of timber in Argyll were the dominant reason for the expansion of the business to the area. He reminds us that at the time, communication with Argyll was almost entirely by sea, which he says was 'easier in many ways than today's circuitous route by land'. Building material and experienced workers were brought in from the Lake District, just as miners had been brought to Morvern and Ardnamurchan, and in the early days at least, the community was almost self-contained. The workers were encouraged to keep cows and there was a church and a school within the community. Sir Duncan Campbell of Lochnell and the 3rd Earl of Breadalbane signed contracts in 1752 to provide timber and charcoal, and Bonawe used 10,000 acres of coppiced woodland over a 20-year cycle to sustain the iron ore production. Seven tons of oak were needed to produce a ton of charcoal. The company's ships ran from Ulverston to Bonawe, taking the ore, and went back to Cumbria and South Wales with pig iron for the production of wrought iron. George Knott, who was by now running the company, said Bonawe's 'wild landed Highland neighbours' were like 'hawks and birds of prey'. Skilled furnace men from Furness, according to Knott's Bonawe housekeeper Anne Tyson, were paid six shillings a week with meat, as their fellow workers in England were. They did not settle well in Argyll and Anne had to dispense wine to sick workers and their wives as well as feed the all-important furnace men. George Knott kept the Argyll wives out of debt by supplying them with up to 50 stones (700 lb) of free wool for spinning each week. He sold the spun wool to Kendal woollen manufacturers. There was perhaps a touch of taking coals to Newcastle about his provision of oatmeal, bought in England, at below retail price. One of his major problems, which seems to have beset the company in all their Highland ventures, was the consumption of alcohol – one agent being sacked for drinking with sea captains, which George saw as setting a bad example for the workers. By the 1780s, not only was the company's Oban quay being seen as 'the principal smuggling harbour' but George was insisting that managers in Argyll stop 'that confounded drinking ... for I believe there is not such another drunken hole in the United Kingdom'. When George died in 1784, a family relative, William Harrison, who had acted as his clerk, took over the management of the company as a trustee and came to dominate the industry. Henry Ainslie came into the equation when he married Agnes Ford, a descendant of the company's founder. In 1812, the company was renamed Harrison Ainslie & Co. and in the summer months at that time employed up to 600 of a workforce in western Scotland.

The ferries across Loch Etive became even busier after the arrival of the new heavy industries. In the past they had, in common with all Argyll ferries, been there for people and cattle, and usually were contracted to take the local laird and his family for nothing as part of the lease. The Connel Ferry in the 1600s was imputed to be linked with cattle stealing, although the ferrymen of the day were seen as very skilled in taking their boats across the turbulent waters of the Falls of Lora (*labhra*, the Gaelic word from which Lora comes, means noisy). In the 1820s, Connel (*a'chonnail* means whirlpool) got a new quay

A steam train crossing Connel Bridge. Now only cars make the crossing.
(Duncan MacMillan collection.)

at a cost of £118. 15s. but passengers who arrived too late were sent off to Oban for the night and had to wait until morning to get across to the Benderloch side because no boat was kept on the south side of the crossing. It took a petition from Donald Campbell of Dunstaffnage to get the local road trustees to keep a boat on the south side. When the railway bridge was built in 1890, passengers still had to use the ferry, while new-fangled motor cars went by rail. Before the First World War, the track running alongside the railway line for cars and pedestrians was opened as a toll bridge. When the Beeching axe fell, the bridge was opened free to motor traffic and the ferry closed. It had started life as a ferry on a drove road, just as the ferry at Bonawe did. The old trails came down Loch Salach from the west and from the Pass of Brander in the east, and met at 'Bunaw' narrows. This was the ferry which got a new status with the arrival of the ironworks on the south side and then, in the 1880s the quarry on the north side. For the whole of the 19th century this ferry prospered, running a large three-ton boat operated by the Campbell-Prestons of Ardchattan Priory and two small ones run by their tenants. The ferry gave work to two men to row the boats. In the early 20th century, a 10-ton boat was introduced which could carry cars.

Hundreds of men worked at the quarry and travelled on the ferry. Many of them were Irish Catholics, brought over for their quarrying expertise, and it was they who funded the building of the Catholic church in Taynuilt. Such was their influence that during Lent, the ferry ran extra services to take them to Mass. Taynuilt (the house on the stream) was not a stranger to the Catholic faith, but the last church of that denomination to have been been built there was Killespickerill in 1228, when the village was the site of the seat of the Bishop of Argyll three centuries before the Reformation. Its ruins were incorporated into Muckairn, the Presbyterian parish church, when it was built in 1829, so the Irish families were starting from scratch.

Taynuilt was the seat of the Campbells of Inverawe. Inverawe House was a fine mansion which grew and diminished in accordance with the economic situation of the day. In the year immediately before the First World War, it was enlarged according to plans drawn up by Sir Robert Lorimer. In the early 1950s, however, that late Edwardian splendour was prudently reduced in the the face of crippling rates which saw many Argyll lairds taking the roofs off their properties to avoid such bills. Inverawe House simply shrank, remodelled by the architect C. L. Norton.

Although thousands of cattle passed this way when the loch was given its Gaelic name of *étibh* – 'loch of the cattle' – the workers in these new industries were producing a far greater volume of traffic than the traditional drove roads

Awe Bridge, swept away by floods, had been a handsome link in a new road chain. (Duncan MacMillan collection.)

could carry. A road and then the railway came through Taynuilt as a result of all this commercial activity on its doorstep, giving it a continued importance. When the railway came in 1879, a smiddy was built to sharpen the railwaymen's tools as well as to shoe the horses. The military road had come through the Pass of Brander in 1756 and in 1780 Bridge of Awe was built to augment it. This, like the much photographed 'Atlantic' bridge at Clach, Isle of Seil, was erected by the Argyll Commissioners of Supply. It lasted until flood waters washed it away in the second half of the 20th century. The ironworks closed in 1876 but the ferry continued for local quarry workers and school children, and for the growing number of tourists travelling around Argyll in their cars. The car ferry named *Deidre* charged 6d. for an adult, 4d. for a child, three shillings for a car and one and sixpence for a motorbike. Mechanisation in the 20th century reduced the number of workers in the quarry but a mail ferry was operating on Loch Etive until the 1970s, with a motorboat taking goods and parcels to remote farms.

These main crossing points, vital in their day because of the industries they served, were not, however, the only ferries in the area. At the mouth of the River Awe was the Penny Ferry and the River Inn (*Tigh-na-h-Aibhne*) where it is said MacDonald of Glencoe took refuge from the snow in 1691 on his way to Inveraray to sign allegiance. His delay led to the massacre. Legend or truth, the inn no longer exists: it was demolished to make way for the hydro scheme built in the 1950s which takes water from Loch Awe to a major power station at Inverawe through a pipe three miles long and 25 feet in diameter. The ferry ran until this hydro scheme and the upgrading of the Inverawe to Bridge of Awe road closed the old ferry road. In its day it had taken generations of Inverawe high-school students across the river to get to school in Oban.

OBAN

By then, of course, Oban was the centre of Lorn's universe. It had not always been so. While Campbeltown and Inveraray were established and developed as towns by the Argyll family, Oban grew organically according to the needs of the area. In 1714 the Renfrew Trading Company built a storehouse there as a local outlet for its goods, but there was no custom house until 1760. One of the many locations which the British Fisheries Society considered as a station for the herring industry was Oban – but it was passed over. Maps from the 1730s show just one track coming in from the east to give access to Loch Etive at Bonawe, which then branched at Tyndrum to Glen Coe and Ballachulish. Trade was carried out by sea, just as it had been in the days of the Mesolithic cave dwellers. In 1793, returning from Mull to the mainland on the last leg of his Western Islands journey, Dr Samuel Johnson merely recorded that he and Boswell stayed at a 'tolerable inn', which can only be assumed was in or around Oban. He certainly did not see fit to name it as he headed south to Loch Awe and on to the Duke's hospitality in Inveraray. In 1800, the eminent traveller Leyden was not much more impressed, calling Oban a 'small straggling village'.

Fish landing at Oban – but other industries would increase the town's wealth. (Michael Hopkin collection.)

Top. The South Pier at Oban before the town's development. (Michael Hopkin collection.)

Above. The interior of Oban railway station with its glittering glass roof. (Michael Hopkin collection.)

If either of those two gentlemen had called back a decade or two later, they would have been much surprised. Perhaps it still straggled – there was a grid plan but this was not adhered to – but there was a new pier to the south of the harbour and a piermaster's house. Several factors led to the upturn in Oban's fortunes. The Stevenson brothers, Hugh and John, who were shipbuilders and merchants in the town, began to establish trade routes to Glasgow, Liverpool and Ireland. The opening of the Crinan Canal at the turn of the 19th century offered safer and quicker journeys. Then came the steamboat. Henry Bell had commissioned the first one, *The Comet*, in 1812 and soon he was sending her through the Crinan Canal, up to Oban, round into Loch Linnhe and north to Fort William. She did not survive – the heavy seas were too much for her – but the technology was there and it developed amazingly quickly. Oban was included in the loop when it was seen how quickly people could travel from Glasgow to Inverness via the two timesaving canals, the Crinan and the Caledonian, opened in 1822. Suddenly Oban was large enough to be a parliamentary burgh with a voice at Westminster. The arrival of Queen Victoria and Prince Albert in 1847 put Oban on the map as so much more than simply a working harbour or a stop-off on the way north. Travelling on the royal yacht north from the Crinan Canal, Victoria said Oban was 'one of the finest spots we have seen'. Just as the Crinan Canal became an instant magnet for tourists wishing to follow the 'Royal Route', so Oban was transformed into a Highland beauty spot. There was rapid commercial expansion aided by the commercialisation of the steamboat by Hutchison and then his son-in-law David MacBrayne. Its hitherto unpretentious old streets made way for much more elaborate hotels and public buildings, such as the great Western Hotel on the Corran Esplanade, built to the Glasgow architect Charles Wilson's designs in 1862.

From such humble buildings and such isolation, Oban's exposure to its new audience led to ostentation of a very Victorian kind. Even the railway

Oban Hydropathic: the opulent health spa dominated the town's skyline but was never completed. (Michael Hopkin collection.)

An overview of Oban railway station, the harbour and town, in 1904.
(Michael Hopkin collection.)

station, built in 1880 with its gleaming glass canopy, clock tower and bright passenger hall, seemed to feel it was in a competition to be the grandest building in Oban.

That accolade, however, would have to have gone to Oban Hydropathic. This was an hotel-cum-clinic built in the Scottish baronial style with many turrets and towers. It was aimed at the wealthy tourists who were pouring into the town and plans were drawn for it in May 1881 by J. Ford Mackenzie for the Oban Hills Hydropathic and Sanatorium Co. At a cost of £75,000, there were to be 137 bedrooms and rooms for the guests' servants. A funicular railway track was to run from the station to the Hydro. The budget was far too high and was slashed to £32,000, but even so, stables, workshops, a golf-course and recreation halls were in Mackenzie's plans. In the spring of 1882, most of the capital had been blown on dynamiting the site, a very rocky one more suited to a castle than a sanatorium. *The Oban Times* did not approve of the results. In July that year, the paper described it as 'huge and ugly' and a detraction to the 'scenic harmony' of the town. It was certainly huge. Three storeys high and with a 300-foot-long façade, it covered the hill-top above what was then Oban cattle-mart and which today is Tesco's car park. With the roof almost finished, the company collapsed and what could have been seen as a folly comparable to the still visible McCaig's Tower was never completed. And just like the dozens of burial cairns scattered around Lorn, it was stone-robbed for the somewhat more modest houses which went up around it.

Although McCaig's Tower is referred to as a folly, it was built by a local philanthropist, the merchant banker John Stuart McCaig, to give work to unemployed masons in 1896 at a cost of £5,000. The tower sits above the town's distillery, established in 1794 by the Stevenson brothers, who rightly have a street named after them. Both tower and distillery survive, but many of the town's glories have gone the way of the Hydro – with far less justification. The most keenly felt loss was that of the railway station, which was demolished in 1985 and replaced by a much more work-a-day construction the following year. The front is now masked by high-street shops. The Bank of Scotland now stands where the Stevensons had a llama park (yes, with llamas) and along the

Top. Well appointed hotels became Oban's keynote, but the town lost one of its finest when the Queen's Hotel burned down. (Michael Hopkin collection.)

Above. Carding Mill Bay to the south of Oban, where wool was carded by the women in a small factory. (Michael Hopkin collection.)

Esplanade hotels have become a little less grand. The Esplanade Boarding House was destroyed by fire in 1973 and ten people lost their lives. The Queen's Hotel was another to go on fire. Built in 1891, it was gutted in 1924 and farmers staying there for the October sales had to be evacuated. The Great Western Hotel, built in the middle of the 19th century and, according to Michael Hopkin, compiler of the pictorial volume *Old Oban*, in 1884 was the first Oban hotel to have electricity installed.[17] This was the place to stay for the Oban Ball, the highlight of the Argyllshire Gathering at which the county's young ladies made their debut. Today it has lost that glittering role and caters more for bus tours of the Highlands. Dunollie Lodge, the octagonal entrance to Dunollie Castle, was built in 1830 but demolished to make way for the Corran hall car park. The Castle, seat of the MacDougalls, Lords of Lorn and once owners of a third of Scotland, was of course in ruins long before that. There is no longer a ferry terminal on Kerrera and nor is there a carding mill in Carding Mill Bay, where from 1800, wool was teased before spinning. The cattle-market is now outside the town to the south and there is a school playing field where once the Argyll Gathering pulled together all the Campbell lairds under the leadership of the Duke.

That Oban became, and remains, such a focal point, despite its losses, is in part due to the advances of technology and in part to the enterprise of the brothers Stevenson and the entrepreneurs who followed in their wake: men with vision enough to create a town of style and flamboyance which could (give or take a few centimetres of rainfall) compete with other Victorian watering

Boxing herring – the backdrop to Oban life into the 20th century.
(Michael Hopkin collection.)

The 'tin cathedral' – the Catholic bishop saw Oban as the place for a new cathedral in the diocese. This stop-gap served the faithful until today's St Columba's Cathedral was finished. (Michael Hopkin collection.)

holes like Biarritz. Trading had been the Stevensons' forte and the fishing had also been a mainstay for the town. The herring fleet attracted gutters – women who followed the boats around the coast and found plenty of work in Oban when as many as 100 came in with their baskets full of silver darlings – and resident coopers kept the industry supplied with barrels. The fish were transported south on trains which left Oban every two hours in the heyday of the herring.

The town's status merited two cathedrals: the Scottish Episcopal Church's St John the Divine and the Catholic Church's St Columba's Cathedral. The first is still there: the first version of St Columba's, however, was lost to posterity, as prosperity demanded a bigger and better testament to the prayer, perseverance and faith of Argyll's Catholics. The Tin Cathedral, as it was called, was on the site of the present St Columba's. It was built in 1886, just eight years after the Catholic hierarchy was restored in Scotland – and more than 300 years after the Reformation. The first Bishop of Argyll and the Isles was the Rt Revd Angus MacDonald, whose choice of Oban as the site of the cathedral and administrative centre was questioned for a number of reasons. This was a time when the County Council meetings for Argyll were held in the Central Station Hotel in Glasgow, because it was as easy (or, perhaps, as difficult) for most representatives to travel there as to any point in the county. The train was new-fangled and certainly didn't reach most people in the hinterland of this Argyll and the Isles diocese and cars, of course, were a thing of the future. Add to this

Above. The fine Victorian station at Oban in 1905 – lost to modernity towards the end of the century. (Michael Hopkin collection.)

Left. The new St Columba's going up around the temporary 'tin cathedral'. (St Columba's collection.)

the fact that, unlike Taynuilt where the Irish workers were centred in their hundreds, there were only four or five Catholic families in Oban itself. The Bishop, however, saw that Oban would become an important focal point of travel and also had in mind that it was close to Iona, the spiritual foundation not only of the diocese but of the Christian Church in Scotland. The Bishop's other main problem was a lack of cash. In a town where rich men were building fancy hotels with electric lights, a wooden hut was all the diocese could manage at first as a place of worship. Then the third Marquess of Bute funded the building of a Pro-Cathedral – the corrugated iron construction with a tower and turrets, lavishly decorated and furnished, which local people called the Tin Cathedral. The Marquess thought it would be a temporary building which would be used elsewhere when a more suitable cathedral building went up. In fact, the Tin Cathedral stayed in place for 50 years, serving a growing Catholic population in the town. Still poor, the diocese made the decision under the Rt Rev Donald Martin, the third Bishop of Argyll and the Isles, to begin the erection of that more suitable building. It was 1919, immediately after a war which had left the country in a sorry state. Bishop Donald turned to Argyll exiles in Canada and America. There were generous donations to meet the estimated £50,000 cost of the new cathedral, but the money dried up as the Depression bit. Even so, the first sod was cut in 1932 and by 1934, half completed, the cathedral opened for public worship on Christmas Eve. The building had gone up around the Tin Cathedral, which was only removed when the new building, designed by Sir Giles Gilbert Scott and built by Oban firm D&A McDougall from blue granite quarried at Kentallen, became watertight. Oban had lost its Tin Cathedral, swallowed up by the magnificent building which today greets every seafarer coming into the bay. The tin building was an integral part of the town for half a century, but unlike the magnificent railway station at the other side of the bay, its loss was replaced by something better.

SOUTH LORN

That is, of course, a subjective view, but it is nevertheless very much a reflection of the evolution of Argyll's land and townscapes: the ugly or the unusual may become beautiful; the beautiful ugly in the hands of each successive generation. To the south of Oban, the Melfort gunpowder works are no more than a memory and workers' cottages have become desirable loch-side holiday homes. The ruins of the works themselves, high on the hill above the tumbling river Oude, are made picturesque by thick cushions of moss. Tranquillity may be the quality which markets this area today, but there was little tranquillity

Map of Lorn. (Michael Hopkin collection.)

Melfort stores served the gunpowder village. (Duncan MacMillan collection.)

about at the height of the gunpowder works' activity. Sulphur and saltpetre were imported by water, charcoal from the neighbouring estates was brought in on 'cars' – the sledge-like contraptions which were the haulage contractor's mode of transport in Argyll until well through the 19th century – and grinding mills were in constant operation. The operation was set up by the proprietors of the Bonawe Iron Furnace, a company which itself had been evolving since the early 18th century. The village of Melfort and the surrounding estate had been in Campbell hands since the 1300s. In 1838, having got their furnace at Bonawe up and running, Harrison Ainslie and Company bought the estate from Colonel John Campbell as an ideal site for gunpowder manufacture. It was seen as remote from population and therefore safe: the estate offered a plentiful supply of scrub oak and the loch was deep enough for a pier for large vessels delivering raw material and exporting the finished gunpowder. Brick buildings were erected over more than a mile of land east and north-east of Melfort House. A tramway linked some of the buildings to the pier at Fearnach Bay and the Tarsuinn burn was dammed above its junction with the river Oude to form a pool for a mill lade. The rock face was quarried out to create the lade and there was a sluice gate. This arrangement powered four mills then flowed into the Oude. Three of those mills ground the ingredients of the gunpowder and the fourth mixed them together. Each of the mills had a change-house for storage. One single boiler-house served the corning house, press-house, glazing-house, packing-house, dusting-house and two storehouses. There were also big storage sheds for the locally manufactured charcoal and the imported sulphur and saltpetre. The biggest of these was over 80 feet long and 30 feet wide and the walls were around 18 inches thick and built against the hillside

Top. One of the ruined gunpowder mills at Melfort. (Author's collection.)

Above. Formerly the court office building at Melfort powder works, converted to stables (now changed further as a holiday property). (Melfort Village collection.)

like their counterparts at Bonawe. The roofs were of local slate. The factory had its own cooperage and there was a local smiddy. The business flourished for almost 30 years, but in 1867 there was a serious explosion. According to the Ainslie history researched from family documents by a descendant, Anthony Ainslie, production did restart. By 1874, however, the days of the gunpowder

The blacksmith's cottage at Melfort, converted to a holiday property. (Melfort Village collection.)

The smiddy is gone – the bellows remain. Melfort gunpowder works. (Melfort Village collection.)

factory were over for good and Harrison Ainslie sold the estate back into agriculture. Sheep replaced the gunpowder works on the hillside about Loch Melfort. Farming continued until the 1970s, by which time most of the gunpowder factory buildings were derelict and former farm workers' cottages were used as self-catering holiday properties. When the estate was sold off in 1982, the part now known as Melfort Village was bought by Charles and Helen Stott who turned the area into a time-share village. They built 32 cottages from the ruins of the gunpowder village and the farm buildings. Stott's house and grounds were sold to the Melfort Club, an association of Melfort time-share owners. The names of the houses reflect their original use ('coachman's cottage', 'blacksmith's cottage') and retain features of the original cottages, including the practical three-feet-thick walls. Housing may be in short supply for local families, but this is a new industry which brings people to the area to explore, to spend money in the shops and restaurants, to visit the monuments of the past and engage in the economy of the present. Melfort gunpowder works is a lost industry: its ruins have created a new one which 'imports' visitors as once the ingredients of gunpowder were imported.

The road to Melfort from Oban is still not an easy one, but at the time when the gunpowder mills were in operation it was a hair-raising byway instituted by the Argyll Commissioners of Supply to improve the infrastructure of the county. Melfort's gunpowder must have been used to blast through the rocks to make this road, which coach horses were not always keen to climb or to descend. Part of this 'new' road was later to be lost under water when the river running through the Pass of Melfort was dammed. Today's A816 takes a less tortuous route.

Melfort Pass, 1904: this dangerous stretch of road disappeared under a reservoir. (Michael Hopkin collection.)

Easdale quay in 1907. These islands exported slate around the world from this quay. (Michael Hopkin collection.)

Loch Melfort goes out to a sea studded with islands – those known as the slate islands where yet another industry has been lost. Seil, Luing, Belnahua and Easdale are to this day rich in slate, and geologists call the slice of slate rock stretching from here to the north-east 'the Easdale Slate Belt'. By medieval times, the slate from Easdale was being used for roofs as far apart as Glasgow Cathedral and Cawdor Castle in Inverness-shire. More locally, Castle Stalker's roof was slated by these islands in 1631 and Ardmaddy Castle's in 1676. The slate was also used on properties throughout the Breadalbane estates, which held the slate islands, stretched across Scotland and took in Nova Scotia in Canada. The family fortune lay in these slate beds. At the peak of production in the mid 19th century, the islands were exporting as many as 19 million roofing slates a year to America, the West Indies, New Zealand and Australia. The islands have also yielded up lead and even gold, but only the slate has been economical to exploit commercially. In 1745, John Campbell, Earl of Breadalbane, Charles Campbell of Lochaline, Colin Campbell of Carwin and another John Campbell who was Cashier of the Royal Bank of Scotland, set up the Marble and Slate Quarrying Company of Netherlorn. Carwin had already been quarrying the slate and his assets were transferred to the new company which planned to do things on a much bigger scale than that effected by one shovel, four picks, two spades and a big mallet – although to give him his due, over a million slates had been made in the year before the Breadalbane consortium took over. Now the most up-to-date equipment and pumps were used and within 20 years Carwin's quota had been more than doubled, and slates were already being exported to England, Norway, Canada and the West Indies. As production on Easdale rose to five million a year at the turn of the century, new quarries were opened on the neighbouring island of Luing at Cullipool, Maryport, Toberonochy and at Balvicar on Seil Island. The only marble extracted came from a quarry next to Ardmaddy Castle on the mainland opposite Balvicar, one of Breadalbane's properties acquired by marriage and linking the Duke's family to the Breadalbane Campbells. The quality of this marble was too poor to sell commercially so it was used for fireplaces in the castle, which had been built in the 15th century and extended in the 18th. Ardmaddy's upper tower was demolished and its lowest storey formed the basement of an early Georgian house.

The Second Marquess of Breadalbane bought out his co-directors in 1842 and modernised the quarries with the engineer John Whyte. Steam pumps were installed in the quarries which had previously been flooded and better equipment was brought in to lift the slate. The quarriers were by then working at a depth of more than 260 feet below sea level. Perhaps not quite a philanthropist, he nonetheless ended the practice of using women and children to carry the slates on their backs by laying rail tracks for horse-drawn engines to transport the slates to the harbours. Workers' cottages were also improved around this time and the Marquess provided a school for the children and night classes for the young men. Medical insurance costing a few shillings was introduced and a medical officer was brought in. This investment in men and machines had to last for some considerable time, because after the death of the Second Marquess in 1862, the succession was disputed and in 1866 the quarries were leased out under separate managements. Those on Easdale Island and at Ellenabeich were leased to Glasgow and Paisley businessmen under the name of the Easdale Slate Quarrying Company, but as no new investment in machinery was made, efficiency and productivity dropped. In 1881, a storm left most of the quarries flooded and there was a change of local management. The Ellenabeich quarry closed and machinery was transferred to Easdale. The quarries at Balvicar and on Luing became the dominant producers at this time as they had not been affected as much by the storm. Under a new lessee, production continued until 1914. Competition from Ballachulish, Wales and abroad had reduced the viability of the slate islands, and although the Balvicar quarry continued sporadically until the 1960s, the last slate was shipped from the Easdale quarries in 1911. On the privately-owned Belnahua Island to the west of Luing, top-quality slates were exported at the end of the 19th century. The village which was built for workers at the edge of the two big Belnahua quarries is now a ruin although some of the machinery is still intact. The last men who lived there were called up for service in the First World War; the women, who had no electricity and no running water and relied on supplies coming by boat from Luing, moved out, and the community died. Today, Ellenabeich, Easdale, Balvicar and the villages on Luing have been placed under a conservation order. This may or may not be a good thing. Plans from the 1850s to improve houses with a porch were never carried out. That means, according to Mary Withal in her book about the slate islands,[18] that the planning rules of the 21st century deny today's residents permission to change the front elevation of the cottages. When the gales sweep in from the sea (and that 19th-century storm was not unique), a porch would give the protection the Second Marquess obviously intended his workers to have. The slate islands' industry has been lost; the quarriers' houses saved in the aspic of unsympathetic bureaucracy. These villages were almost deserted like the one on Belnahua, even though workers had been offered their houses for a year's rental when the quarry company folded. Those who bought moved away nonetheless – what work was there for them around abandoned slate quarries? When the Breadalbane estates were wound up in the 1930s, the cottages were sold to a wider population, but by the 1950s many on Easdale were let out by their owner Donald Dewar (not the first First Minister of Scotland), and others had their roofs removed to avoid paying rates – a trick not confined to the owners of fine mansions. The subsequent owner, Peter Fennel, reconstructed many of the houses and today most are renovated and inhabited. Bizarrely, those reconstructed before the conservation order rarely have slate roofs in an area which once roofed the world.

But then, the buildings constructed in the early days of Christianity here did not conform to any building regulations, and although most of the chapels built here from the 6th century to medieval times are crumbled ruins, we can see the stamp of individuality. St Brendan had preceded Columba to Argyll from their native Ireland and had already developed little pockets of Christianity up the west coast. His monastery on Eileach a' Naoimh in the Garvellachs was probably his first stop, followed by the church of Kilbrandon in Lorn. West of Loch Seil to the south of Oban, Brendan boldly set up shop beside an ancient stone circle. On Seil Island, another church said to have been established by Brendan was built near the site of Kilbrandon House. Kilchattan church on Luing dates to the 12th century, the earliest of the medieval churches and chapels in Lorn. Luing had been the site of very early occupation, with earthworks dating from the Iron Age, and would have been an inviting fertile place for the missionaries who came later. Today it is the home of the world famous Luing cattle owned by the Cadzow family. The slate workings are confined to a few craftsmen, and any evidence of the former agricultural regime is recalled in the crumbling ruin of a grinding mill on the east of the island – the wheel and querns a mere whisper of the past.

The proliferation of 'kil' names in this south-west corner of Lorn (Kilmore and Kilninver among them), indicate that when the Christian missionaries came, they did not move on quickly – but names like Easdale let us know that before Kilchattan church was built on the island to the south, the Vikings had been in residence. This is only the throw of a roofing tile from Kerrera, of course, where a Viking burial was said to have taken place near what became Mount Pleasant House; and an earth house was discovered at the north end of the island where a bone pin with an animal head displayed a fusion of Norse and native traditions. A ship-burial was said to have been discovered near the site of Oban railway station.

Go east and you reach Loch Awe, which along with Loch Avich, Loch Ba, Loch Nell, Loch Scamadale and Loch Tulla formed the southern boundaries of the kingdom of Lorn as gifted to Loarn Mor, son of Erc. Lorn stretched more than 30 miles from Rannoch Moor to the tip of Luing and some 20 miles from Duror to Tyndrum. This south-western section was valuable if for no other reason than that the wealth of water made it a route for man – whether he was seeking food, taking his cattle to market, or moving his armies. Depending on their place of origin, cattle heading south to those great trysts at Falkirk grazed the lush glens and were swum or ferried across the water which made the glens fertile. Those drovers from the islands who came by boat to Kerrera crossed to a point south of Oban on the mainland and then came down to Scammadale, over to Loch Avich and crossed Loch Awe at Dalavich. Those who came from Appin and further north travelled via Loch Etive through the Pass of Brander and crossed Loch Awe at Kichrenan.

Beaker pottery, flint and jet beads have been found in the hills above Loch Awe and many cairns were sited around the loch. When Brendan and then Columba came, monastic cells and small chapels were built across this area. Most chapels from this time have fallen into almost unrecognisable ruin and even post-Reformation churches in this part of Lorn have not fared well, although the one at Kilchrenan, built in 1771, is a fine exception.

A very modern reason for the loss of visible evidence of the past was the arrival in the 20th century of the Forestry Commission. The Commission's more recent commitment to conservation and the environment was not part of its earliest remit. However, another cause for the great loss of archaeological and historic remains charting the course of man through this area is the fact that it has been such a busy thoroughfare. Throughout history it has been well protected: by the 13th century, there were at least two tall houses protecting island sites – Fraoch Eilean and Inch Chonnell – on Loch Awe. Archaeological divers have found evidence of many crannog fortifications dating from earlier centuries and island defences were used across the whole of southern Lorn: an islet was constructed in Loch Nell with a timber defence in the 14th century while the island in Loch a' Phearsain was natural and had a simple stone defence. There was a crannog in the bay of Rubha nan Eun and another north of Innis Chonnell, south-west of the chambered cairn above Ardchonnell which is now under forest. A fort lay to the south of Portinnisherrich and in the bay of Barr Phort on the opposite shore of Loch Awe was yet another crannog – while on Innis Sea-ramhach a pre-Reformation chapel, once 70 feet long but now little more than the substance of the schist rubble and lime mortar from which it was built, testifies to the fact that this was not simply a backwater used as a quick route south by cattle drovers. Kings and war lords trod this way, accounting for the wall of defences around Loch Awe and all the way to Oban. Innis Chonnel was one of the earliest, built in the 13th century and remodelled in the first half of the 15th century. Although the building lost its roof, the courtyard buildings and first-floor hall remained identifiable. Fraoch Eilean, the 13th-century tall house built for Alexander III, was granted by the king to Gillechrist Macnachdan (MacNaughton) in 1267. Macnachdan had an allowance to keep up the castle and to provide hospitality when it was required. In the Wars of Independence, the MacNaughtons fought with the MacDougalls against Robert Bruce and the supportive Campbells were given Fraoch Eilean in the spoils. The MacNaughtons sensibly tugged their forelocks to the Campbells and stayed on in the hall house as tenants. The original house had two storeys and a garret built from locally quarried stone. It had an unvaulted cellar below a big first-floor hall which may well have been surrounded by a walkway. There was a mural stair going down to a dungeon and another going up to the first-floor hall, which was very wide and lit by windows on the north and south walls under which were stone seats. Its floor joists may have been on timber piers or masonry posts and there was a central hearth with the smoke escaping through a louvre in the roof. A curtain wall was built later. After the MacNaughtons left for Loch Fyne, the castle fell into ruin but in the early 17th century – a brave time for anyone in this area to make domestic changes – the Campbells built a small three-storey house in the north-east corner of the original hall house. There was just one room to each storey and by the late 17th century this had been extended out to the south-east corner of the original defensive building and a courtyard created out of the remaining hall foundations. It was sold to Robert Campbell of Monzie, husband of a

Campbell of Loch Awe daughter, in 1765 and then went to the Campbells of Dunstaffnage. Uninhabited, it fell into disrepair, but some restoration was carried out by one of the descendants of the Campbells of Inverawe.

Another Loch Awe side defence was Caisteal na Nighinn Ruaidhe on Loch Avich, probably another built by the MacDougalls, who were the dominant war lords in Lorn until 1308. Three storeys high, it was similar to Finchairn Castle on the south-east shore of Loch Awe, seat of the Lords of

KILCHURN CASTLE, LOCHAWE.

Top. Kilchurn Castle on Loch Awe, one of the many ruined castles on this strategic stretch of water. (Duncan MacMillan collection.)

Above. The island on which Kilchurn castle stood merged with the shore when the waters of Loch Awe dropped several feet in the 19th century. (Michael Hopkin collection.)

Glassary. But in terms of major defences, Kilchurn Castle is probably the oldest surviving tower-house in the Loch Awe area. It was built by Sir Colin Campbell, first of Glenorchy, around the middle of the 1400s. It was remodelled by the family over the next 200 years until the First Earl of Breadalbane, who continued the Glenorchy line through marriage, made the final alterations to the building in the last decade of the 17th century. This was one of the last attempts at private fortification in Britain and Breadalbane did it in style with cylindrical angle towers that allowed for firearm defence and barrack blocks which could hold over 200 men. After 1688, such private defences were not encouraged and after the Uprisings of 1715 and 1745, even less so. Breadalbane, an entrepreneur in the arms industry as well as slate and minerals, offered Kilchurn to the Government in 1747 at what he saw as the going rate for a permanent Highland garrison. The Government did not take him up on the offer, however, and the castle was abandoned. Its ruins are extensive.

Who, then, apart from the drovers, followed the routes which crossed Loch Awe? Who needed palaces in which to stay and fortresses in which to seek protection? This was, of course, the route of the kings – dead Scottish kings going to their resting place on Iona. As far back as the days when Dunadd in Mid Argyll was the capital of the kingdom of Dal Riata and the cradle of Christianity in Scotland (it was there that Columba anointed the first Christian king in the islands that are today's Britain) the mortal remains of its leaders and priests would no doubt have crossed Loch Awe on their way to the sacred isle. The crossings were used by living kings seeking to subdue this fretful western flank of Scotland; by the leaders of armies in the civil war; and by a new generation of travellers with enlightenment in mind when peace eventually filtered there. The ferrymen saw the tears of those leaving the country, too poor to stay; and they they saw the spilled blood of those fleeing from their enemies. Was the Port of Peace really so in those turbulent times? That is the meaning of Portsonachan, the southern side of the ferry crossing to the House of the rocks (*Taigh na Chreagan* or Taycreggan as it is today). And this 570 yards boat-ride was part of the ancient road to the isles. Whoever else travelled this way, the bread and butter for the ferrymen came from the drovers taking cattle from the Western Isles through Oban to Portsonachan and on to Crieff and Falkirk. After 1313, Sir Neil Campbell, that supporter of Bruce, was given a large portion of Loch Awe lands and in turn he granted some land and the ferry rights to a gentleman called MacPhedran after he saved his son Duncan in a storm, an act of gratitude recorded over a century later. Of course, however grateful the Campbell family was, it still demanded ten shillings of silver a year, barley, oats, cheese and a sheep, for the privilege of running the ferry and tenanting the Portsonachan lands. The MacPhedrans, who continued to run the ferry for centuries, were also contracted to carry all infirm, lame or blind passengers free – and of course, the Campbell family went free as well. By 1627, the goodwill of the 14th century had somewhat dissipated and when the last MacPhedran died without sons and left Portsonachan to his neighbour Duncan Campbell, the Earl of Argyll put out a contract and had Duncan killed because he felt the lands should revert back to the estate. In 1645, who knows what the contemporary ferryman witnessed of the blind fury of Alasdair Colkitto MacDonald when he crossed Loch Awe and marched his men over Leacann Muir to Loch Fyne and Inveraray to sack the town and then burn the Campbells out of Loch Fyneside all the way down Kintyre?

A dozen years later, with the civil war still raging, the first and only Marquess of Argyll gave the feu and ferry rights to Ian Campbell of Staffnage, who was presumably seen as a safe pair of hands. By the next century, when black cattle traffic was on the increase because the markets in England had been opened up to drovers from the north in an attempt to improve the Scottish economy, Portsonachan was the principal crossing point for cattle and Rob Roy MacGregor, whose regular stamping ground was to the east around Lochearnhead, used the route. The troubles for the ferrymen were not over, however. Government forces came this way to quell the 1745 Uprising, but even then, a military road was being built between Inveraray and Tyndrum which had – eventually – the desired effect of opening up Argyll from the east. Plans to move the ferry north towards Cladich were abandoned, and eventually

The Portsonachan steamer replaced earlier wooden ferry boats. Now it, too, is only a memory. (Duncan MacMillan collection.)

A stagecoach met travellers from the Loch Awe steamer outside the hotel at Ford.
(Duncan MacMillan collection.)

bridges were built in the 1770s which were the beginning of the end for the
ferry. In 1773, however, Dr Johnson described travelling through 'cataracts' of
rain before joining the new military road from Cladich, where the fords were
flooded, to Inveraray on his way to his visit to the Duke. At the turn of the
century the ferry and feu were bought from the fifth Duke by Robert Campbell,
but it wasn't a sound investment. The steam era was about to invade Argyll,
and as the century progressed steamers on Loch Awe damaged trade for the
old ferries. New roads, a railway passing the east end of the loch and the need
for an efficient mail ferry after the introduction of the penny post made this a
century of struggle. By the 1840s, after tenants had gone bankrupt because of
the lack of traffic, there was a demand for better boats. In 1850, at the height of
their wealth and fame, the Malcolms of Poltalloch in Mid Argyll bought up the
Sonachan estate. They were building a mansion on their Mid Argyll estate to
which they would invite royalty and all the celebrities of the day. Some would
travel there via the steamer to Ardrishaig and stay at a purpose-built hotel
there, while others would come by rail to Loch Awe and take the steamer to
Ford, perhaps stopping at the Portsonachan Hotel, which Malcolm also built
for his guests. Naturally, the ferry boats across the loch from south to north
were upgraded to a large 22-footer and a smaller ten-foot boat for passengers
only. A four-wheeled carriage could travel for five shillings while a bull could
cross the loch for a mere eightpence. Letters covering the resignation of the
poor-board inspector of the time (he seems to have cooked the books) show that

the crossing had to be made at four o'clock in the morning in mid-winter. It was no easier by the 1920s when the doctor and district nurse complained about the inefficiency of the ferry. Argyll County Council put it out of its misery in 1953 as road transport improved.

The other main ferry on the loch was from Portinnisherrich – a name which reflects the antiquity of the crossing. Innis Sèaràmhach means the island of the six oars or the six-oared galley, and the medieval chapel on the island suggests that a ferry was running from at least the time that it was built. In early times, this was the route used for the royal cortèges, travelling on to Loch Feochan past the chapel of Kilmore to the Rock of the Dead, the jetty for Iona and their resting place. It continued to be a chosen route for the Campbell hierarchy and Campbell soldiers chased after the Marquess of Montrose across this ferry after his 1644 attack on the 8th Earl at Inveraray castle. The following year the Covenanters' army crossed by it when Colkitto marched into Kintyre. It remained a useful route to the Western Isles in times of peace before the building of the Crinan Canal, but in the 18th century the north shore of Loch

The ferry is gone, the jetty is unused and crumbling and New York is just the name on a modern cottage. (Author's collection.)

Awe became a destination in itself. Passengers asked the ferryman to take them to New York – where they found no skyscrapers but one of a number of 'New York' settlements of workers' cottages built by the infamous York Building Company. One was on the banks of the Crinan Canal, another near Strontian and the third here on the north shore of Loch Awe.

This had headquarters at York Buildings in London. In 1719, following an Act of Parliament, the company acquired a joint stock fund of £1,200,000 to buy forfeited and other estates through a system of life assurance policies. The lead mines in Morvern became one of its many Scottish investments and a village called New York for 500 workers was created near Strontian from timber frames manufactured in London. No traces of that New York remain – it was abandoned when the mining stopped in the 1740s. Another New York was erected by the York Buildings Company on the north shore of Loch Awe and still another on the banks of the Crinan Canal, sometimes also called The Tile Houses. These were in a small valley (NR791941) running up from the canal to Kilmahumaig and may have been built for the canal or for workers in a nearby slate quarry. John Stevenson, manager of the slate works at Ballachulish, bought up lands in Knapdale in 1791, at a time when the engineer John Rennie was surveying the area for different routes for the Crinan Canal. Stevenson and the York Buildings Company shared their mining and quarrying interests. All three New Yorks were lost as the management of the York Buildings Company properties in Scotland became the subject of much litigation. There were massive debts, parts of the forfeited estates were sold to pacify creditors and by 1818, after several decades of controlling huge tracts of Scotland and involving dukes and baronets in major industrial projects, the company's only asset was its original waterworks, now claimed by a rival. It was dissolved by an Act of Parliament in 1829 and creditors received the crumbs remaining from this strange venture.

At the time all of this was being played out across Scotland and in high places in London, the ferry from Portinnisherrich to New York (where the ferry inn has been replaced by a modern bungalow and the jetty lies abandoned at the entrance to one section of the vast Loch Awe forestry plantations) was in the hands of Donald Campbell, the tacksman of Innisherrich, who paid £60 rental for the ferry-boats, which carried cattle and carriages alike across Loch Awe. On the south side of the loch at this point, the onward journey to Loch Fyne went from Durran, a little distance to the west along Aweside, across Leacann Muir to Auchindrain. Fine for cattle and rugged drovers, it was never a road suited to carriages. When the Malcolms of Poltalloch bought up the Loch Awe lands, the push to join up all their lands by road was on. Having

Ben Anea, Dalmally, was the site of traditional cottages now lost to forestry. (Duncan MacMillan collection.)

acquired the rights to the Portinnisherrich ferry along with the lands, they eventually made moves to close it in 1870, but there were complaints from Dalavich and the neighbouring townships. John MacIntyre of New York took on the ferry at £10 a year and the council and road trustees match funded this. When John died in 1902, however, the ferryman's allowance was discontinued and so was the ferry. The ferry was 870 yards wide and led north to the Streng of Lorn, a drove road which divides at Loch Scammadale. The cortèges of the kings took the track going north of Kilninver to the natural pier in Loch Feochan known as Carraig nan Marmh ('the rock of the dead'). The other spur went via Kilmore to the Kerrera ferry. On the south side of the Loch stood a 16th-century thatched ferry inn but this was replaced in the early 1800s by a slated house. Portinnisherrich boasted a shoemaker, a smith and two ferrymen – Duncan and Donald Turner – at the beginning of the 19th century, as well as the ferry inn-keeper, all paying rent to the Malcolms' Poltalloch estate.

As elsewhere in Argyll, it is the evidence of the lives of tenants which has been lost. The documents relating to kings and dukes – and even to tacksmen – survive and their substantial residences are hard to erase even when they have been attacked or simply abandoned to the elements. It is far harder to see where and how the families who served these landlords lived out their lives. Allan Begg of Lochgilphead was no formal historian, but he felt passionate enough about recording the status of such lives to produce publications for Argyll library service. His starting point was always the churchyards, where sometimes hard-to-decipher grave-slabs give a name, a place, an age and a date of death. Many of those places have been lost: some in clearances or less violent changes of land use; some because of famine or disease; some subsumed into the forests of the 20th century. Deserted or lost townships and villages are nothing new. When Montrose burned out the Dunstaffnage estate tenants in 1644 leaving the smouldering ruins of byres and dwellings, he was following the example of invaders throughout history. On Kerrera under the shadow of the imposing ruins of Gylen Castle, a late 16th-century L-plan tower-house lived in for just 65 years by the MacDougalls of Dunollie before it was burned down, there are the remains of township buildings at Upper Gylen Farm. In so many townships, improvements in the agricultural systems which joined land together into single farms instead of runrig units co-worked by several families meant dwellings became outhouses, stood empty and fell apart, or were cannibalised for new buildings. From Duror in Appin to Kilchrenan on Loch Awe, the remains of cottages with square rather than rounded angles and steeply-pitched hipped roofs can be found in many stages of dilapidation. Traditional thatched roofs were also lost because of farming advances. The factor of the Breadalbane estates complained in 1804 that it was difficult to introduce a proper crop rotation plan because of the amount of corn grown to provide straw for thatching. Breadalbane divided the township of Stronmilchan into crofts as early as 1784 to improve his land and tenants were moved around to suit the needs of the landlords. Those on the joint farm of Ardnahua were shifted to Tigh Cuil in 1790, yet a century later the township was abandoned, and the coming of the sheep meant the hundreds of shielings used throughout Lorn for summer grazing of cattle disappeared in the 19th-century. Above Cladich in Glenaray – along the river followed by the modern A819 from Loch Awe to Inveraray – Boccaird was a village lost to the 19th century sheep boom. Two centuries ago there were 11 houses, a school, a church. Today they stand roofless and abandoned. This had been cattle land for centuries, held in the 16th century, according to historian Mary MacGrigor, by MacArthurs of Tirrevaddich.[19] The family faced financial problems in 1751 and mortgaged Boccaird to a John Lindsay. The tack was then sold to John Campbell of Airds in 1802, when it and Accurach farm were made into one for sheep. By 1817, there were over 1,500 sheep on the land and six milk cows for the shepherd of Boccaird. The tenants had been dispersed and the village became a scratching post for passing sheep.

At the other end of Loch Awe, Allan Begg's search for the dwellings of those recorded only on a cold headstone in a parish churchyard have uncovered in the north of the parish of Kilmartin the ruins of Upper and Nether Kintraw

Kilbride kirk was a medieval chapel south of Oban, now a picturesque ruin. (Michael Hopkin collection.)

and Salachary, townships on part of an old drove road which flourished in the 18th century. Kintraw's meal mill is now augmented into farm buildings and there are the remains of an old stone bridge which took the old road south to Kilmartin. This is a corner which was inhabited from the very earliest times, with a cairn, duns, forts and standing stones having stood the test of time perhaps better then their much younger neighbours built at least one millennium later. Patches of 20th-century forest hide so much, but the Forestry Commission cannot be held to account for all the ills of Loch Aweside. Native woodlands have been destroyed successively by the Irish, the Norse and every subsequent user of the land. Much of the Loch Aweside forests were destroyed to get rid of the wolves (Legend has it that the last wolf died near Auchindrain, having tracked a woman over the moors from Loch Awe. In the snow, she turned to face it, stabbed it with the spindle she carried but died herself from fright.) Remaining woodlands brought a fine price from the furnace on Loch Fyne. Today's Commission is planting native trees and conserving long-lost villages: a walk in the woods around Dalavich not only takes in a beautiful landscape but offers information about a lost past.

CHAPTER 4

ISLAY, JURA, COLONSAY, ORONSAY, SCARBA AND THE GARVELLACHS:

BOATS, BLESSINGS AND *UISGE-BEATHA*

They came by boat and they brought their blessings with them. Very sensibly, they incorporated the culture of the Druids into the teachings of Christianity. On Eileach a' Naoimh ('the rock of the saints'), and its near neighbour, the

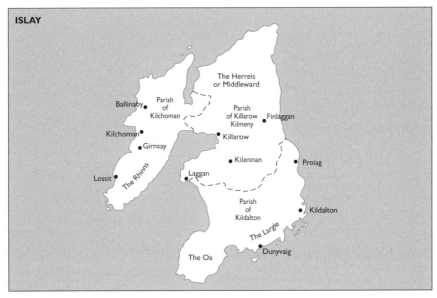

Map of Islay.

craggy Scarba, which has at its feet the wild Corryvreckan (*Coirebhreacain* – 'cauldron of the speckled seas'), the Celtic monks came to live out their contemplative lives, farming, fishing and praying. On the island of Scarba, there were half a dozen beehive cells built together as a hermitage in a sheltered place above a bay named Iurach, or a group of yews – always the sign of a holy contemplative place in this part of the world. While Scarba's north-eastern neighbour, Luing, has its share of ancient fortifications, Scarba seems to have had a peaceful and religious past. Perhaps the sheer cliffs, threatening caves and fearsome whirlpools around the west and south of the island were protection enough. In later centuries, when the monks had long abandoned their cells, a church was dedicated to the Virgin Mary – Kilmorie. It has stood the test of time less well than the beehive constructions, although neither can compare with the good state of preservation of those on Eileach a' Naoimh. The church has gone and the graveyard has become overgrown. The last burial took place in the middle of the 20th century. The island, which in 1797 was home to over a dozen families, became a deer forest and is home only to gamekeepers and their families. The Garvellachs to the north-west of Scarba were more exposed to danger and Don Chonnuill, the most northern of the islands, has its royal castle while Garbh Eileach ('a rough rocky place') has a dun above a bay on its eastern coast. Eileach a' Naoimh has its own cliffs to rebuff the curious. The remains of the monastery here suggest a much smaller settlement than the one at Skellig Michael off the Kerry coast of Ireland, where a whole village of cells was established around AD 600 and remained occupied for two centuries until a bloody Viking raid in 823. The monastery on Eileach a' Naoimh is accepted as having been established by St Brendan in 542 which, it has been suggested, makes them the oldest ecclesiastical buildings in Britain. The earliest written record of the monastery was not made until 300 years after the death of Columba in 597. Columba is said to have visited the island and his mother Eithne is reputed to have been buried here. Brendan was in his fifties when he came from his home in Kerry and set up a number of religious establishments around the Argyll mainland and islands. Eileach a' Naoimh was said to have had excellent pasture for grazing cows, which could have been a reason for choosing it as a contemplative site. Or was it just that, like Columba's friend Cormac, Brendan was looking to 'find a desert place in the ocean'? The beehive cells are found in a pentagonal inner enclosure with two outer walls blocking the approach from the boat landing in the rocky inlet below. Outside this enclosure there is another beehive cell with two rooms, and there are three Early Christian crosses marking graves and a circular 'special grave'. The earlier of the two chapels on the island is rectangular and clay mortared, and

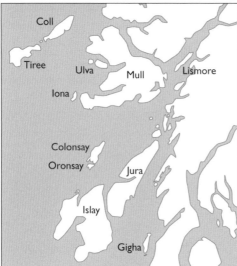

Above. Dun Bhoraraic, site of an ancient Islay fortification. (Graeme Winter collection.)

Left. Map of Islay, Jura, Colonsay.

probably dates to the 11th or 12th centuries, at least half a millennium after the island was colonised by Brendan.

These southern Hebridean islands were in sight of Ireland. Islay, Jura, Colonsay, Oronsay, the Garvellachs, Scarba and Luing were settled from around BC 7000, some three thousand years after a change in sea level. The Beaker people settled on Islay, Jura, Oronsay and Colonsay, bringing their new-look ceramics and tools and changing lifestyles.[20] A Bronze Age hut circle on Colonsay shows that there was little difference between these settlements and the earliest 'modern' black houses on the island. The earliest settlers scattered their defences everywhere – 80 forts have been identified on Islay alone and

Dun Bhoraraic is the southernmost broch in a county where brochs are in short supply.

We know that the Irish Celts made their way through at least some of these defences – but there was no keeping the missionaries out. They founded monasteries, built chapels and converted the people to a very different form of Christianity to that experienced around the Mediterranean. They became the teachers and doctors and protectors of the communities in which they settled – or which settled around them. We have seen that Brendan's followers had their contemplative monastery on Eileach a' Naoimh, and on Nave Island off the north-west corner of Islay there was a similar but smaller set-up where – as often was the case – a later medieval chapel was built, in this instance ovoid in structure. There was possibly a monastery at Kildalton and there are the remains of at least 15 cills and their neighbouring burial grounds throughout Islay, which suggests even more missionaries working here than in mainland Argyll, blessed as the mainland is with such chapels. None of the Islay chapels was large (up to about 20 feet in length and 16 feet in width) and some stood within small oval enclosures about 40 feet across. There were splendid crosses marking burial sites and much bigger ones claiming the territory as Christian just as the standing stones claimed it as Druid. Kilnave and Kildalton had crosses in the Iona style dating from about the 8th century, and a total of 11 have been found on Islay, with another eight identified elsewhere in Jura, Colonsay and Oronsay. With such evidence of the concentration of mission work in these islands, it isn't too great a leap of faith to suggest that many more crosses and much other art work is lost to us. These monks came from the stock which

Castle at Finlaggan Loch – part of the Lord of the Isles' power base on Islay. (Michael Hopkin collection.)

produced the Book of Kells. The Iona brothers were highly educated and highly artistic. St Columba is said to have infringed copyright when he duplicated the written and illuminated work of a brother – how much more was written and painted?

The Lords of the Isles based themselves on Islay, with a residence at Kilchoman and the seat of power at Finlaggan. This latter was where new lords were inaugurated, where the Council of the Isles met (causing great unease for the royal household on the mainland), and where there was a chapel and a family graveyard for the Macdonalds. The Kilchoman residence was lost long ago but there are substantial ruins showing the extent of the power house at Finlaggan. For a hundred years annual councils were held in a hall the size of that at Linlithgow Palace with a sprung wooden floor and the councillors left behind them midden heaps containing the 'empties' of French claret and leftover delicacies that speak of much sophistication.[21] The lordship passed down through Donald, son of Ranald, son of Somerled from the early 1200s and its power was at its height in the 14th and 15th centuries. There were family allies in Antrim and property throughout the islands and mainland of Argyll. A Gaelic charter from 1408 signed by Donald, Lord of the Isles, as 'McDomhnaill' and he was known simply as The MacDonald. Donald's brother John held Dunivaig, which became a military stronghold for the lordship, and it was his descendants who became Islay's most powerful family in the 16th century. In 1493, however, came the Forfeiture – to this day always referred to with a capital letter, possibly because it had such far-reaching repercussions throughout Argyll. John II Lord of the Isles went a step too far and his lands were confiscated. He lost his head in 1499, as did his son, and the vast property was redistributed among families who seemed more likely to be peaceable and toe the official line. John MacIan of Ardnamurchan, who had been Bailie of Islay, was rewarded for arresting the two doomed MacDonalds and delivering them up to Edinburgh for execution with the gift of lands on Islay, including Dunivaig castle. MacIan was murdered by MacDonald of Lochalsh, and in 1545 MacDonald lands were restored to James MacDonald of Dunivaig. An effigy of MacIan's great grandson in armour lies in the old parish church of Kildalton. Not content to be at odds with the king, the MacDonalds did not always play fair with their own kinsmen. The MacLeans of Duart on Mull claimed evidence of his inheritance of Islay lands has been destroyed by Angus Og, heir of the second Lord of the Isles, and in compensation, James V gave Hector Maclean of Duart much MacDonald territory in Islay, including Loch Gorm with its island castle.

This was just one of ten island fortifications on freshwater lochs on Islay.

Dunvaig Castle, Lagavulin – the defence system of the MacDonalds. (Michael Hopkin collection.)

Most date from the Late and Post Medieval period and most were quite substantial with two or three buildings. One at Ballygrant had at least six constructions on the island, all round-angled with thick drystone walls. Although most of these island fortifications are in a very decayed state, half of them show traces of enclosure walls. Some, like Eilean Mhuireill on Loch Finlaggan, were artificial islands. Glen Gorm Castle itself remains as it was in the 17th century with just the turf-backed curtain wall, probably built by Sir James MacDonald after he recaptured Islay for the MacDonalds in April 1615 and three rectangular buildings from around that same period. In the largest of these buildings there were cruck slots for the roof in the side walls.

In tandem with the development of the MacDonalds' defence system was their network of power within the church. The local MacDuffie and Mac Mhuirich families provided leading figures for the Augustinian priory founded on Oronsay (some say it was named by Columba for St Oran, others that this is a derivation of the Norse name 'ebb-tide island' which describes the fact that the island is accessible on foot at low tide) in the 14th century. Although the buildings were similar to the nunnery on Iona, there were no links with the Benedictines there despite John of Islay's patronage of Iona. A simple style, there was a church and detached living area. There was a stone-carving workshop here where top craftsmen were employed to carve the tombstones, which can still be seen in the Prior's House, and the Oronsay Cross. Columba is reputed to have rejected Oronsay, as he is said to have rejected so many other Argyll locations, because Ireland was still in view from Ben Oronsay. Whether he stayed long enough to lay the foundations of an establishment before going on to Iona is 563 is not clear. The present ruins date from the mid-1300s and the church, dating from 1400, is parochial rather than monastic. The roofs are gone, but compared with so many other religious buildings of that period, it is remarkably well preserved, having escaped the rigours of the Reformation and been cared for by the MacNeills of Oronsay – even a stone altar with its original slab has survived. The inside walls have succumbed to seven centuries of weather but still show where an upper floor was in place. A new roof covers one building to house the remaining carved stones, which rival those of Iona but are also weather-beaten and damaged by acidic bird-droppings.

There were many contemporary churches built on these islands, but only the early 13th-century one at Kildalton on Islay and parts of a small church at Kilchattan on Colonsay are preserved. The earliest churches had been modest and unadorned and Kildalton indicates the period at which more grandiose plans began to be drawn up – perhaps coinciding with the spreading influence introduced by Queen Margaret, who directed Scotland towards Rome and away from the Celtic tradition. Those which are now only memories and stones are the early 13th-century chapel on Nave Island; Kilmory Chapel on Scarba; Cill Challum Cille chapel at Tarbert on Jura; Cill Chaitriona chapel at Balnahard and Teampull a' Ghlinne chapel on Colonsay; Cill Challum Chille chapel at Keills, Kilnave, Orsay, Nerabolls, Kilchiaran, Ciadh Eilsteir, Kilbride, Kilnaughton, Texa and Finlaggan chapels on Islay; and Eileach a' Naoimh church. There was an important parish church at Kilchoman but only late medieval grave slabs remind us it was ever there, while the parish church at Kilarrow may have been as large as that at Kildalton. Kilarrow medieval stones include effigies of priests, and they have been identified as having been carved by the Iona school, as were those at Kilchoman, Kildalton and Nerabolls. The Loch Awe school of carving is represented at Kilarrow, Kildalton and Kilmeny, while the Loch Sween school has examples at Oronsay and Kildalton. Not surprisingly, most stone carving was done by the Oronsay schools, and while this industry was lost when the Reformation condemned decoration, the depiction of Christ and other forms of iconography as idolatry, evidence of its finest hours in these islands has been damaged more by the elements than the iconoclasm experienced elsewhere in Argyll. Even physical evidence of those Franciscan friars who came to Argyll and tried to reclaim Catholics lost to or suppressed by the Reformation has lasted longer here than on mainland Argyll in the form of crosses on the walls of the King's Cave on Jura. The churches built after the Reformation have perhaps fared no better than those much older and more primitively built. Many 18th-century churches were built in places difficult to reach by both parishioners and the sparse number of ministers available. While the Bowmore church on Islay, designed by William Adam and his son John, stands as proud as they intended it, the parish church built on Jura almost two decades later in 1777 was remodelled considerably and the Risabus Parliamentary church in the Oa, Islay, one of the Thomas Telford designs, became derelict by the 20th century.

Looking at Islay's history and the MacDonald compulsion to retain power down the centuries, it is surprising that the island itself was not sunk without trace in some bloody battle of retribution. Instead, forts and castles kept bouncing back and the land on which they were built survived for more peaceful and profitable pursuits than warfare. Fortifications were recycled, so that a prehistoric fort such as Dun Éibhinn was refined and redesigned to meet the latest defence strategies right through to medieval times. The result is that the earliest layouts are difficult to disentangle from the later ones. Much easier to define are the 14th- and 15th-century remains of the principal seat of the MacDonalds on Eilean Mor, the biggest island on Loch Finlaggan. Was this Islay residence ever a defended castle – or simply a palace with a power message built 'according to their auld fassoun' as Dean Munro described it in 1549? The chapel and remains of domestic buildings along with the foundation of the ground floor hall reveal no sign of fortification and apart from its situation on an island, there seem to have been no security measures. Dun Chonaill, one of the properties which passed to the MacLeans of Duart, was described by Fordun in the late 14th century as a 'great castle', so there is no question about its purpose. How successful it was is another matter. Also built on an island, it was protected by steep cliffs and its landing places were dangerous. Rubble-built curtain walls around the main summit were strengthened with lime mortar but the remains of around 30 buildings had drystone walls Some of these, scattered near the landing place and higher in the lea of the summit, may have been part of the 14th-century deal achieved by Hector MacLean. Jura had always had its own island defences, from an Dunan at Ardmenish dating from the early prehistoric age through to Claig Castle – probably built in medieval times – on an island offshore from Jura House, which was to become the island's main estate headquarters in later centuries. The experts have found it difficult to date and what remains may be from buildings which went up in the 15th century. Claig Castle was neither hall-house nor tower-house, according to its shape and size; it had the thick walls of a defensive building, a rectangular floor plan with the suggestion of two separate rooms and an inside straight staircase climbing one wall.

Dunivaig Castle was built in defiance as well as defence. To declare oneself Lord of the Isles was to make a statement which expected an aggressive answer – and throughout the centuries, this stronghold was attacked again and again. It has been described as a 'shattered fragment' of the MacDonald fortification it once was. Most devastating was the siege of February 1615, followed in 1647 by another drubbing. Its origins were 14th century or perhaps even earlier and the earliest remnants include a lime-mortared curtain wall which may well have completely surrounded the rocky summit on which the castle once proudly perched. The most visible remains were probably built in the middle of the 16th century and indicate a two- or even three-storeyed hall building which extended over the earlier building. There was a hexagonal external courtyard in which five buildings stood, as well an an interior courtyard with a stairway. When the inspectors from the Royal Commission for Ancient and Historical Monuments made a survey for their 1984 volume, they saw evidence of a retractable footbridge. The MacDonalds were careful about who came to visit at Dunivaig. Thick walls and narrow embrasures from which to fire cannons were the main means of defence but there may have been extra defences built from which to defend the February 1615 rebellion. The MacDonalds had a big defence bill that year, rebuilding the island castle on Loch Gorm and creating corresponding fortifications on Colonsay on Loch an Sgoltaire. Each stood solid and square against all the king's men, but each suffered in the retribution meted out against the Lord of the Isles. Sir James MacDonald got his Gorm Island stronghold back two months after the February attack of 1615, but worse was to come later in the century. From north to south, Islay shielded itself from attack, with A'Chrannag trying to stave off the enemy in 1598 with the help of a ditch during the battle of Traigh Ghruineard at the head of Loch Gruinart, and Dun Athad, which was thrown up on a promontory near the Mull of Oa.

With peace came later generations of the Argyll protagonists who were more domestic in their architectural aspirations. Industry – carried on in a desultory way since the arrival of the very first settlers – began to be developed. The Campbells who took over in the 17th century were not content to sit in draughty castles on rocky promontories or in island fortresses. As early as 1631, John Campbell of Cawdor was saying he wanted a 'more commodious hous ... in a more proper pairt of the yle' than the castle of Dunivaig' which his father had won for him. Not surprisingly, that being the century of remarkably bloody civil war throughout the whole of the British islands, this building of a 'commodious hous' did not happen for some time. Sir Hugh Campbell of

Cawdor made plans in 1677 for a place at Kilarrow – what was a good enough site for a medieval chapel was good enough for him – and brought in outside masons to build for him.

Islay House was built in the last quarter of the 17th century when peace was still a precarious commodity and to build for comfort was a brave deed. It was styled on a traditional domesticated tower-house in an L-shaped plan with three main storeys and a garret. This original design is not entirely clear as an extension was built in the next century which turned the place into a half-H. In early Victorian times, the famous architect, W.H. Playfair, was commissioned by Walter Frederick Campbell to add Scottish Baronial style offices but these were never built. Eventually, when Hugh Morrison inherited the house from his uncle in 1909, the Playfair plans were altered by Detmar Blow of the Arts and Crafts Movement to give a frontage which was felt to be more in keeping with the older parts of the house.

Although the title 'Lords of the Isles' has a romantic ring to it in the 21st century and many an Argyll bungalow proudly bears the name Somerled, there is no doubt that later proprietors of Islay paid more attention to development than to accumulation. The MacDonalds had held onto Islay, Jura, Scarba and Muckairn lands until the reign of James VI when they went to Sir John Campbell of Calder. His feu duty for Islay was £500. All these lands were sold on to Campbell of Shawfield for £12,000. If Campbells were considered outsiders in previous centuries, the 19th century brought yet another change of lairds and of tenants. Morrison of Islay had 67,000 acres worth £16,440 a year; Ramsay of Kildalton (the member of parliament John Ramsay) had 54,250 acres valued at £8,226; Finlay of Dunlossit held 17,676 acres worth £2,882 a year; and Campbell of Ballinaby had 1,800 acres worth £378 a year. According to the records of the agricultural societies of the 1870s, most of the 'old native race tenantry' had gone and the land was being used for dairy farming by tenants from Ayrshire and the Lowlands. The hill districts were 'covered with thriving flocks of black-faced and Cheviot sheep'. Land cultivation had improved since the 1840s, when many natives of Islay were heading for Canada and America for a better life, and since the new excise laws in the 1820s, the distilleries had prospered, turning Islay towns and villages into famous names the world over wherever whisky was drunk. John Ramsay of Kildalton was ready to build a fine house on his 54,250 Islay acres. This was a man who has been accused, like so many other lairds in Argyll, of sending his tenants off to the New World to give him room for expansion. Whatever the subjective viewpoint may be, there are records showing that he funded the passage of some of his tenants and he did visit Canada in 1870, making a point of visiting the Islay émigrés and taking news of their families. He also built Kildalton Castle in the Baronial style. It had a four-storey crenelated and corbelled tower with an angle-tower adding yet another storey. The gabled wings were crow-stepped and there was an arch over the main entrance. Inside it was more classical in style, with spacious rooms. Ramsay took his role as laird seriously, donating a silver replica of the intricate Celtic cross at Kildalton as a trophy to the local golf club. But in 1922, the estate was sold to the Cliftons, who let the place run down. John Talbot Clifton spent more time exploring the world than in his island home, and during Henry de Vere Clifton's proprietorship in the 1970s, the place was vandalised and put on the market in a dilapidated state.

The Campbells of Ballinaby had bought their acres from the Duke of Argyll as far back as 1650, but by 1895 this property was in different hands, too. The MacLachlans lived in the mansion house at Ballinaby, which burned down in 1932. The MacLachlans still owned the lands and the farm until they sold up to the Ministry of Agriculture and Fisheries at the end of the Second World War.

There were no other extravagant houses on Islay or its neighbouring islands. Colonsay House was a two-storey laird's house in 1722, but that original simplicity was lost as the house gradually grew to become more like the mansions on the mainland. The vernacular houses, particularly on Islay, have perhaps a better rate of survival than elsewhere, especially those in the planned villages. Although the thatched black houses have disappeared, the Campbell lairds of the 18th century left behind them a lasting monument – Bowmore, built in 1786 by Daniel Campbell (the Younger) of Shawfield and Islay on the grid pattern with its round church to keep out the devil still standing; Port Ellen, built in 1821 by Walter Frederick Campbell on a semicir-

Kildalton Castle, left a ruin by its latter owners. (Michael Hopkin collection.)

Top. The black houses – here at Erabus – which were the homes of most Islay folk. (Michael Hopkin collection.)

Above. Jamieson Street, Bowmore – a planned town, but the planning didn't offer plumbing. (Michael Hopkin collection.)

cular plan and named for his first wife; and Port Charlotte, which was also on the grid pattern and went up in 1828, called after Walter Frederick's mother. These villages – seen as a model way to progress – were built as centres for agriculture, fishing and distilling. The Bowmore distillery was built in 1779 and the two-storey houses survive from the earliest part of the development. As this book concerns itself with what has been lost rather than what has survived, it is more appropriate to look towards the ruins of townships and shielings found throughout these islands, evidence of populations which were manipulated during the late 18th and much of the 19th centuries. The townships had existed long before the fine plans for model villages were drawn up. Some, like Tockmal on Islay and An Carn on Jura, both sites of cup marks, and at Dun Nosebridge on Islay and Dun Éibhinn on Colonsay, had grown beside ancient settlements; some, such as Kilslevan on Islay, were built near medieval chapels.

Kilarrow Old Township at Bridgend on Islay was in existence in the last quarter of the 18th century, as were shieling huts on Jura. These townships were not able to sustain the increase in population which lasted until the 1830s, but at the same time the lairds were reducing the number of multiple tenancy farms and giving leases to single tenants. In the Oa pensinsula of Islay, there are many townships which were abandoned at this time, like the large one at Lurabus. But agricultural changes were not the only reasons here for townships being deserted. At Knocklearoch farmstead there had been a lead-mining settlement at the start of the 1700s. When it was abandoned at the end of its working life the workers moved on.

Many of those workers were seasonal and itinerant. Like those who worked the lead mines of Morvern, the slate quarries of Ballachulish and Easdale and the ironworks and gunpowder factory at Melfort, they weren't locals but men who had gained expertise in other parts of the country. John Taylor, who was born in Cumberland (now Cumbria), was left fatherless at the age of four. When he was nine, he was sent to work dressing lead ore for twopence a day. After much mining experience, he went in his 30s to Islay to make a report on the mines and he worked there on and off until 1730. His career ended in the Leadhills mines of Lanarkshire. Like his fellow miners, he worked shifts and ate irregularly and like his fellow miners he ended up with scurvy because of drinking whisky and eating salt provisions.[22]

Mine washings at Finlaggan farm, one of the lead-mining centres on Islay. (Craigard Holidays collection.)

Lead mining had been the earliest industry on Islay, stretching back at least to the Late Middle Ages. From early in the 17th century to 1880, a succession of proprietors and lessees extracted the ore, though there were never mining operations to the extent seen in North Argyll. Lead and silver mining went on around Ballygrant – *Bail' a' Ghrana* means 'village of grain' – from Viking times, and during the last major spell of production which lasted 18 years from 1862, there were 14 mines working. To the south-west of Ballygrant quarry, a mine at Gartness produced most of the area's 18,424 ounces of silver. A row of miners' cottages was built to house 16 families at Ballygrant – like John Taylor, the workers often came from other mining areas. This row of houses has not been lost – but today in a much modernised state houses five families in the same space. The building which today is the Ballygrant Inn was once the house and grounds of the manager of the Mulreesh lead mines. It was known as Robolls House and itself was built on the site of Robolls Crofts, indicating a three-stage evolution over the period of two centuries. Today, instead of mining, Ballygrant families like the Grahams, who run the Inn, and the Bells who tenant a farm and run Craigard Holidays, rely increasingly on tourism for a living and the remains of the mines – a machine house and mine hole remain on the Bell's Finlaggan Farm and there are 'washings' still visible on the neighbouring Achnaglach Farm.

Ballygrant is reputed to be the longest-established village on Islay and

House and grounds of the manager of the Mulreesh lead mines.(Graeme Waters collection.)

Left. The wheel-house of the mine on Finlaggan farm. (Craigard Holidays collection.)

Below. Ballygrant mill – built to serve one of Islay's oldest settlements. (Craigard Holidays collection.)

certainly it must have been an agricultural centre for many centuries, with tenants like the Bells' predecessors being thirled to the water-powered meal mill. The main part of this building was demolished in 1991, having been converted into a sawmill for the previous 60 years.The last major revival of the Mulreesh mines was in 1862, and up to 1880 they produced 1,919 tons of lead ore and some silver. There is still a small mining operation, but along with the bog iron ore mined on Jura and Islay in the 1700s, it is consigned to the past as a viable industry.

Slate, marble, siliceous sand, iron, lead and silver all provided a level of income for Islay lairds in the 19th century. The sand was shipped out for glass making and there were brick and tile works to meet the demands of a

The old mill in the process of demolition. (Craigard Holidays collection.)

Government Drainage Act. Clay at Forland made good land-drainage tiles and along with the burning of lime for fertiliser was an industry which evolved from the farming developments of the second half of the 19th century. Slate quarrying was profitable for some time at Kilchiaran and Esknish on Islay, and at Tarbert and Inverlussa on Jura, but none created as big an operation as the abandoned quarry on the island of Belnahua. By comparison with this one-time little power house of industry, Islay, Jura, Colonsay and Oronsay were in the main agricultural islands. There were meal mills and markets and fairs at Bowmore, Port Ellen, Bridgend and Ballygrant. The introduction in the 19th century of the steamers connecting with Glasgow every day in the summer and twice a week in winter did not only make communication for people easier: it also improved freight transport and contributed to the growth of the main industry which was a by-product of that agriculture – distilling.

Pot-still malt whisky was produced for over 200 years from the water, peat and barley, but after new legislation was introduced between 1816 and 1823, Islay was able to take advantage and create a new legal industry. Once, pot stills were probably run in every settlement. Ballygrant had its quota of illicit distillers, including Baldy a'Chladdaich who was deported to Australia as a result of his activities. The village also had a legal distillery, now closed, on the site of Lossit Kennels. Throughout Islay today there are seven working distilleries out of an original 12 built in the 19th century. By 1830, there were 16 licensed distillers but some were very small and very short-lived. During that new decade, the flourishing distilleries were at Port Charlotte, Octomore, Newton, Daill, Lossit, Bowmore, Tallant, Port Ellen (a converted malt mill), Laphroaig, Ardbeg and Lagavulin, where there were two. By the 1880s, Bowmore, Port Charlotte, Laphroaig, one of the Lagavulin distilleries, Port Ellen and Ardbeg were still flourishing and new distilleries were built at

Ardbeg distillery still produces one of Islay's well-loved whiskies but many of the original buildings have been lost. (Michael Hopkin collection.)

Bruichladaich, Bunnahaibhainn and Caol Ila. Today, Port Charlotte and Port Ellen have also been lost.

The Port Ellen distillery was built in 1825 by James Ramsay. It was on the seashore about half a mile from the village and had three barley lifts and three malting floors. The lifts ranged between 100 ft by 36 ft and 135 ft by 30 ft. The two kilns were 56 ft by 26 ft and 36 ft square. A malt store and a mill room also went up and the mash tun was 14 ft in diameter and 5 ft deep. There were also six warehouses capable of holding 240,000 gallons of whisky and the distillery produced 140,000 gallons a year. Water for the distillery came from two local lochs and peat was used for drying. At Port Charlotte, J.B. Sheriff was the proprietor of the Lochindaal Distillery, built opposite Bowmore. Loch Octomore fed the Bruichladaich distillery, built in 1881 two miles from Port Charlotte. The water was presumably freed up after the closure of the Octomore distillery – a small farm-based distillery like the other early ones which by the 1880s had fallen before the market forces of the major purpose-built businesses. Where distilleries have closed, fine buildings have been lost. Port Ellen distillery was demolished after its closure in 1983; the Port Charlotte buildings have become warehouses for Bruichladaich and a bed and breakfast establishment; and even distilleries like Ardbeg, which still flourish, have lost some of their original buildings. The methods of shipment have also vastly changed. In the 19th century, whisky from several distilleries was shipped from Port Ellen, some of it floated out in its barrels to waiting ships, while whisky

Port Charlotte Distillery buildings are now warehouses for Bruichladaich, another fine whisky, and incorporate a bed and breakfast establishment. (Michael Hopkin collection.)

from Bruichladaich was shipped from Bruichladaich pier every Tuesday to Glasgow. The barrels were towed by a boatman and they were floated to the ships lashed together with iron pins and chains called 'dogs'.[23] Puffers delivered the coal which fuelled the distilleries.

By the 1880s, each distillery was exporting up to 250,000 gallons of the water of life each year to Glasgow, Liverpool and London. The distilleries employed between 50 and 70 people in the 19th century and some built workers' houses and recreation halls – the latter an innovation which must have impressed those used to working at the fishing or on the land. Even so, people continued to leave Argyll during the later part of the 19th century. The potato famine of the 1840s, which affected their near neighbours in Ireland so badly, also forced many from these islands (266 people drowned when the *Exmouth*, carrying emigrants to America, foundered off the north-west coast of Islay in May 1847). The immense changes in the use of agricultural land also created deserted townships such as Tockmal, Grasdal and Lurabus on Islay. The population fell from 15,000 in the 1830s to 8,000 at the end of the 19th century. This was nothing new for the people of Islay, who in the early 18th century had suffered a small-pox epidemic, famine and poverty in the wake of the civil war. People died or drifted away like John Taylor to seek work, but occasionally vast numbers would leave. It is recorded that between 1738 and 1740, almost 500 people left Islay for the British colony of New York. The rise and fall of a variety of industries has meant that this loss of people has continued and those who stayed in the 19th century were often condemned to the poorhouse – as many as 80 were dependent on the authorities in the late 1880s, ranging in age from six to 87 years. Sometimes a whole family was taken in, such as the six MacIntosh children aged between two and 13 who presumably had been orphaned.[24] The loss of the Islay poorhouse is not one to be regretted. In retrospect, the opportunities for work seem many, but the fishing at Portnahaven was precarious (the fleet no longer exists as such), the salt pans at Portnahaven and Ardlarach were worked in the late 17th century but disappeared with little trace, and the woollen mill at Redhouses, built on the east bank of the River Sorn in 1883, may have retained some of the last water-powered wool-processing machinery to survive in the UK, but as an industry offering jobs, it ceased to function in the 20th century. The first proprietor was James Christie of Bridgend and his 'manufactuary' processed wool from the raw state to the finished product in a three-storey building in which the powered machinery was driven by a low breast-shot iron water-wheel with an unusual chain drive mechanism.[25] The tile works which made farm-drainage systems had been built in the early 1840s near Foreland House on Islay. It comprised a drying shed with ten bays, an engine house with a cast iron cylindrical horse-driven clay-mixing machine and a vaulted kiln, but having provided a handful of men with work until the drainage system was installed, it became a roofless shell. In the late 18th century a smelting furnace had existed at Freeport, probably near a later Caol Ila distillery site, but although it was illustrated in the 1770s account of Pennant's Tour there are no traces today and the 322 lead mines on Islay which provided work for so many English miners between 1708 and 1730 are now the object of archaeological study by the Council for Scottish Archaeology summer school work parties. Much of the lead workings seen on Islay by Pennant during his 1772 tour of Scotland were open-cast with six-foot deep trenches but in later years shafts were sunk south-east of Ballygrant. Kilslevan had seen copper mining in 1760 but that, too, was overtaken by the quest for lead. The mining papers from the Islay Estate documents show that mining ceased in 1880 and the plant and machinery were sold after the termination of the final lease in 1904.

Jura, too, had its mines but never to the extent seen on Islay; but both islands, as well as Colonsay and Oronsay, had historically lived on their black cattle, as had so much of Argyll. The drove-roads and the ferry routes were important links from the earliest times. Some of these routes were circuitous and dangerous – and could never have been comfortable. Some of the routes, with their stone piers and slipways, are still intact; some were built by that very busy engineer Thomas Telford. When Telford first travelled there himself in the early 19th century to make surveys for roads, bridges and piers, he found the ferry inn at Lagg on the east coast of Jura crowded with hard-drinking drovers who had to wait for better weather to take them to Keills on the Mid Argyll mainland. Some of the drovers took matters into their own hands. The cattle, tied by their heads to the ferry, kicked to get free and the journey was a perilous one with the head drover himself taking the helm. It is likely that such hair-raising crossings were not unusual. There was no regular ferry from Jura to the mainland for many years but mail came out from Crinan to Kinuachdrachd in the north-east of the island – saving a very difficult land journey from the south.

The Reformation had taken place in 1560 but change was slow. The new church believed it could only move things along if all the islanders were able to go to church on Sunday. As we know, Dr Samuel Johnson found that there were too few churches and ministers for the potential congregations and people were travelling long distances to church. Regular ferries meant ministers could go to the people. At the turn of the 18th century, Donald MacNicol of Jura asked for his stipend to be raised from £139 6s. 9d. because £50 of it was used to pay his assistant who ministered on Colonsay. The ferry fares took up a large portion of the £50 and Mr MacNicol explained that the assistant had to travel nine miles by land and then make a dangerous ferry crossing (this was probably the route between Kinuachdrachd to Scalasaig). Although Kinuachdrachd now seems remote and cut off by land and sea, in the 19th century it was quite a bustling place – no doubt because it was on the route of the cattle ferry from Colonsay to Craignish on the mainland. Cattle boats also went from Scalasaig to Loch Tarbert on Jura, a slightly longer journey of 11 miles. John MacNeil, the laird in the early 1800s, improved Colonsay's main centre at Scalasaig by building a new stone harbour wall and slipway, much admired as the best place in the Hebrides for repairing boats by Lord Teignmouth during a visit in 1836. He was a hard man to impress, having dismissed the Kyles of Bute as lacking in scenic beauty. These improvements remain, having replaced nothing more than rocks from which it was dangerous to embark. In those days, people travelled from Colonsay to Islay while the cattle took the Jura routes. The nearest point on Islay was Rubha' a Mhail Point but the ferries of later centuries came down through the Sound of Islay to Port Askaig. Those cattle which came in to Port Askaig crossed to Feolin and took the drove road to Lagg. The northern Jura sail meant the onward drove would be via Loch Awe and Dalmally.

Colonsay was – and is – an island where community means much. In 1841, a thousand people lived there. Today, fewer than a hundred remain. During the 18th and 19th centuries, many people left for North Carolina, Prince Edward

Island, Bruce County, Manitoulin Island and Saskatchewan – all destinations which offered hope to people whose homes were being denied them. When Thomas Pennant visited the island in 1772, he said that the two islands of Colonsay and Oronsay were the property of a MacNeill laird who was popular and fair with his people. But in September 1791, almost a quarter of the population (28 men, 28 women and 86 children) left Colonsay and sailed directly from the island for America on a ship called the *General Washington*. Mr Malcolm Campbell, the Islay customs officer, reported that this ship went to Colonsay from Islay to take passengers and all their effects 'which consist only of wearing apparel, as they are poor labouring people who have been deprived of their farms by their landlord and they will not be stopt by him'. On the same ship were 40 adults and 31 children from Islay, a Jura man, four men and women and 125 children from Mull. Archibald MacNeill of Colonsay was the landlord of the day. On 17 August 1792, the *Fortune* left Bowmore on Islay with 73 men, 60 women and 47 children from Jura and others from Coll, Islay, Knapdale and Luing. With 417 passengers on board and not all accounted for, it is believed that a proportion were from Colonsay. As Jura and Colonsay were a joint parish, the people described as coming from Jura may have included Colonsay families. In 1806, all the passengers on the *Spencer*, bound for Prince Edward Island, were from Colonsay. This was said to have been a voluntary exodus of the MacMillan and Bell families and their tacksmen. It is likely that these people were not all the 'poor labouring folk' who were forced out in the previous decade but perhaps people making the decision to seek a new life. The population of Colonsay grew again to that peak in 1841, but then came more hard times and more migration and emigration.

A lost population and lost homes: although houses from the 16th century survive at Scalasaig, Dunan a' Chullaich and Dun Ghaillionn, only 89 houses remain from that larger population and of those, only around 50 are occupied all year round, with Colonsay Estate owning 44 properties, including all those in the settlements of Kiloran and Machrins and many in Kilchattan and Scalasaig. Colonsay House, the heart of the Estate, dates from 1772. It was sold, with the rest of the island, to Lord Strathcona in 1904 and at the time of writing is owned by the Howard family. Ruined townships and shielings are found on all this group of islands as we have seen, but on Colonsay the distances between the winter town and the summer shieling were far shorter for simple geographic reasons. What remain are signs of the single herdsman's stone hut to groups of more than twenty structures. On Jura in 1772, Thomas Pennant thought the 'sheelins' were 'grotesque': summer huts for the goat and cow herds were low structures, some rectangular and some conical, with entrances covered not with doors but birch-twig faggots. Some of these were made from branches covered with sods – true 'benders' in modern parlance – and the beds 'heath, placed on a bank of sods'. While they were living in the shielings, the women made cheeses and stored them in hanging wicker baskets. Some of the more isolated ruins of huts on the coast of Islay may have been where men stayed when they hunted sea fowl. The winter houses were very substantial on all the islands: they had to protect against violent storms. Most roofs on Colonsay, Jura and Islay seem to have been constructed using end crucks and scarf crucks (a cruck is one of a pair of curved timbers supporting a roof; the scarf crucks overlap) but in recent times, the only remaining examples have been at Keils on Jura. Lord Teignmouth said during his late 18th-century tour that the tenant farmhouses on Colonsay had two or three rooms, a storehouse or barn and a byre, but that despite the fact that the laird of Colonsay had given between £10 and £12 to any tenant who built a chimneyed fireplace, the people were still insisting on setting their fire in the middle of the floor so that the 'wee things' could get round it. Thatching continued in crofting townships at Keils on Jura, at Conisby on Islay, and elsewhere well into the 20th century, usually made from reeds or straw and heather. Many of these townships had corn-drying kilns and kiln barns and threshing mills, sometimes horse-driven like the one at Cladville Farm on Islay. But with the move towards single-tenanted farms and the introduction of sheep or shooting, the populations dropped and townships like Islay's Kilchiaran were abandoned.

We cannot regret the loss of houses where people lived in conditions likely

Peat-cutting was a necessary intrusion into the farming year for a population which even in 1912 could not afford coal. (Michael Hopkin collection.)

to be responsible for high infant mortality and the generation of life-threatening disease. The Reports of the Medical Officer of Health for Argyll in 1882 said that on Islay, an inspector found a house with seven occupants in a kitchen and small bedroom. The family shared the kitchen with five cows, a calf, dogs and chickens. A child in the family was suffering from convulsions because of congestion of the lungs. An aunt in the same room was in the last stage of consumption [tuberculosis]. At Bowmore in 1893, a large part of the village depended on water from the distillery for domestic use. The aqueduct which brought the water down three or four miles went through fields where cows and horses had free access to the water. In summer, these animals spent a large part of the day cooling themselves by standing in the water. To add insult to injury, a drain from a dwelling house emptied into the aqueduct just before it reached the village.

Today's population of Islay is around 4,000. Machinery, skills, cultures and communities have been lost, as they have been in the neighbouring islands. They leave no greater shadow on the landscape than does Dun Éibhinn Iron Age fort on Colonsay. There is often far less to be seen of their past presence than the well-preserved ruins of Oronsay priory. But while we can regret the loss of language and customs we can only rejoice that people no longer have to share their homes and their drinking water with the cows and chickens. The harsh realities must disabuse us of any romantic notion of the rural island past.

Oronsay Priory – lost, but leaving behind some of the best preserved ruins from the Western Isles' past. (From Thomas Pennant's A Tour of Scotland and Voyage to the Hebrides, *1772.)*

CHAPTER 5

MID ARGYLL AND KINTYRE:

OLD AS TIME, NEW AS
TOMORROW'S ENERGY

The surprise factor in the Mid Argyll and Kintyre story is not how much has been lost – but how little. This stretch of southern Argyll has been occupied by foreign forces, battle scarred, industrialised and marginalised. It has pioneered the most modern forms of transport of the day, been subject to agricultural experiment and today is not only host to a growing number of wind farms but manufactures the blades for the windmills. And still there is clear evidence of the past: standing stones, henges, cairns, cists, chapels, monasteries, duns,

Dunadd Fort – once the hub of secular and spiritual power in Scotland.
(Author's collection.)

forts, castles and baronial mansions may not be in pristine condition but their remains generously inform us of our ancestry. That is not to say, of course, that the landscape from the Mull of Kintyre to Rubh a' Chnaip at the mouth of Loch Melfort is set in aspic, a Disneyland of the prehistoric, the historic and the near past. Stonerobbing, torching, evicting and neglect have wrought their worst here as throughout Argyll; but perhaps because there were such riches to squander, there are signposts to the past at every turn. It says much about those riches that in researching the ancient and historical monu-

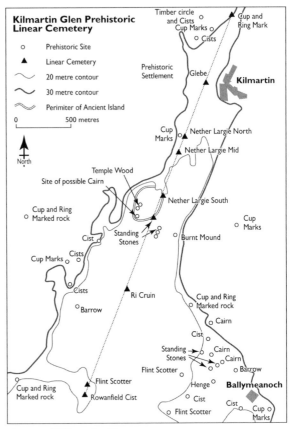

A map of Kilmartin Glen.

ments of Mid Argyll, the late historian-archaeologist Marion Campbell of Kilberry, FSA, and her companion, Mary Sandeman, visited a thousand sites in the area. Although that research may have been exhausting, it was not exhaustive, as Miss Campbell would have admitted herself, and in the intervening half century since that survey was made, many more sites have come to light. To cross the border into Kintyre – once a foreign country under an agreement made with the Norse king, Magnus Barefoot – is to magnify those riches threefold.

Forts and duns sprinkle the coastline from Melfort to the tip of Kintyre. Some are almost on the shore, like those to the north of Duntrune Castle at Ardifur or Dun an Garbh-Sroine to the south of Arduaine. Some are on islands (Eilean an Duin on the outer rim of Craobh Haven marina is named for its purpose), and some are high in the hills – above Ardfern, above the still tricky

Bealach Mor, above Loch Ederline, above Kilmichael Glen. Perhaps the most famous is Dun Add fort, protruding from the Moine Mor to the north of the Crinan Canal. There is a carving of a boar, a footprint in a rock. The summit of the hill still shows signs of the stone defences, but a bigger community lived here in wooden houses long gone. This was a special place. It looked north up Kilmartin glen across five major burial cairns. In the hills above the cairns, many stone cists have been found with burnt and unburnt human remains and grave gifts. On a clear day, the mighty Ben Cruachan comes into sight. To the west, the Druidic standing stones align with the solstes. The river Add is thought to have once been able to bring large craft farther inland than today is possible. The early artists had decorated numerous rock faces in the area with the swirling cup and ring carvings: at Achanarnich on the Craignish peninsula, near Ormaig on the mainland opposite, in Kilmichael Glen, at Cairnbaan, at Slockavulin, Achnabreck and several sites on the Moine Mhor ('the great moss)' itself. All this and much more would still have been clearly visible and perhaps intact when St Columba anointed Aidan the first Christian king of Scotland – and first in the British islands – in the year 574. The early missionaries like Columba were careful to inculturate their Christianity; to graft it onto the spirituality of a people who already had beliefs in the power of the earth and the heavens. Unlike the Conquistadors who destroyed the cultures they found in South America in order to impose a new religion and order, the Celts nurtured what they found present and added to the layers of art and knowledge.

Many keys have always been evident in Mid Argyll, sometimes unappreciated, often vandalised. In his report for the *Statistical Account* of 1792, the local minister said there was nothing of interest in Kilmartin Glen. Some have remained hidden for millennia. MacLeods, owners of the quarry above Kilmartin village, are obliged to call in archaeological experts to assess the land for every new phase they work, and in that process, a number of important cists and artefacts have been uncovered. A farmer who slept out in the hills of Kilmichael Glen stumbled across another cist. Peat, moss and leaf mould are as much responsible for the loss of Argyll's past as the stone robbers, the land clearers and the iconoclasts. But water, of which there is so much in this county, has also played its part in hiding from view or simply destroying evidence of structures built in other ages.

In 1972, the waters of Loch Awe dropped to the lowest level in living memory, revealing many crannogs which had been lost to view. These island dwellings and fortifications, found mostly in Ireland and Scotland, and often man-made, were used in prehistoric times but also through to the second Christian millennium. When the waters of Loch Awe went down, so did the archaeological divers, and visiting 60 sites in the loch, they found twenty crannogs, all except one a stone-faced structure with easily visible criss-cross beams and radiating timbers. One crannog had a broken saddle quern and there was a broken rotary quern on the shore opposite. Whetstones were found and there were visible harbours, jetties and, in three instances, causeways. One of the crannogs had a midden.[26] These sites included Keppochen, Larach Ban, Inverliever, Ederline, Finchairn, Sonachan and Kilneuair. This being a dangerous loch and these crannogs holding precious detail of a lost past, the archaeological divers were not keen to encourage amateur divers to visit the sites. The sheer numbers involved, however, confirm the importance of Loch Awe throughout history.

It can't all have been about defence, of course. The monks who settled there from the earliest times must have found peace and solitude. The traders heading for the Tay Gap must have found it a convenient highway. The drovers taking cattle to the major trysts must have found it not just easier going than the difficult hills and dangerous passes, but a place where the cattle could find grazing. The lands towards the west end of the loch were first in the hands of the powerful Lords of Glassary, a family called Scrymgeour. Their seat of power was a castle at Finchairn and nearby there was a church at Kilneuair (*Cill an lubhair*, 'chapel of the yews') which was a major focus of Christianity in this part of Argyll. The ruins of the church are about two miles east from Ford, on the footpath from Loch Awe to Loch Fyne, and it was in use by the second half of the 13th century. The original work of the chancel survived. A piscina (the stone niche near the altar into which is emptied the water in which sacred vessels have been washed) and a font also endure from the earliest times. The font disappeared but was discovered and restored to the church by 1916. The main walls of the earlier church, however, and the sandstone and epidiorite dressings were worked into the walls of a newer version of the church which went up some time in the earliest 1500s.[27] Part of a 16th-century tomb chest is in the church and in the graveyard there are other carved grave slabs of the Loch Awe school which depict knights in West Highland armour of the style used in the 14th and 15th centuries. The Scrymgeours lost their power to the Campbells and by the first decades of the 17th century Finchairn and Kilneuair were in the hands of Campbell of Ederline. The power of the church shifted too: Kilmichael Glassary became the major church in the area and Kilneuair, which had been the site of huge cattle markets for centuries, fell into disrepair. By 1563, the church was in ruins, the cattle market had shifted to Kilmichael Glassary and the local community was under threat. Above the church on the hillside, Kilneuair settlement in time became deserted.

Above. Kilbride chapel above Rhudle farm – myth says screams can be heard there at night. (Author's collection.)

Right. The fine windows of this medieval chapel have stood the test of time. They looked across what was once a busy glen before townships were cleared. (Author's collection.)

The name Kilmichael suggests an Early Christian chapel and on the other side of the hills which run between Kilmichael and Kilmartin glens is another chapel, this one dedicated to St Bride. Kilbride is a tiny derelict chapel in the hills above Rhudle Mill, now a dwelling house. The east wall of the medieval chapel has survived well and its two fine tall narrow windows are intact. Across from the chapel are the hidden ruins of Achayerrran, one of the many settlements wiped out in Kilmartin and Glassary parishes by the cholera outbreak of 1854. In Rhudle Glen, site of a busy working farm, there is an early 18th-century house which later became a hunting lodge for the Malcolms. It is now used with great respect as a farm building.

Top. The 18th-century Rhudle hunting lodge now respectfully used as farm storage. (Author's collection.)

Above. Carnasserie Castle, built by a bishop, torched in the civil war. (Author's collection.)

Light up the indicator in Kilmartin Museum to check out the position of important prehistoric sites in the area and the Christmas tree effect is blinding. When Kilbride, Kilmichael and Kilmartin chapels were built, this had already been an area of immense activity for at least three thousand years. The fact that the kings of Dalriada centred themselves here in early Christian times suggests

The first Gaelic translations of the Bible were instigated at Carnasserie by Bishop Carswell. The language struggles to survive in Mid Argyll. (Author's collection.)

that it was still a place of great importance and the move of religious and economic power from Kilneuair to Kilmichael in late medieval times picked up the threads of that status – although by then there were no kings and no saints in permanent residence. There was, however, a bishop (or a superintendent of the church, for he was styled in several different ways) resident in the area just beyond Kilmartin Glen high above the crossroads of the modern A816 and B840. The building of Carnasserie castle, itself sited on land bearing not only prehistoric standing stones and cairns but evidence that ancient physicians cultivated a physic garden there, began in 1565, just five years after the Reformation. The castle was completed in 1572 and was unusual in that it had a tower and an adjoining hall wing. Its first resident was John Carswell, under whose direction the first translation of the Bible into Gaelic was begun. A century later, this castle was blown up during the civil war and its substantial ruins show evidence of the blackening of gunpowder.

At Kilmichael church and more especially at Kilmartin, evidence of the military atmosphere which existed in Mid Argyll is present in the graveyards, where armour-suited effigies are carved on grave slabs; fine examples of the carving schools of their day. Both churches are later versions of their original selves. There is no evidence of the medieval Kilmichael chapel, although a Celtic iron bell in a medieval bronze case bearing a representation of the Crucifixion , identified as having been cast in the 12th century, was found in 1814 – either at nearby Torbhlaren Farm, or at the back of the manse on the site of the old church. This may have come from Kilneuair or may have been in use in a very early chapel at Kilmichael. This type of bell was used in the Early

Christian chapels but the Romanesque encasement was from a later era. The artefact survived the Reformation but is lost to the area because it is now kept safely by the National Museums of Scotland. Many of the treasures found in the burial cairns of Kilmichael Glen have also left the area for museums in Edinburgh, although many more, it may be assumed, must be in private collections, in attics or long since consigned to dustbins by those who rifled through the grave gifts of the dead of previous millennia.

As in every corner of Argyll, agriculture and land improvements are the culprits for the disappearance of many prehistoric and historic relics. Stone-robbing to build houses and in more recent centuries, enclosure walls, must have obliterated many more cairns than have now been excavated and recorded. We treat such places with a degree of sensitivity today, ploughing around standing stones, laying aside land on which burial cairns were erected. There was no such respect at Kilmichael Tryst Fair, the huge cattle market held on land west from the church to Leacach Luaine ('the dancing stones') near the two-arched Bridge of Add built in 1737 by the Argyll Commissioners of Supply. There, a fallen standing stone was used to measure fabric, a measure which became standard throughout the area. Contemporary local farmers clearing their land of stones to grow bere and oats were equally prosaic about their surroundings.

If Mid Argyll has been fortunate in retaining so much of its ancient past, there has perhaps been a greater loss of detail of Mid Argyll's more recent past, involving as it did the poor and therefore unrecorded. There is little record of the congregation of Kilmichael Glassary, with its mix of ploughmen and fishermen beholden to their feudal landlord. We know, however, that there was a church in Kilmichael Glassary in 1423. The rector, a member of the still powerful Scrymgeour family, was moved on because he did not speak or understand the Gaelic language of his congregation. We know that in 1647, the poor fishermen and farmers of this area lost their nets, their ploughs, the blankets in their kists, their lobster pots and the very houses themselves because there is a record of the slash-and-burn policy of Alasdair macCholla [sic] – Sir Alexander MacDonald, a descendant of the Lords of the Isles – who left no house untouched the length of Loch Fyne, ostensibly in the name of the imprisoned King Charles but more likely in retribution on the House of Argyll for past Campbell wrongs against MacDonalds. He was know as *fear tholladh nan taighean*, 'the house burner,' and was responsible for the disappearance from the landscape of a generation of vernacular houses, as well as a few castles. Further depredations were carried out in 1685 against the Campbells, when the parish of Kilmichael – then a 94-square-mile territory – lost cattle and other farm animals, tools and clothes. In this instance, the records do detail the affairs of the common man, but mainly because the document known as the 'Depredations Against the Clan Campbell' was instigated by the Clan chief in an effort to seek compensation.

By the end of the next century, many more townships were to disappear without the excuse of civil war, but so too would more substantial landmarks. The church at Kilmichael was in a state of disrepair after a century during which that war was played out literally on its doorstep, with macCholla marching his men past its door, Covenanters hiding in the hills behind it, and troops marauding down Kilmichael glen, raping and looting as they went. By 1760 some work was carried out, and repairs continued until 1790. They were to no avail, and in 1827 the centuries-old church was demolished and replaced by a new building with an ambitious 1,300 sittings. In 1830, lightning struck the new building and it was never the same again. Yet another new church was built 40 years later, this time with just 300 seats to suit Kilmichael's status as a 'mere church hamlet', as described by the Ordnance Gazetteer of Scotland in 1885. There was still a market and fair at Kilmichael at this time, and farm servants were still hired there, but the market had suffered badly because of a campaign started as early as 1762 by Dumbarton traders to shift the cattle market there, and by now the population had dropped considerably because of the combining of farm tenancies and the continued dominance of sheep. In the

Old Poltalloch House was never completed and became a ruin before the Malcolm family built their new mansion on the Moine Mhor. (John Campbell of Kilberry collection.)

*The lodge of the Malcolms' original family home at 'old' Poltalloch.
(John Campbell of Kilberry collection.)*

New Statistical Account of 1792, sheep were already outnumbering the traditional black cattle, with 12,000 of the former by then on sheep-walks throughout the parish compared with just 3,200 of the latter. Lairds had already begun a system of enclosure to improve farming and increase the value of their land. Trees had been planted on previously arable land and pasture to meet the needs of the furnace on Loch Fyne and to provide timbers for the Crinan Canal. These were both lucrative business ventures for the landlords but like the incursion of sheep and combining of farm tenancies they meant that people had to leave their homes. If the women of Arichonan had not protested and the ensuing rammy had not led to a court case at Inveraray recorded by the legal system, it is doubtful if we would have known much about the eviction of Poltalloch estate tenants in the summer of 1848 from this little township to the south of the Crinan canal in North Knapdale. This was at a time of much migration and emigration from Mid Argyll, as from elsewhere in the county. The Malcolms, who had bought Duntrune from a bankrupt James Campbell in 1792, were the new breed of investors in property rather than feudal landlords and they wanted a good return from the land. They had been the Malcolms of Poltalloch, a small estate to the north of Duntrune. Alexander Malcolm had farmed there since 1719 and through marriage to a lady from Kilmartin he inherited property in Jamaica in 1746. Although this venture was not initially successful, a new generation led by Neill Malcolm invested the profits well and was able to buy the Duntrune property from James Campbell. Old Poltalloch

House, which had never been finished, was abandoned and the family, which by now had extensive properties in England, earmarked Duntrune as a summer residence.

Looking at the Duntrune land, fought over, trampled over by soldiers and neglected during the post civil war economic depression, Malcolm must have shaken his head and wondered what this could bring other than status within the local community. There were too many tenants using that land and such subsistence farming was never going to augment any investor's fortune. In time, as the Argyll estates sold off parcels in Mid Argyll as elsewhere in the county, the Malcolms expanded until they had probably the most extensive property in the area. It included lands on Loch Aweside, in Kilmartin and Kilmichael glens and south into Knapdale. On their doorstep, of course, was the Moine Mhor, the great moss, and with the help of of a bright young man called James Gow, employed in 1797 to oversee agricultural improvements, the Malcolms set out to improve their situation. Neill Malcolm had invested in the new Crinan Canal and wanted to drain the 3,000-acre moss and turn it into arable farmland. James Gow had previous experience of drainage operations, having been involved in the improvement of Trafford Moss near Manchester. Now he set about bringing Crinan Moss into cultivation. Experiment Farm was built by 1801 as the headquarters of the drained areas (it has now been rebuilt as Barsloisnoch) and the engineer John Rennie was pulled in from his work on the Crinan Canal to advise on drainage and the installation of water-powered threshing mills. The investment was a good one from the Malcolms' viewpoint. The value of the estate's crops rose from £200 to £1,000 in the last four years of

The chimney of the Poltalloch Estate brickworks was on the outskirts of Slockavulin village. (Duncan MacMillan collection.)

the 18th century. Fields were enclosed with stone walls and townships were turned into single tenancy farms. A brickworks was built at Slockavulin, one of the oldest villages on the estate, along with a sawmill, and in time a gas-works to power the magnificent mansion a succeeding generation was to build. There were also lime kilns built on the estate for agricultural improvements, which the Malcolms had been quarrying on Island MacAskin in Loch Craignish since the 1770s. There was a kiln at Turnault, north of Craignish, where in the days of steam power a puffer delivered coal to fire the furnace. Others stood at Finchairn on Loch Awe, at Glasvaar north of Kilmartin, at Kilmartin itself, at Nether Largie , and at Ri Cruin, which became the Malcolms' factor's house. The remains of this kiln, south of Kilmartin, were removed when the large cairn there was restored. Yet another Poltalloch estate lime kiln was at Meall Cottage north of Kilmichael Glassary. More stretched across the Poltalloch and other estates from Kilmory above Lochgilphead to the island of Danna, near Keills on the Tayvallich peninsula.

In the 19th century, the Malcolms built many brick, slate-roofed houses for workers carrying out the new order of things, but many workers lost their homes and the old cottages were left to crumble. In some ways, this was not entirely a bad thing. Even in 1955, 2,178 houses were seen as unfit for habitation in Argyll. A century before that, workers' houses were in the condition reported by the 1792 *Statistical Account* and by the agent employed by the contemporary Duke of Argyll to assess his estates: earth floors, thatched roofs, chickens sharing the living quarters (and sometimes larger farm animals as well), no chimneys, smoke-filled rooms, inadequate doors and windows. Antiquarian Anne M. Kahane has researched the history of gutters and drainpipes and says that when it rained (as it frequently does in Argyll) it would have been impossible to enter the vernacular houses of that era without being soaked in a deluge from the roof. Sanitary reports that some houses had a floor level lower than the area outside indicate that many tenants must have lived in a sea of mud.

Had each and every one who was moved from a cottage been compensated by a move to one of the modern red-brick houses so reminiscent of the Malcolms' southern estates, leaving home would not have carried the same trauma. The Malcolms did offer assisted passages to the New World in the mid 19th century, but many more simply drifted away to the factories of the Scottish industrial belt to sink or swim in the textile factories and dye-works. When Allan Begg undertook his valuable research into the deserted townships of Kilmichael and Kilmartin glens, he discovered 56 ruins and former house sites in Kilmartin parish and 41 in Glassary parish. Many more mentioned on grave slabs going back to the 1600s were untraceable because of afforestation. Like the work of Marion Campbell of Kilberry and Mary Sandeman logging the ancient and historic monuments of Scotland, such work has become increasingly important because so many vestiges of the past have been swamped by afforestation. While the Forestry Commission today is fully sensitive to the value of the past and encompasses preservation in its work, it was not always so.

So many ancient monuments were once seen either as personal acquisitions or as complete nuisances to be removed. The view that Kilmartin had nothing of interest to offer was not a quirky view held only by a minister of the Church of Scotland who perhaps saw pagan relics as an embarrassment rather than an embarrassment of riches. Grave-robbing, let along stone-robbing, destroyed much of the evidence of the major cairns in Kilmartin Glen. It was only in the late 19th century that the first properly recorded excavations of this area were carried out by Canon William Greendale, Canon of Durham Cathedral, and the Reverend Reginald J. Mapleton, Dean of Argyll and the Isles. The men did not work together, but their findings were recorded by the Society of Antiquaries of Scotland.[28] These men found the stones from the cairns had been used for walls and drains and there was little left in the cists. There had been an investigation of the cists in the cairn at Ri Cruin around 1830, according to Michael Davis, Sheena Carmichael and Eleanor Harris, who researched these excavations for an edition of the local antiquarian society magazine,[29] and there was precious little left in them when Mr Mapleton came to excavate four decades later. Later still, Sir Ian Malcolm and J. Hewat Craw discovered an Early Bronze Age jet necklace in the roots of an elm tree where a burial cist had been uncovered. Today, the Moine Mhor is classified as one of the most important bog or raised mire sites in the UK and the prehistoric remains of Kilmartin glen are seen as of huge archaeological importance. Much of each has been lost, but late rescue operations have managed to conserve what remains.

There was scarcely more respect for the castle and the mansion house than there was for the ancient monument, the vernacular cottage or the environment. As property began to change hands at the end of the 18th century, the names of houses also changed. The Malcolms of Poltalloch abandoned their plans to build a better house at what is now referred to as Old Poltalloch when they bought Duntrune. In 1829, as their fortunes improved, they also took on Largie House, which they were to rename Kilmartin House. They were to split their time between the two properties and then spread themselves ever more thinly as properties in London, Norfolk and elsewhere clamoured for their attention. Largie House was relatively new when the Duntrune estate was sold to the Malcolms in 1792. Built at Largie Farm, just half a mile north of Kilmartin, it was a fairly modest but elegant Georgian house which must have been very much more comfortable than Kilmartin Castle, which it replaced as the Campbells of Kilmartin seat. It had been built by Neil Campbell, who was rector of Kilmartin between 1574 and 1627, and his Bishop. A semi-fortified residence, it remained in the hands of this branch of the Campbell family until the 1670s, when the Campbells of Inverawe took it over. By 1800, the first floor was being used as the parish school and in 1826 it was the residence of a 'female pauper'. The Kilmartin minister described it as a ruin in 1844. This ruin of Kilmartin Castle would be bought in the 1980s by the Clarke family who restored it as a family residence under the guidance of Historic Scotland. By the mid 19th century, the burgeoning Malcolm family had taken to inviting politicians, diplomats and other celebrities of the day to stay at their Scottish estate. Duntrune castle had been refurbished when it first came into Malcolm hands and was altered yet again in 1833-4 by the London architect and builder Joseph Gordon Davis. Mr Davis travelled to Argyll initially to work on Kilmory Castle for the Campbell Ordes, who were friends of the Malcolms. The Malcolms must have been impressed with what they saw because they asked him not only to do quite extensive work at Duntrune Castle but in 1834-5 to design a new church at Kilmartin to replace the 1601 church. Kilmartin House was much changed at the same time: views were becoming important and the stables were moved to allow a panoramic one of Carnasserie Castle.

Kilmartin House had been the home of Neill Malcolm while his father lived at the castle. The number of guests was increasing, and Davis was also involved in building the Royal Hotel in Ardrishaig so that they could be accommodated there when they came off the steamer. The Royal Hotel is now the Grey Gull, much altered internally but still with an imposing exterior which must have impressed first-time visitors to Argyll.

In 1837, Neill Malcolm succeeded as laird. His first wife had died and he continued to live at Kilmartin House until he remarried in 1843. It was his new wife who lobbied for a new house with a view over Loch Crinan, and Poltalloch House was planned. Kilmartin House was at first used as a home for the factor, but perhaps it was more convenient to have him even nearer at hand and Ri Cruin was built near the village of Slockavulin. A retired factor moved in but there was no room for sentiment and in the 1870s Kilmartin House was demolished. While Poltalloch House was being built, the throng of guests stayed at the Royal, Kilmartin House and Eredine (when Poltalloch House was up and running, some guests came north to Loch Awe and were brought by steamer to Ford and then by a horse-drawn brake to the estate).

Poltalloch House was designed by the architect William Burn in 1849 and built at a cost of £100,000. The grounds were landscaped and a Scottish Episcopal chapel (where amateur archaeologist Mr Mapleton became rector) was built beside it. Although the Neill Malcolm who bought Duntrune had been an elder in the Church of Scotland at Kilmartin, his successor had his own ideas of religion. And while this was a time when the Scottish Gothic castle was coming into its own, this house, at first known as Calton House, was English neo-Jacobean. Most of the workers' houses which were built on the estate had a very English red-brick look to them, and the laundry house at the top of the Long Walk, with its tall chimneys, looks as if it had strayed from a village in the south of England. The magnificent front sweep of the house included a conservatory which produced blooms for the Malcolms' London home. There was a domed clock tower and a balustraded front terrace. Inside, the house was designed so that the mechanics of the building never intruded on the guests. There were 25 guest rooms with six bathrooms, a staff of over 20 women, five footmen, a butler and a number of men working in the stables and other offices to the back of the house. The village of Slockavulin became the power house of Poltalloch House, with workmen of every sort to run the house and the estate. It was grand beyond belief, but just a century later, the house was a ruin. The 20th-century Malcolms were hit by two world wars, the Depression, and then in the post Second World War days by crippling rates and legislation to improve the property of tenants to modern habitable standards. For some years, the house which had echoed to the laughter of Lillie Langtry and the then Prince of Wales (Sir Ian Malcolm was to marry Miss Langtry's daughter) was flatted and let out. But the bills were too high, and to solve the problem, the roof was taken off, a solution so many other lairds were to adopt in the mid-1950s.

Within a century and a half, the Malcolms had seen off three rather splendid houses: Old Poltalloch on the shores of Loch Craignish which was started as a replacement to the existing farmhouse but never completed; Kilmartin House; and Poltalloch House. They were back in the ancient Duntrune castle which had stood watch over Crinan Loch since medieval times. As Allan Begg found, the houses of the estate workers had disappeared in far greater numbers. Kilmartin graveyard is the resting place of blacksmiths, builders, carpenters, a contractor, a cooper, farmers, farm-workers, a forester, gardeners, gamekeepers, merchants, millers, tradesmen and wrights, as well as wealthier men and women. A similar story is told by Kilmichael Glassary graveyard. All of them had their homes in the hills and glens of the two parishes. A cooper at the mill at Achavan made barrels for the oatmeal. In 1825

Bellanoch was a farming township with thatched cottages on the banks of the Crinan Canal even in 1904. (Michael Hopkin collection.)

there was a mill and eight other buildings. Achachrom, where there were still occupied thatched cottages at the start of the 20th century, housed MacVicars, MacColls, Campbells, MacLeods and MacFadyens. The settlement is deserted today. On the hills above Glassary there were at least 23 settlements. One of them, Lag, which sat above the River Add on the road which once led from Kilmichael Glassary to Lochgair on Fyneside but has itself now disappeared, was where a private school accommodated all the children from the old farms: Achlee, Tunns, Dalnerach, Creagans and Monunernich (now all under afforestation) and Barrachuile, Knockalva, Lecuary, Kirnan, Fearnach, Socach, Ceann-Loch Leithan and Leacann-na-Muilt.[30] Each child was required to bring two peats to school for the fire. Some settlements in these two parishes were deserted because the tenants were evicted; some because the tenancies were consolidated. The coming of the forestry has made many too difficult to trace, but the names remain on headstones which date back to the 17th century.

Opposite top. The very grand mansion built by the Malcolm family in the 1840s, first known as Calton Mor and then as Poltalloch House. (Sheena Carmichael collection.)

Opposite middle. A lost lifestyle: the rich, powerful and famous came to stay at Poltalloch; some were picked up in carriages from the pier at Ford. (Sheena Carmichael collection.)

Opposite below. The ruined Poltalloch House, which had served the family less than a century when its roof was removed. (Author's collection.)

Uilean, opposite the village of Kilmichael, dated back at least to the 16th century, when it was marked on Timothy Pont's map, and the graveyard shows that a tacksman, a shepherd and a farmer lived there. Most of the houses in these and many more settlements have disappeared, sometimes leaving little more that a trace of steadings or a sheep fank.

Apart from farming and fishing, there were other industries which exercised Mid Argyll. Mr Malcolm had a lead mine on his land and there were others. None was as developed as those in Morvern or even those on Islay, but their history was long. In Kintyre and Mid Argyll, copper, lead and silver were mentioned in documents as far back as the 13th century – and of course, the archaeological evidence is there to prove at least another millennium or so of mining activity. The Constable of Tarbert was making payments for coal supplied to local lead mines in 1326. Copper ore was noted in the hills of 'Cantyre' in 1683 and by 1747, lead mining in Glen Shira to the north-east of Inveraray was an established cog in the Duke of Argyll's estate machinery. This continued to run contemporaneously with the Malcolm lead mine on the road from Kilmartin to Old Poltalloch. Mining at Inverneil, south of Ardrishaig and heading across the hills towards Kilberry, had been in operation from very early times, too, and in 1790 Sir Archibald Campbell of the Inverneil Estate brought in experts to assess the possibilities of developing the estate's mineral resources. Despite favourable reports, Sir Archibald did not develop the Inverneil mines. Copper, nickel, zinc, silver and gold have been mined across Mid Argyll but small investors usually went bust after a couple of years and big companies made no investment in machinery and shafts. It is said that lightning causes so much damage in Mid Argyll because of the quantity of minerals in the earth – but when companies weighed up how much it would cost them to extract the minerals and ship them out from what they saw as this far corner of Scotland, the effort was seen as too costly. Local historian Sandy Rankine reported that most Mid Argyll mines had gone out of business by 1912.[31]

These mines rarely scarred the Mid Argyll earth as they did in Morvern, and there were few factory chimneys to blot the landscape. But at Crinan harbour and Tayvallich there were plants making pyroligneous acid for the dye-works in the Vale of Leven. These were known as 'vinegar' factories locally. The one at Crinan harbour, where the tall red-brick chimney is all that remains of a short-lived industry, was leased by Neill Malcolm of Poltalloch to Timothy Philips. At the end of the 1870s, the lease went to Messrs Turnbull and Co., who kept the factory going until 1888. At Tayvallich, another 'vinegar' factory has left no sign of its presence on the road to Carsaig. Tayvallich had little claim to fame other than as a stopover for drovers coming from Islay via Keills or Carsaig.

The pyroligneous acid factory at Crinan harbour which served the dye industry in
Alexandria. (Courtesy Mike Murray, from a collection by Jim Souness of Edinburgh.)

Then Turnbull and Co., Manufacturing Chemists and Vinegar Makers of
Camlachie, saw that the birch woods on this Argyll peninsula were a perfect
source for their pyroligneous acid production. The process used in these two
'manufactories' involved the dry distilling of wood. Birch, alder, oak and beech,
the best woods for the job, were all found in the remnant of ancient forest
which today is protected on the Tayvallich peninsula. Tar, a by-product of the
process, was exported to meet the needs of the colonial rubber trade while the
acid was used in paint dye. The charcoal industry has left more trace in this
area – there are charcoal platforms throughout the Taynish peninsula which
date at least to the 18th century when the iron ore smelt industry came to Loch
Fyne at Goatfield (later to be known simply as Furnace). Today, the Taynish
forest is recognised as one of the last and largest oak-dominated woodlands on
the west coast of Scotland, particularly in Argyll, and as such were declared a
nature reserve in the late 1970s. Fuel, charcoal for Bonawe and Furnace, oak
bark for the tanning industry and wood for the 'vinegar' factory must all have
depleted woodlands which now are confined to an area of just under 900 acres.
Areas of the woodland were cleared for cultivation and a corn-drying kiln once
stood on the western slopes of Barr Mor, the highest point of the stretch of
Dalriadan schists. Wood was also used for the kelp industry which flourished
briefly in Knapdale. In 1794 over 31 tons of kelp was manufactured on the
Taynish peninsula. This was when the price of kelp had risen from £6 a ton to

£10 a ton. During the Napoleonic Wars, when the chemicals which kelp produced could not be obtained from Spain, the industry earned the equivalent of £1.7 million a year in the Hebrides alone and the Taynish peninsula played a small role in that short-lived boom.

The Knapdale peninsula had earlier sustained yet another industry. The chapel at Keills, once known as Kilmaharmic, survives in better condition than many contemporary chapels and houses fine post-Medieval examples of the Loch Sween school of stone carving. Stone was quarried in the area from the earliest times and was sometimes exported for work elsewhere. The Campbeltown Cross was carved by the Iona school from bluish-green calc-chlorite-albite schist quarried at Doide between Castle Sween and Kilmory Knap. Of the mainland schools, the Loch Sween masons were most highly rated.

Castle Sween itself was considered to be the oldest stone-built castle on the Scottish mainland by those who claim all records for Argyll. It probably dates back to the late 11th century, contemporaneous with the Norman invasion of England. The 16th-century Book of the Clan Sween (*Leabhar Chlainne Suibhe*) says the builder was Suibhe, whose son Dugald held Skipness Castle. The MacSweynes were in charge until the 13th century. It was built near an older defence, Dun a' Chasteil, which was occupied from the third to the first millennium BC, probably by Mesolithic hunters and fishermen. A succession of inhabitants left behind them a polished Antrim axe and a Bronze Age sharpening stone. The castle itself had an arched door and flat buttresses similar to Castle Duart. In the 13th century, an extra level of battlements may have been added. A hall wing was added by James III and the MacMillan Tower was added in the 1400s when the MacMillans were custodians of the castle under the Lords of the Isles. This was a castle which was a pawn in the early Scottish power games. Robert I captured it twice. It was then forfeited in the 1490s when the Lord of the Isles was accused of arming Castle Sween treasonably. The Earl of Argyll put in his own men when he was given the castle into his keeping. In 1647, it came under attack in the civil war and was destroyed. The dignity of the past, however, has been lost as the castle has become swallowed up within a caravan park and making it difficult for the public to access.

It was agriculture which left the most significant traces of its history, however. The Tayvallich Inn, now a dwelling house, was a stopping point for the drovers. Cattle from Taynish itself – considered to be of a very high standard – were walked to market at Lochgilphead until the beginning of the Second World War. Those which came from Islay and Jura landed at Keills or

Castle Sween was among the most important of Argyll's defences. Today its ruins are swamped by a holiday park. (Author's collection.)

Carsaig – ferry routes which were lost with the coming of the steamers. From Keills, the drovers often took the cattle across the sea loch to Castle Sween. Others went up to Tayvallich, joining those who had crossed to Carsaig and heading on to Kilmichael Tryst or much later, to the Lochgilphead market. Flax was grown here, the women were involved in weaving and MacNeill tenants were thirled to the mill at Taynish. It was built in 1650 when the MacNeills also built Taynish House; today its picturesque ruin is incorporated into Nature Reserve walks. The mill was two storeys high, built of rubble masonry, with an

Tenants from the Taynish peninsula were thirled to this mill, dismantled by scrap dealers in the mid-20th century. (Author's collection.)

outside stair to the upper floor. In 1724, oats, bere and rye were ground here and at mills leased by other lairds at Oib, Danna, Keills and Taynish Loch. Tenants like Peter and Archibald Brown were contracted by their landlord Duncan Campbell of Taynish in 1803 to bring their grindable corn and bere, seed and horse corn to the Taynish mill. It had a pair of millstones on the upper floor, one to shell the grain and the other to grind it into meal. Downstairs, the milled grain was graded, milled and bagged and stored on the premises. The water which powered the mill ran from a mill-pond above the building down a lade to turn an iron-framed water-wheel with wooden buckets and an iron shaft. The bed for the millstones was wood and the stones were adjusted by means of a horizontal beam for different gradings of grain. Adjoining the mill there was a drying kiln with a furnace in the bottom with an iron frame and iron doors. There were perforated tiles on the drying floor and the grain was carried down the kiln stair and up the mill stair when it was dried. The mill was converted into a house or byre in 1870 but was later abandoned and became derelict. In the 1950s and 60s, the last waterwheel was removed by scrap metal merchants.

During the industrial revolution, there was an odd mix of the very latest technology (sometimes actually being tried in Argyll ahead of its use in more densely industrial areas) and the most primitive. The ironworks on Loch Fyne and at Bonawe used the latest technology but there had been bloomeries in Scotland, and particularly in Argyll, for centuries before the invasion of English companies in the 18th century. Point of Knap had one of these bloomeries and 17 others were recorded in Argyll. Iron slag deposits were smelted in hollow clay 'beehive' furnaces which used the prevailing winds to achieve enough heat. According to the Society of Antiquaries of Scotland,[32] small-scale iron smelting took place at Skipness, Benmore in Cowal, around Loch Goil, 'Bunawe' near Taynuilt and at two series of bloomeries – one in the Strathlachlan area on a six-mile stretch of the east coast of Loch Fyne; the other further north around Strachur. The quantity of oak wood available to make charcoal for these small furnaces was, of course, one of the attractions when the Duddon Company from Lancashire set up a a large-scale smelting operation at Inverleckan – the mouth of the river Leacann – which came to be known as Furnace. It operated from 1775 to 1813 using an early blast furnace. Charcoal, that ever-present commodity throughout Argyll, fired the furnace and it had water-powered bellows.

After the iron smelting ended at Furnace, there was a lull in industrial activities, but the lure of the availability of charcoal brought a gunpowder works to the west side of the Leacann Water (the iron works had been on the east side on the site of Craleekin Farm) in 1841. An explosion there brought work to an end, but the contracts for timber, or the sale of entire woodlands, signed by lairds in Mid Argyll, Knapdale and Cowal brought them excellent fringe benefits for almost a century. The down side of such contracts was that they deprived tenants of rights to fallen firewood and led to the loss of native woodland.

The building of the Crinan Canal also called for much timber and this waterway from Ardrishaig to Crinan was to change much in this part of Argyll. Its raison d'être was to take the fishing fleet safely from Loch Fyne to the west coast without the lengthy and sometimes dangerous voyage around the Mull of Kintyre. It was conceived at a time when Loch Fyne was rich in herring and the busy herring fleet comprising vessels from all over Britain and Ireland regularly anchored at Crinan harbour. Cod, ling, turbot and oysters were Crinan bay specialities. In the early 1790s, herring brought a shilling a hundred and between 20 and 30 boats reported making £500 in a month or so. This was an enormous sum for the time but bad weather frequently stopped the men from earning at all. James Watt and John Rennie, eminent engineers of their day, surveyed the canal route and Rennie put a price of £63,678 on the job. James Campbell, 5th Duke of Argyll, was elected to run the Canal Company in 1793 and appointed Rennie chief engineer. The canal first opened in 1801 at a cost of £141,810 and the castellated Tawes of Dun-ArdRigh, the seat of the MacTavishes, had to be demolished. Forts, cairns, and cup-and-ring marked stones also disappeared as the nine-mile waterway was made and then repaired. Built against a backdrop of steep hills, the water run-off from the lochs above caused the canal walls to collapse a number of times in the coming decades.

The canal, of course, is still with us, a stunning leisure attraction carrying pleasure craft on its waters, and walkers, bikers and horses on its towpaths. But the fishing fleets have diminished and the steamer traffic has disappeared completely. The Crinan Canal was a victim of the steam era. Scarcely had it been opened when the first steamer was launched on the Clyde. Henry Bell, who launched the first steamship to take his hotel guests from Glasgow to Helensburgh, saw that this short cut could mean big business. He enlarged the *Comet* and set her on a regular route from Glasgow to Fort William via the Crinan Canal until she foundered in seas too big for her. When the Caledonian Canal opened, the quickest route from Glasgow to Inverness was via the two canals and many people took advantage of it. Queen Victoria and Prince Albert sailed along the canal in 1847 in a flower-bedecked boat and created a tourism industry in Argyll. Increased traffic turned settlements like Bellanoch into bustling villages with an inn and a post office and Crinan had two inns for a while. A ferry ran across Loch Crinan, giving the Malcolm estate access to lands in Knapdale. But while visitors were coming with their sketch books and having picnics in picturesque places, the people of North Knapdale were suffering badly from famine and cholera and migrating or emigrating from the

Bellanoch

Bellanoch grew in importance with the advent of the canal, acquiring shops and inns. (Michael Hopkin collection.)

Top. The Linnet, *seen here in 1928 at the end of her career, was the most famous vessel to sail the Canal, taking thousands of trippers from Ardrishaig to Crinan. (Michael Hopkin collection.)*

Above. Coal was landed from puffers at estates around Argyll. Boys were called from school to load the carts on the beaches. (John Campbell of Kilberry collection.)

area. Throughout the 19th century, work craft and pleasure boats, including the famous *Linnet*, sailed the canal, but the fishing industry was dwindling and the steamboats were getting too big to negotiate the narrow and shallow canal with its 15 locks. In 1854, 35,000 passengers, 27,000 sheep and 2,000 cattle travelled the canal (the two latter being telling figures in terms of the downturn of black cattle and the upsurge in sheep farming with the accompanying loss of tenants and their houses), but takings were always less than expenditure because the banks had to be repaired frequently. The day trippers did not bring in enough to make the canal pay its way, but the delightful *Linnet* continued to offer a thrilling day out for half a century until she was taken off the run in 1929. Today, after many renovations and improvements and a 21st-century makeover, it is mainly private yachts which head out to the Sound of Jura through a sea lock. The last surviving puffer – the cargo boats which used the canal to take goods to remote areas on the mainland and to the islands – sits at Crinan waiting for enough funds to be raised to make her seaworthy again.

Coal was delivered onto the shore and collected by tenants in horse-drawn carts in so many areas of Argyll. Lairds like the Campbells of Kilberry and villagers in Newton in Cowal waited with excitement tinged with anxiety for the next delivery of coal to be made. It would last for months and be shared among tenants. But that coal usually came from Ayrshire rather than from Kintyre's coal mine at Drumlemble, and most of the poorer families still made do with peat, cut and dried during the summer months and stored to feed fires in the coldest months. Peat was also used to fire the Glendarroch distillery on the banks of the canal half a mile from Ardrishaig. The Darroch burn falls from a height of 70 feet down to a tunnel under the canal and emerges in Loch Fyne at the foot of Robber's Glen, where tradition says smugglers once made their own illegal whisky. It was the Ard burn, however, which fed the legal distillery in the 19th century and was filtered through gravel at a number of points on its three-mile journey from a loch in the hills to the plant. The distillery was built in stone on a three-acre site and had a 500-ft-long frontage onto the canal. Barley was brought by the canal and discharged at the granary doors. This 19th-century enterprise was built on the site of an ancient fort. Now it, too, has gone, but in its day it produced 80,000 gallons of whisky a year. The granary and the maltings were two-storey buildings and there was a concrete steep where huge quantities of barley were wetted. The proprietor in the 1880s was William Gillies and according to Alfred Barnard,[33] it had a new kiln which was 'the

The Glendarroch distillery at Ardrishaig. (From The Whisky Distilleries of the United Kingdom, *by Alfred Barnard, first published 1890.)*

finest in this part of Scotland'. It was 51 feet square, floored with wire cloth and heated with peats, and the peat shed always carried 500 tons of peat, ready for firing the kiln. The still house was also state of the art. The distillery had its own cooperage and stables and Mr Gillies lived in Glendarroch House as a summer residence. He had formerly lived in Glengilp House but gave this over to his manager and there were eight houses for workmen with a small plot to cultivate vegetables.

Further north on the canal was Auchindarroch or Oakfield House, near the junction of the modern A83 and A816 in Lochgilphead. This was built in the late 18th century and the grounds were laid out by John MacNeill, Younger, of Gigha, who owned the estate until 1830. It was he who developed Lochgilphead from 1815, a village which literally had not been on the map until MacNeill began to sell feus and brought in Sir John Rennie to advise on laying it out. Kilmory and Kilduskland, two ruined ancient chapels on the north and south of Loch Gilp, were the landmarks from distant times. Settlements grew up at each within the sprawling parish of Kilmichael in Glassary and the tenants lived by fishing and farming. In 1750, Roy's map shows a small settlement with one single house at Masnacur on the north shore of Loch Gilp. In the 1770s, however, it became the juntion of the new roads from Inveraray, Oban and Campbeltown, giving it a sudden importance. As more buildings went up, it became convenient for public bodies to hold meetings in this increasingly accessible place. In 1801, John MacNeill of Gigha developed the lands of Druim on his Oakfield estate and a small village was laid out by Peter Campbell of Kilmory in the area of Cossack Street, the quay at Paterson Street and

Fishing nets were still dried on the shore in Lochgilphead at the turn of the 20th century. (Duncan MacMillan collection.)

Whitegates, which was then the entrance to the Kilmory estate. By the 1820s, Lochgilphead had a dye-house and water-powered mills. Crinan Moss provided domestic fuel for Lochgilphead in the form of peat until a gas-works was built. Kilmory estate was developed by the Campbells and then in the 19th century, architect Joseph Gordon Davis was called in by the Ordes (who became Campbell Ordes by the end of the century) and he altered Kilmory Castle between 1828 and 1837. Sir William Hooker, the famous botanist, was employed to create the estate gardens. Today, the castle is the headquarters of Argyll and Bute Council, unrecognisable internally but with the gardens developed in the 1830s now open to the public. It is interesting that John MacNeill, the Lochgilphead developer, lived in a delightful but relatively modest two-storey mansion. His house, according to Michael Davis, had a flat-roofed portico, pilasters on the front wall and a rusticated doorway onto the garden.[34] On the other hand, Campbell Orde, the major employer in the area, lived in an increasingly grand castle. John MacNeill was revered by local people: successions of Ordes were unpopular enough to have instigated myths which to the later 20th century were still perpetuated. Records confirm that Sir John Orde was not responsible for the death of a child when he grandly rolled through the village in his carriage – but grass roots opinion wanted it to be so. He was in fact tried for injuring a child in Ardrishaig, but was acquitted. A Campbell-Orde did, however, build a causeway across Loch Gilp. It was alleged he did it so that he could drive straight from his clock-tower entrance (today a dilapidated building earmarked as a site for the county archives) on one side of Loch Gilp to Ardrishaig on the other without going past riffraff to be found in burgeoning Lochgilphead. It is more likely that he built it to accommodate Queen Victoria when she travelled the length of the Crinan Canal on her Highland journey, but despite his best efforts she did not go to Kilmory Castle or cross his causeway. He was an autocratic laird who increased his unpopularity by objecting to fishing nets being dried within 20 feet of the centre of the road. Eventually, the silting which the causeway encouraged made it impossible for the village's fishing boats and the steamers which had become an important link to the Clyde to come into the loch. Part of the causeway can still be seen at low tide. The dangerously dilapidated ruins of the Kilmory estate home farm at the rear of the castle are buildings which imaginative investment could turn into premises for valuable social and educational community projects, but are in danger of following the more modest estate properties which are now scarcely able to be traced into the surrounding forrest.

John MacNeill sold Oakfield House to Alexander Campbell, who restored the house's Gaelic name of 'Auchindarroch' and continued to act as MacNeill had done as a patron of both Lochgilphead and Ardrishaig. In time, Auchindarroch House was altered, with the addition of dormer windows. Then, despite it being a List B building, it was demolished in 1969 and a small modern house was built on the site. So many of Mid Argyll's big houses suffered a similar fate. Ederline House and Inverliever Lodge at Ford were both demolished in 1966. The former was a Scottish baronial mansion built in 1870 for the Warde-Aldams. Michael Davis suggests it may have been designed by the architect David Bryce, and it had large Victorian windows and a series of fantastic castle-style features, including turrets. Inverliever Lodge was an established residence in 1748, when Archibald Campbell of Inverliever paid 6s. 6d. window tax on his 13 windows. A second house was built in the following decade and in the 19th century this was yet another estate which came to be owned by the Malcolms of Poltalloch. The Malcolms built a lodge around the time that their other building work was going on in the 1840s. The lodge, with its Tudor-style chimneys, looked to be the work of William Burn, was demolished and then the house was also dismantled. Hayfield House, which sat on the north-west shore of Loch Awe, was built in the 1790s by Allan MacDougall of Gallenach as a small Georgian mansion with a hipped roof and two tall chimneys. A Glasgow merchant called William MacNeill owned it in the early 19th century and it was then bought by Sir Richard Grierson, 7th Baronet of Lag. In 1912, the house burned down. And yet another house to succumb to flames was Inverneil House at Ardrishaig. Once in the hands of the MacNeills, the Campbells had their eye on it and were promised the estate as a dowry, but the marriage never took place. Sir Archibald Campbell then bought the estate in 1773 after it had changed hands during bankruptcy proceedings. Sir Archibald's older brother James moved from Killian farm between Auchindrain and Inveraray to Inverneil House and inherited the estate when his brother died. A modest laird's house, it was James's home until it was destroyed by fire. The second house was a Georgian mansion with a fine garden and a look-out tower nearby where the laird and his guests could admire the views with the aid of a telescope. During the 19th century, the house was much altered and when it was sold off in the mid 20th century, the Georgian section was demolished, leaving the crenelated Victorian addition. Although the Georgian house may have been lost, the 20th-century owners restored the garden, a well and an ice-house.

At this time, Ardrishaig had become the biggest village in the area and the seat of local government in South Knapdale. It had become important and had grown with the arrival of the canal. Throughout the 19th century it was a

Left. Steamer trips were a favourite pastime for people living on the industrialised Clyde. (Courtesy Murdo MacDonald, Argyll and Bute Archivist.)

Below. RMH Columba and Iona delivering hordes of tourists to Ardrishaig in 1917. (Michael Hopkin collection.)

bustling port where freight and passengers were loaded and off-loaded in increasing volume. But while it may have seen itself as a workaday village of fishermen, the growing tourist industry had different aspirations. By 1877, a report into the sanitary defects of the village of Ardrishaig revealed that not only were the houses insanitary but there were no public privies to accommodate visitors who disembarked from Glasgow steamers to sail the canal. At P. McArthur's property, inspectors found that the 'ashpits' were neither floored nor drained (ash was used in outdoor trench lavatories), the walls leaked and there were six families which had no 'privy' at all. At R. Thomson's property, 16 families had two privies, 'of which one is nailed up and the other has no door'. The ashpits were described as being very foul and offensive and 'containing much liquid sewage'. In 1894, the medical officer of health reported that many of the Ardrishaig houses were still not provided with water closets, privies or ashpits and all the refuse was thrown over the breast wall of the quay. The windows of the houses along the shore were permanently closed in summer because of the offensive smell coming from the refuse on the shore. Although the old illustrations of Ardrishaig village, when there were houses on both sides of its main street, look very picturesque, the reality was that the houses were insanitary and a health hazard, like so many properties in the county in which the poor lived. Typhoid and tuberculosis were rife and there were even villages destroyed by cholera in the 19th century. The parochial board which was responsible for Ardrishaig's sanitary arrangements was well aware of the difficulties. During the fishing season, the village was host to a large fleet of fishing boats. In 1867, the parochial board erected three privies in different localities in the village at a cost of over £62. Today's public lavatories stand where the lochside row of houses once lined the road: not only have the old privies gone but the insanitary houses and the fishing industry have also

Chalmers Street in Ardrishaig looks picturesque but many houses were unfit for habitation. (Duncan MacMillan collection.)

Ardrishaig was one of the many Loch Fyne ports where herring was landed. (Duncan MacMillan collection.)

disappeared. Instead of being modernised, the houses were replaced by concrete car parks in the mid 20th century. One may regret the loss of industries and insensitive planning but one cannot regret the passing of conditions which led to infant mortality and life-threatening adult illnesses.

There was another '*Clochemerle*' decision taken by the authorities in neighbouring Lochgilphead in 1864. The Lochgilphead Feuars Committee erected a 'No 3 MacFarlane's iron water closet for three persons' at a cost of £16 (was Ardrishaig overcharged?) which was de-mountable and moved to different locations on two occasions. It first went up near the entrance to the public gardens off what is now Lorn Street. New improved public privies and a store were built in 1872 in what is now Smiddy Land. The cast-iron privy,

made in Glasgow by Walter MacFarlane and Co, architectural and sanitary iron founders at the Saracen iron foundry, whose cast-iron work was very decorative, was re-erected in Cossack Street. By 1889 this was in what was described as a deplorable state and condemned as a serious annoyance to the neighbourhood. The privy had one division for men and another for women and children but was 'hardly consistent with decency'. Little changes. The public lavatories which sit on the green in Lochgilphead today are under threat as a public nuisance because too many young people congregate there, vandalise the property and make a noise. Buildings may come and go; human nature rarely changes. Lochgilphead's late 18th- and early 19th-century buildings remain, some in less than perfect condition. It has lost some of its industries – the gas-works, the rope-works, the Wilkie distillery, the woollen mill which stood where the Co-operative is now sited, and the fishing. Its stone quay on the east shore only ever allowed high tide usage for steamers, but it

Top. The growth of Ardrishaig and Lochgilphead took religious and political power away from Kilmichael Glassary. (Duncan MacMillan collection.)

Above. In rural areas, increasing numbers of settlements, like the Glennan township shown here, fell empty because of evictions or cholera. (John Campbell of Kilberry collection.)

has gained the centre of local government and a headquarters of the forestry industry. The villages of Loch Fyne have all lost their once famous kipper houses: now only the co-operative Loch Fyne Oysters smokes and sells local fish and sea food at the head of Loch Fyne.

Both Lochgilphead and Ardrishaig grew, and took religious and economic power away from Kilmichael Glassary, because of the coming of the canal and the new roads. These were the new major stopping places at crossroads and

Lochgilphead's broad main street was built with a new centre for cattle in mind – the new market was held on Lochgilphead's green. At the same time, however, what had been similarly-sized settlements simply vanished from the map. The bleak sums done by Allan Begg show how many communities have been wiped out. One of them was Achnaba, where in 1803 the men were all listed as fishermen, even though the settlement was inland. It has been suggested that they kept their boats at Silvercraigs, then a fishing township. Their access was from the old road on which stood the long-since-ruined Cossack Inn, a drovers' stop-off, and followed a line west from Lochgair close to Kilmory Castle at the Lochgilphead end. To make this road more direct, a loop was made in 1828, but promptly closed by Sir John Orde of Kilmory Castle. Then in the 1830s, Achnaba was cleared of inhabitants for sheep. Those turned out of their houses included Crawfords, Fergusons, MacColls, MacEans and Kerrs. What upheavals did little Archibald Ferguson experience before his death at the age of just ten in 1833? By 1865 the Ordnance map marked the site of the settlement as 'ruinous'. The outside walls are visible but there is no sign of a chimney or fireplace in any of the houses. A 'knocking stone', a small circular basin in the rock used to catch the ears of corn as they were knocked off the sheaf before going into a corn-drying kiln, is visible near the Achnaba ruins. Corn-drying kilns have gone the way of the settlements – at Dun Dubh near Ford, at West Barravullin where there were probably two (NM816077), Finchairn (NM902033), Dun Dubh (NM864041) Upper Moneydrain (NR865896) Scotnish (NR679682) and at Auchindrain. Water mills also fell into disuse as communities disappeared: the lintel at Kilmartin Inn is a millstone from the Carnasserie mill, while evidence of mills at Old Poltalloch, Temple Wood, Carsaig Bay, Point of Knap and Kilmory Oib is sparse. What is always noteworthy in such settlements is that where timber (planted in the 18th century by local lairds to feed the furnace at Inverleckan, now Furnace, or in the 20th century by the Forestry Commission) has not swamped the land, the evidence of kailyards, ridges of lazy beds and runrig systems survives when the buildings have long gone. It was because centuries-old runrig plots were still visible around the settlement of Auchindrain that historian Marion Campbell of Kilberry pushed for it to become a folk museum when the last of the tenants moved out. The township, on the old Loch Awe to Loch Fyne road and now at the side of the modern A83 between Inveraray and Lochgilphead, has some fine examples of vernacular houses which elsewhere throughout the county have disintegrated. Neighbouring Killian is a case in point. This estate, between Inveraray and Auchindrain, was bought in the late 18th century by a rich Indian merchant and his brother. The small tenants were cleared to make a modern farm and the settlement of Auchindrain took the people in. They were required to go back to their former homes to help with the harvest and although they were allowed to keep one sheaf in four, their old houses were cleared. In the 1970s, the Duke of Argyll was keen for the land around the Auchindrain houses to be afforested, but the influence of academics, archaeologists and historians saved at least some vestige of ancient agricultural methods. The Duke was merely following in the economic footsteps of his ancestors. The Argyll Estate, Taynish, Kilberry, Stonefield and many other smaller estates planted thousands of trees in the late 1700s and on into the 19th century.

The Earls and Dukes of Argyll have, as we have seen, shaped the social and economic landscape of Argyll. Its physical landscape was perhaps most visibly changed in Inveraray itself, where the old castle and town were rebuilt to suit the estate. Today's castle is a fine Scottish Baronial building and the town has a chocolate-box frontage which entices every visitor to stop on an unfortunate bend on the A83 approach road to capture the view on camera. It is described as one of the earliest and best-preserved planned towns in Scotland, dating as it does to a building period stretching from 1753 to 1776. What we see today, however, is a complete replacement of an earlier town and castle which were a little the worse for wear when the 3rd Duke of Argyll decided to do a little housekeeping. Inveraray (the name means 'mouth of the river Aray') had been well enough established by the 15th century for James III to make it a Burgh of Barony in 1474. The motivation of Charles I in making it

The old town of Inveraray was removed along with the castle to create a new planned town and modern castle. (By permission of his Grace the Duke of Argyll.)

a Royal Burgh in 1648 is questionable. He was desperate for support during the civil war and the Argylls moved back and forth across the political and religious spectrum in that century. It must have been a poor specimen of a Royal Burgh. The old castle had been besieged and many houses torched by the Montrose forces four years previously. It seems to have been something of a wild frontier post, with 43 taverns counteracting its church and school. There was a tollbooth, a ferry, some substantial houses and workers' houses for a fishing industry which was sometimes much more profitable than others, depending on the movement of the 'silver darlings' chased by the fleet.

The end of the 17th century found an exhausted Argyll and an exhausted population. Inveraray had suffered badly because of its proximity to the seat of the Earls. Who could blame those fencible men for coming home and piling into one of the 43 taverns the old town had to offer? But a new century brought new intentions. Instead of warmongers in the castle, there was the dawning spirit of the Enlightenment: improved agriculture, better-run estates, and finer buildings were to be the order of the day. In 1743, Archibald, Earl of Islay, became 3rd Duke of Argyll and instigated many such plans. There was just one small problem with constructing a fine new building to replace the battered old castle. If it were to have the landscaped gardens around it which its architects proposed, something would have to go: Inveraray. The old town, with its market and fairs, stood where today's castle gardens lie. A new town was

Inveraray had been created a Burgh Barony in 1474. Tenants were moved to make way for the landscaped castle grounds. (By permission of his Grace the Duke of Argyll.)

designed half a mile to the south. This was one of the first planned new towns and eviction orders went out to tenants so that their homes could be demolished and the Old Burgh obliterated. In 1746, a Summons of Removal was taken by Archibald, 3rd Duke, against 126 people in the Old Town, including many prominent townspeople. In the next two decades, people like Margaret Campbell, widow of Robert Murray, an Inveraray merchant, William Douglass, a mason, smith James Johnston, innkeeper Patrick McArthur, Marion McAulay, widow of the tailor Hugh McPaill, and Donald McIlmauag the boat carpenter from Fisherland, were moved around like pawns on a chess-board. Whitsunday was the usual deadline day for evictions. Cooper John Stewart, Angus Sinclair, a wright, Blind Archie McNocaird and Robert McKellar, a fisherman living in Fisherland, were among those still in their houses in 1758, when another summons of removal was made against people on the east side of Laigh Street and 22 more tenancies were terminated. The lists included tenants from as far outside the Burgh as Killian and Stuckscardan. Whether this was simply an excuse to remove people from other properties while the building of the New Town was going on is difficult to judge. After all, this was a time when His Grace was signing instructions for his Oban factor to remove tenants from Glenshellach to accommodate settlers at Oban and similar orders were endorsed around the county. Some of the Inveraray people went to the new tenements of Relief Land and Arkland and there were houses built by the more affluent in the Main Street to the north of what would be the New Town's parish church. Others went to the outlying farms of Glen Aray, Glen Shira and along Loch Fyne. There were just 11 Campbells on the removals lists, including the minister and a lawyer who was later appointed Chamberlain of the Lands of Argyll, Bute and Inverness, which perhaps pacified him for having been evicted. The mason William Douglass [sic], whose name was on the eviction list, was the man responsible for building the Doocot and Watchtower in 1748. Perhaps the psychology of giving evicted people good jobs was a good one. By 1799, the last of the old houses had disappeared and the people had been dispersed. It was not as traumatic as the clearances but lives were irrevocably changed, as was the landscape.

The 15th-century castle had been a fortified tower-house. The 3rd Duke commissioned English architect Sir John Vanburgh to draw up plans for the castle and new town and brought in an expert in Palladian style, Roger Morris, to work with William Adam, and later his son John, as the supervising architects. Influences for the new building may have come from Blenheim Palace and Castle Howard, where architect John Vanburgh had included a major central tower, lit from large upper windows, similar to that incorporated

The 15th-century tower house at Inveraray had suffered many attacks and by the late 18th century it was time for a new building. (By permission of his Grace the Duke of Argyll.)

into the plans for the Inveraray castle. The stone was local: a greenish blue schist. The interior was designed by Robert Mylne for the 5th Duke and completed between 1770 and 1789. All this, of course, was almost lost in two separate fires a century apart. In the 1880s, the upper floors of the new castle were burned out and Anthony Salvin, known as an expert in castle architecture, suggested conical roofs on the external corner towers. He also designed the Armoury Hall, a central tower seen by thousands of visitors today. Then in the autumn of 1975, fire caused £1 million worth of damage. The 12th Duke was able to call upon Campbell supporters around the world to donate towards the sensitive reconstruction work which included painting the interior in an authentic 18th-century manner.

It was perhaps a good idea to move people from dilapidated and insanitary hovels into a new planned town, even if that did involve eviction notices and much worry and inconvenience. The conditions of tenants, however, were not vastly improved. This was, after all, before the automatic inclusion of water closets in domestic properties: some tenants would not have such luxury in Argyll for another 200 years. Garderobes (lavatory provision) may have been built into castle turrets for centuries, but tenants had to be content with throwing their 'ashes, filth and other nastiness' on the street in front of their houses, as they did in this shiny new town of Inveraray. They also threw pails of household 'filth' over the little old jetty from which the ferry sailed. The tide did not always wash away the resultant stinking mess. Add to this the fish refuse thrown from boats onto the streets and the shore and the fact that domestic animals were free to roam the streets and it perhaps isn't surprising that the ever-critical Dorothy Wordsworth said in 1803 that the backs of the Inveraray houses were a doleful example of Scotch filth.[35] The estate erected dung pits, but in 1869 the estate accounts said that Philip Kelly had been paid £3 for cleaning the breast wall of the jetty over a period of six months. Little wonder then that disease was a constant companion of the Inveraray citizens through the 19th century.

Fresh water was, however, a priority for the Duke. And not only was it to be sourced but its source was to be beautified. Behind Inveraray on the hill Creag Dubh is a spring known as Bealach an Fhurain (NN088085) which was a main supply of fresh water to the town. A plan was drawn up by William Adam around 1747 which enclosed the site of the spring within a semicircular wall. A small classically-styled building of the same schist as the new castle was decorated with a ball finial on the apex of the roof and had a flagged stone floor. The paving probably continued outside the building, as shown on Daniel Paterson's 1756 plan for the new town. Walls have disappeared as well as the exterior paving, probably removed by those who felt they had better used for the stones. In 1803, iron gates were made by Robert Napier, the smith to the Duke of Argyll. They were to keep out those who had already stolen lead piping and removed the iron plating through which the water was fed into the pipes. Wooden pipes from the spring were a conduit to a lead tank near the school, and then to the town well near today's Cross. The wooden pipes, lead tank (thankfully) and well did not survive, except as fragmentary souvenirs because the building continued to be vandalised down the years. There was also a well-head known as the Physic Well near Maltland, but it was demolished in 1775.

Despite the fine concept of the new town, which included such handsome buildings as the George Hotel, built in 1770 and with a renovated interior, and the Argyll Hotel, where the Duke lodged his guests, the surrounding territory was still unimpressive in the eyes of Lord Cockburn. In 1838, he complained that upper Loch Fyne's 'little Indian wigwam-looking hamlets' looked quaint at a distance but were an 'utter abomination' up close. He remarked that 'until the lairds be civilised and cease to be all regularly and systematically bankrupt' it was useless to expect their tenants to be housed decently and comfortably. As for Inveraray itself, he found the new castle 'abominable' and too near the town for comfort. What would he have said of the bell tower, considered by local people to be a disaster, cutting out light from the the town?

The old town, of course, relied on ferries to reach the outside world. Of the seven ferries which once linked Cowal and the rest of Argyll, the most important served the House of Argyll and its visitors. This ran between St Catherine's and Inveraray. The name Ferry Land serves as a reminder of the service. Two miles south of Inveraray was the Wester to Easter Creagans ferry used by Mary Queen of Scots in 1563 to visit her half-sister, who was Countess of Argyll, and return to her castle in Dunoon. Despite the introduction of the military road through Glen Croe over the Rest and Be Thankful, the perceived approach to Argyll remained by water down the years. In 1856, the steamer *Argyll* took an hour to cross Loch Fyne, but despite carrying 4,000 passengers a year in the 1860s, none of the many contrators made the crossing a financial success. Eventually, road improvements made the ferries unviable and service was withdrawn in 1963.

To the north of Inveraray stands Dunderave Castle, built in 1560 by the MacNachtans of Glen Shira. Their former seat was on Fraoch Eilean on Loch Awe, but too many feuds led to a move to Dubh Loch, north of Inveraray in Glen Shira. After plague was brought to the castle by a chapman selling infected linen, the family moved to the castle at Dunderave across Loch Fyne from Cairndow and Glen Kinglas. Plague graves are said to exist beside Dubh Loch but they are no longer visible. Dunderave was a ruin within 200 years. Used by Neil Monro for his novel *Doom Castle*, it was bought at the beginning of the 20th century by Sir Peter Noble who employed the architect Lorimer to restore it. The emphasis was placed on following the tenets of the Arts and Crafts movement. New wings were added but with a view to harmonising with the original. *Dun da Ramh* translates as 'fort of the two oars', which suggests a fort was on this spot before the MacNaughtons came and entertained guests such as the Thane of Cawdor, and also perhaps another lost ferry. Neil Monro was not the only artist to be inspired by the castle. In recent times it has been used as a film set, as have other locations in Argyll, sometimes disastrously destroying important ancient landmarks. Mid Argyll's Dun Chonnallaich on the coast road to Oban was a fort with unique features until a film unit used the walling to build huts. At Barnakill on the Crinan Canal, an old lime kiln was reconstructed to represent a dwelling house for another film crew. The deserted settlement of High Barnakill was also reconstructed to create a slave-drawn cart with five-foot solid wheels, which certainly does not fit the orthodox view of historians (a sledge or 'Jura carr', which was made from birch saplings, was the transport of Argyll until recent times) and scandalised the local historical society which feared a documentary confirming this as 'authentic'. Film crews cannot be blamed for the ruination of carvings at Barnakill and Dunadd, however. An over-enthusiastic but ill-informed public has rubbed away at both until they are beyond recognition.

But there are so many reasons for the loss of a landscape. Today's farmers may very occasionally be offered the chance of making a bit of a living from a film crew, with or without disastrous results, while more conventionally they may make enough to keep the wolf from the door by selling off a field or two for domestic building or a new quarry. When Lord Cockburn was travelling on his circuit, bankruptcy was the stark reality of the economic situation in Scotland for so many: hence the conceptual success of the New York company. To look at the situation again in microcosm, a number of small lairds like the MacNaughtons had lived in Glen Shira from late medieval times. They left when rents began to plummet, prices for sheep dropped and cheap food imports made it hardly worth their while to farm at all. Remains of houses such as Stuckagoy, family home of Munros, Kilblaan, home of the MacKellars and an ancient chapel site, and Coulfochan, home of the Sinclairs, become harder to find as the years go on. Some of these minor lairds may have removed their tenants before their own turn came, and scores of deserted settlements in Mid Argyll bear witness to that, as do the records of Lochgilphead poorhouse residents which show children as young as seven and elderly people in their seventies and eighties from Kilberry to the south of the poorhouse catchment area to Inveraray in the north.

It is not only because people leave houses that they become dilapidated. Modern though the 3rd Duke's new town was in its day, by the mid 20th century, many of the properties intended for fishermen and other workers were among the 2,000 or so seen as unfit for habitation in Argyll at that time. Some of these properties were sold to tenants at low prices. Others were left to decay as they became empty because landlords could not afford to make the necessary upgrades. The 11th Duke had inherited in 1949 when the building stock of the whole town was in a very poor condition. The cost of the repairs was beyond the Argyll Estate and the properties were put in the hands of the Ministry of Works, and ownership was given to the Town Council. Ian G. Lindsay and Partners, who had restored 17th-century east-coast domestic properties for the National Trust, were commissioned to design an improvement scheme for the Inveraray properties known as Relief Land. Between 1958 and 1963, 103 properties were improved to modern standards. Lindsay also planned to rebuild the spire of the parish church. The church had been built in 1802 by Robert Mylne. It was divided internally to provide a Gaelic and and English service, and it is a very pertinent and poignant indication of one of Argyll's biggest losses – its language – that the Gaelic segment in time became a store. The spire was taken down for safety in 1941 and Lindsay's plans to restore it were not carried out because of lack of funding. A gas-works, installed around the time the church was built, continued to light the town until 1964, when electicity finally came to Inveraray.

The population of Argyll has changed its composition many times over the centuries. From the 1500s, the House of Argyll brought in people from Ayrshire and the Borders to improve agricultural practice and create a politically favourable climate. From the 1700s, people migrated and emigrated for economic reasons. In the 20th century, villages like Lochgilphead have become towns because of the relocation of political and economic power, while Inveraray has lost the larger role it held historically. Here were the court and the jail: remember the accused from the Morvern lead mines brought to plead their case all the way to Inveraray. This was the principal county town of Argyll for centuries, with the courts meeting in the Town House on Front Street from the middle of the 18th century (in a less civilised time, lairds held their own courts and their own executions and evidence of gallows is recorded around the county). The ground floor beneath the court room was the county prison, exposed to the view of passers-by. Because of the number of escapes from the prison, judges threatened to move the courts from Inveraray unless better premises were found and the old prison abandoned. Plans were drawn up for a new courthouse and prison in 1807 by Edinburgh architect Robert Reid. Advanced for their day, with separate blocks for men, women and debtors, the plans were too costly and it wasn't until James Gillespie Graham adapted the plans in 1816 that work went ahead. The courthouse was smaller than Reid envisaged and the new architect made just one eight-cell block for the prison. The work was finished in 1820 and in 1843 exercise yards were built. A new men's prison was opened in 1848 which had twelve individual cells, a water closet on every floor, accommodation for warders, a store-room and indoor exercise gallery. It was lit by gas and well heated. By August 1889, however, Inveraray had lost two jails since the turn of the century. County jails were seen to be too costly to run compared with the big city prisons. What by now was seen as Inveraray's 'inaccessibility' (the County Council met in Glasgow) and its diminishing economic importance as the herring industry drastically waned, combined to take its 'badges of office' away. The Circuit Court would meet just twice in the town after 1900. The Sheriff Court was moved to Dunoon in 1954. In this instance, however, only status has been lost. The revenue which comes to the town from tourists visiting the well-restored courthouse and jail, eventually recognised a century after its closure as the finest 19th-century county courthouse and prison in Scotland, must well surpass that brought by the ceremoniously grand meetings of the Circuit Court. This was, however, a very fancy affair when judges held a reception and dinner attended by the

Town Council, leading citizens and the attendant lawyers. On the first day of the court, a formal procession progressed from the Great Inn to the courthouse, led by two halberdiers in red, yellow and black uniforms and followed up by the Town Council, lawyers, the sheriff, the Lord Lieutenant, trumpeters, mace bearer and the judge himself. The mace was carried ahead of the judge to symbolise the royal power invested in him. This happened twice a year in spring and autumn, and in between the sheriff court met in the courthouse. When the courts moved away from the town, so did the lawyers, procurators fiscal and sheriff officers.

Although ease of access has often dictated the site of an Argyll castle, a monastery or a settlement, the choice of ferry routes was not always based on the shortest distance between two points. Tides and currents, rocks and spits of land have most often been the main influences on such sitings. Brainport, also known as Chapel Ferry, situated on Loch Fyne between today's Inveraray and Minard and running across to Kilbride Chapel on the Strathlachlan side, is a good example. It was in existence from pre-Medieval times, perhaps for many centuries before the building of the ancient chapel above a still-visible slipway on the east side of the loch. Excavations at Brainport suggest this was an important site in prehistory. The astrological alignments of ancient stones, the presence of a large cairn and cup-marked stones pinpoint it as yet another hub of major activity in Mid Argyll. The route across the loch is two and a quarter miles and was a good route from Kilmichael Glassary to the Holy Loch: across the hills from Kilmichael to Brainport, a ferry-crossing to Cowal, another drove along the track through Glendaruel, brought drovers to the ancient ferries from the Holy Loch to the Clyde settlements. By the 1770s, there was a sizeable settlement around the Brainport ferry slipway. The remains of a long house are that of the ferryman's house and near it there was a store or possibly a smoke-house. Loch Fyne kippers are now an expensive speciality which Deputy Prime Ministers and Chancellors of the Exchequer go out of their way to buy at the Loch Fyne Oyster Bar. Then, they were ten a penny and every settlement on the loch was doing its own smoking. A large square building stood in what is now woodland and there were several other structures, including one known as the milkmaid's house. Fishing and farming, and the quarrying, dressing and exporting of rotary quern stones seem to have been the main industries of the community. While other settlements across this stretch of land – Achnaba, the Cossack Inn, Achnalephen, Drimgarbh, Drim-fuar and Lagnahuleidh – were the subject of evictions in the early 1860s and in April 1894 were the subject of an inquiry at Tarbert into the state of crofting, Brainport had already been burned out because of a cholera outbreak in 1832.

By then, although the 18th-century ferry house remained, the ferry had closed before the turn of the century. The new roads which were built on either side of the loch detracted from ferry traffic, and in 1790, landowners petitioned Argyll Road trustees to be allowed to close the route across the loch. The ferry never reopened. A route which survived for almost a century and a half beyond that was the Otter Ferry. The delightful name conjures up *Ring of Bright Water* images, but the mammal was not the derivation of the word. *Oitir* means a spit of gravel or sand running out into the water, and there is a mile-long spit south of this crossing at the entrance to upper Loch Fyne. The ferry ran one-and-a-half miles across the loch from Otter Bay on the east between Strachur and Kilfinan, and West Otter Quay north of Glas Eilean and east of Port Ann. This was formerly part of the Silvercraigs Estate on the edge of the Asknish forest and it was valued by Robert Lamont of Silvercraigs, who said in 1561 that it was precious in peace and war as a means of access. The links between the Lamont estates were vital, and the 1600 Timothy Pont map showed a crossing on 'Loch Fynn' from Kerry Cowal (Ardlamont) to the north end of the Carricks, Lochgilp (Silvercraigs). Kerry was the old name for this corner of Argyll, a corruption of *ceithir* or four, and indicating one of the quarters of the kingdom divided among the sons of Erc, the powerful Antrim prince who colonised this land in the third century AD. Kerry Cowal later came under the feudal lordship of the Lamonts from medieval times and some of their territory spilled over the west side of the loch. By the 1700s, this was no private route but a public highway and in need of attention. The quay at East Otter was completed in 1744 by a Mr Douglas, appointed by the Commission of Supply for Argyll, while at West Otter, local tenants and their horses were required to give two days of their labour to build a quay. Ten pounds was paid to Dugald McTavish of Dunardry for this work, but by 1748, Dunardry still had not handed over the money to Provost James Fisher of Inveraray and the work was not completed. In 1761, the money still seems to have been languishing in the hands of Dunardry, because James Campbell, an Inveraray merchant, complained that the West Otter ferry had no quay or landing place, and horses had to get on board by jumping from a slanting rock into the boat. Another £12 was allocated to build a quay and the Silvercraigs tenants were to provide the labour. A new quay, however, did not guarantee a good crossing and in 1769 there was a complaint of bad service. This was yet another place where cattle crossed, and in the 19th century it was a provision of the lease of the ferry that the ferryman would carry cattle. But by then, the boat had a different role. With steamers now travelling up and down the loch on a daily basis, the Otter ferry did not simply cross Loch Fyne but also acted as a ship-to-shore ferry, carrying up to 15 passengers in the 1890s.

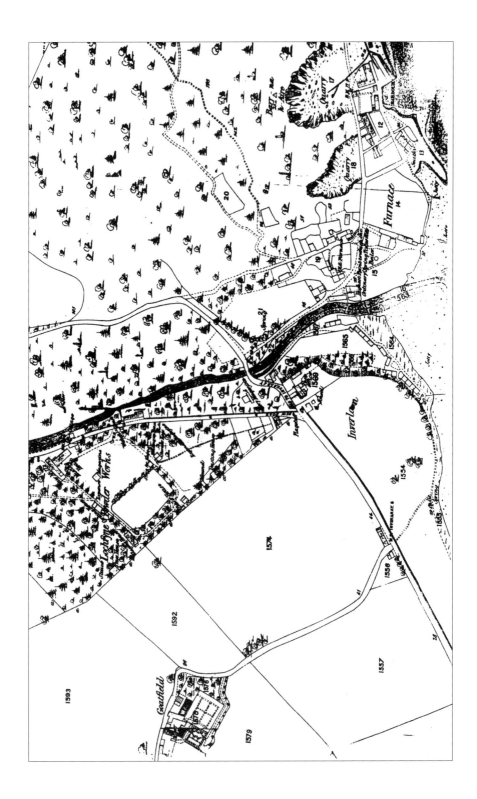

In fact, it was rarely used actually to cross the loch, as the steamer traffic (six days a week except in winter when it was curtailed to four days a week) was more popular. At the start of the Second World War there was a halt, and in 1948, the Ministry of Transport Committee on Ferries decided not to make this a vehicular ferry, which in effect killed it off. The old jetty, which took so long to come into being as the funding stuck to the hands of those intended to pay the contractors, still survives at West Otter Ferry, but not the houses, although people were still living there until the mid-19th century.

So many settlements between Inveraray and Lochgilphead disappeared, but Furnace remains a thriving village with one aspect of its industry still intact: the quarry thrives. The iron foundry, while not restored as a museum like its counterpart at Bonawe, still shows conserved evidence of its existence. The furnace itself and the remains of a former charcoal shed capable of holding 600 dozen bags of charcoal are evidence of the size of the 18th-century operation. A cast-iron lintel bears the inscription '1755'. Craleckan, as the works were originally known when the Duddon Furnace company set up here, had a casting house, a blowing house, and aparently incorporated a forge between the casting and blowing houses where basic pig iron was turned into wrought iron. The lining of the furnace hearth lay undisturbed after the furnace was finally damped down. The exact outline of the works has not been easy to define because production ceased in 1813. The third industry based at Furnace was more disastrous for the village because it ended with an explosion. The gunpowder works were set up to provide gunpowder for the local granite quarry in 1841. The ruins stand north of the village between Goatfield and the River Leacan. This was the last of four gunpowder factories to be set up in Argyll: the others were at Glean Lean (1832), Melfort (1838), and Kames (1839). The factory was water-powered from a mill-lade which ran from the Leacan Water a mile above the works. This fed a mill dam and a large waterwheel was sited at sawmills close to the road to power six incorporating mills. A long shaft went uphill to the mill range. There were individual waterwheels for the press, corning and glazing houses.

A licence had been granted at Inveraray Quarter Sessions as early as 1772 to the Sheriffs, father and son, under the terms of the Gunpowder Act. They ran the Glen Lean factory until 1840 and then started the Furnace factory the following year. It was run by Carl Hauser of Glasgow, then by the trustees of Robert Robin of Glasgow, and finally by John Hall and Company, who already

Map of the furnace and gunpowder sites at Goatfield, now Furnace on Loch Fyne. (Author's collection.)

had a large gunpowder works in Kent. In 1875, before the trustees of Robert Robin took over, the new Comprehensive Explosive Act came into force. This specified the distances which there should be between buildings, the limits on the weight of explosives and the number of people who could work in each building, as well as the distances between the factory buildings and dwelling houses and public roads. The four Argyll factories had to apply for a Continuing Certificate, but were allowed to carry on their work. The inspectors who came to Furnace on 24 October 1876, saw that the stove was too near the dusting house, that the heading-up house was too near an expense magazine, the glazing house too near the press and corning house, one of the expense magazines and the heading-up house were too near some cottages and the road and that the factory needed permission from the Secretary of State to rebuild. A magazine in which the most gunpowder was kept had been erected in 1867 on the far side of the main road, apparently without building permission. Rules seem to have been bent to allow 80 tons of gunpowder to be stored, a reduction in the quantity normally kept there. The magazine was just 100 yards from the village school, the post office and three houses and only feet from the main road. As a compromise, a blast wall was built a few feet from the magazine gable end, but the 1874 Act said that the magazine should have been three miles from such buildings and the road.

It could be said that accidents were just waiting to happen, and when they did, the thick granite blocks which formed the walls became missiles. The first occurred on 11 May 1877 when a cart with a large hole in the bottom, used to transport powder, crossed the road from the charge house to the press house several times during the day. Eventually, the sparks from the horse's iron shoes ignited the gunpowder and the horse, driver and cart went up in the explosion. The manager of the factory was prosecuted and fined £20: a small price for the lives of a man and a horse. The second accident took place at ten minutes past three on the afternoon of Saturday, 29 September 1883, and involved two-and-a-half tons of gunpowder exploding in the drying house, known as 'the stove'. The manager, William Robinson, was struck by a heavy stone from the building. Some weighing up to 250 lb flew as far as 300 yards from the site of the explosion. Robinson died two hours later. Ten men working in the factory somehow escaped injury. Again, a stray spark was said to have caused the explosion. The latest restrictions within the industry meant there could be no more compromises and no more blind eyes turned. The Furnace factory had to close, and in 1888 the business was wound up. The buildings, however, remained the property of John Hall and Company and then their successors, Curtis and Harvey, until the 1920s.

Whether by accident or design, fire has so often been the instrument of destruction in Argyll. The spark of a horse's hooves igniting gunpowder, the flames carelessly lit by bored boys playing in a factory where today they would be too young to work, the flames of retribution meted out by enemy troops, or the flames of evicting officers making sure tenants could not return to their homes. On Loch Caolisport, Stronefield was once an important crofting area until in the 19th century police and keepers came and torched tenants' houses to make way for shooting and sheep. With the loss of the crofters, the mill was no longer needed and so it would also fall into disrepair. On a steep hillside, west of Ellary in Stronefield Glen, the mill had a seven-foot-wide archway where bere and oats used to be ground. Inside was an inverted conical kiln once covered by thatch but by the time of the evictions by woven hair (the mills on the island of Luing were the first to use woven hair on which to lay the corn to dry). It is difficult to imagine how the tenants got their sacks of corn up to the mill, and even more difficult to see how they pushed the great 4 ft 7 ins diameter grinding stone up there. But they were obliged to take their produce to this particular mill, however hard the journey, just as they were obliged to leave their homes when their landlord said they were surplus to requirements.

The Ellary Estate was owned by Henry Rogers, who seemed more interested in pleasing his guests than in preserving communities – or indeed archaeological remains. On his land was what tradition calls Columba's cave. Whether the saint ever set foot in it or not is impossible to tell, but it was certainly used as both a dwelling and as a place of worship. In the late 19th century, it was partially excavated by amateurs who disturbed the layers of the millennia and left a rubbish tip outside and a mess inside the cave. By the 1960s, another generation of Rogers wanted to prettify this site (and establish Columba as a visitor if not an inhabitant if that was possible). Marion Campbell and Mary Sandeman, recorders of so much of archaeological importance in Mid Argyll, were called in to look at the cave and persuaded the Rogers to hold off their prettification. Although it was impossible to sort out the stratification, some valuable work was done over a period of several years. One of the major finds during that time was a rare Viking balance. The abundance of prehistoric and Early Christian remains throughout Knapdale will probably never be fully investigated. Even the medieval monastery ruins within the much diminished Kilberry Estate grounds are likely to remain no more than a footnote in history, their presence noted in the diaries of the late 19th-century laird John Campbell and the letters of his granddaughter Marion.

Knapdale was from the time of the Reformation until 1965 part of Kilberry and Kilcalmonnell parish, which crossed into Kintyre. Parishioners from

Left. The shaft of the Kilberry carved stone cross, broken like so many during the Reformation. (John Campbell of Kilberry collection.)

Middle. The side of the cross which the iconoclasts would have found less offensive. (John Campbell of Kilberry collection.)

Right. The medieval Kilberry cross with its depiction of the Crucifixion. (Author's collection.)

Knapdale had to cross West Loch Tarbert to Clachan at Communion times until 1821 when the church at Lergnahension was built at the head of Loch Stornoway. The late 16th-century church with pink sandstone corners built by the Campbells at Kilberry had collapsed in 1788, having been dilapidated since 1733 because of lack of funds for its upkeep. One ferry ran between Ardpatrick and Portachoillan (Clachan) and was the main land link between Kintyre and the rest of Argyll until the Sliabh Gaoil route along the Loch Fyne shore was built with great difficulty in 1776. The other route was over high ground to Avinagillan, where the Dunmore to Kilchamaig ferry ran. Known as the Whitehouse ferry, it was a half-mile crossing known in later years as Kintyre ferry No. 1, while the Ardpatrick route was known as Kintyre Ferry No. 2.

It was the Dunmore ferry which was used by the supporters of James VII and II to meet William of Orange's troops heading up from Ayr in 1689. They met at the Battle of Loup and the Jacobites escaped to Gigha and to Mull. No doubt both ferries had been used throughout that century to transport both Royalist and Cromwellian supporters as they trailed the length of Argyll, pillaging as they went. It was the MacAllisters of Loup who ran the Ardpatrick ferry and their salmon and birlinn family crest with the date 1620 was carved at Portachoillan on the lintel of a building which may have been the old ferry house. By the end of the 18th century, this had become an illegal drinking den for the ferry's passengers, which no doubt offended the sensibilities of those using the ferry to attend Communion. By the late 1740s, the quays on both sides of these ferries were in such a dilapidated state that funding and manpower were sought from the Commissioners of Supply to repair them. From 1800 until 1860, three generations of MacPhails ran the Portachoillan ferry and the family link continued right up until 1922. On the Ardpatrick side MacAllisters, who were also farmers and lobster men, ran the ferry. There was a mix of sailing boats and clinker-built rowing boats as well as passengers who paid one shilling a ticket or 6d. a head for parties. Cows and bulls went over for one or two shillings each, calves and pigs cost 3d to 6d. and the ferries carried everything from bags and parcels to furniture. The Dunmore ferry charged a flat rate of 6d. It wasn't always easy to get people to run the ferries, however essential they were to the well-being of the community. In 1877, an advert sought a good shoemaker who would also run the Ardpatrick ferry. In 1908, a ferryman said he lost much farming time attending to the ferry. On the Portachoillan side, the ferry was owned from the middle of the 19th century by Sir William MacKinnon, who was laird of Balnakill and the founder of the British East Africa Company. From the 1920s, the council took over, building a ferryman's house, now known as Tigh na Leven. Because the village at Clachan was 'dry' (as so many places were in Scotland until the 1960s) Irish labourers working there used to cross by ferry to use the pub at Lergnahension. Now there is no ferry, no pub and no labourers. In the severe winter of 1947, the ferry took mail for Kilberry, Ardpatrick and Clachan and groceries for the Islay ferry. But the last ferry was in 1954, by which time it was no longer crossing the west loch but taking passengers out to the Islay boat, which from 1830 had provided extra work for the No. 2 ferry.

For decades, people from Kilberry and Clachan, from which the roads to Tarbert were very poor, used the ferry to join the Islay boat to get into Tarbert. The ferry house at Portachoillan had an additional role in the 1950s as a lighthouse for the Islay steamers until a light was built at Corran Point. The Dunmore (No. 1) ferry had closed in 1926 because there was no longer a demand. The pier at Portachoillan was never repaired after the time of Sir William MacKinnon. From East Loch Tarbert, a ferry still runs to Portavadie on the Cowal peninsula despite many interruptions over the centuries, and a ferry runs from Tayinloan to Gigha.

The 19th century may have seen seen much faster means of transport than ever before. The first steamship to reach Inveraray was the *Dumbarton Castle* in 1815, just three years after the *Comet* made its debut, and in 1826 the *Maid of*

Horses taking off freight at the West Loch Tarbert quay. (John Campbell of Kilberry collection.)

Islay was running routes which took in Portree, Tobermory, Oban, West Loch Tarbert and Askaig on Islay. A paddle-steamer service was established between Islay and West Loch Tarbert in 1856.

But people had been travelling to Tarbert by boat for millennia. Its excellent harbour made it a place to be coveted and protected and there had been forts overlooking both east and west lochs from the earliest times. Romans and the Phoenicians knew the area and there were traders in Cornish tin, French wines and other consumer products when Ptolemy was putting Kintyre on the map. When the Irish princes came in the first centuries of the Christian era, followed by missionaries and settlers, this became a desirable strategic place to be and a fortification was established in the 8th century overlooking the East Loch. The Ancient Annals of Ulster record that a fort here was destroyed in 712 and again in 731. By 1292, a royal castle was in place, granted to John Balliol by Edward I of England. The MacGilchrists held the Tarbert lands after the Vikings had gone home in the mid 13th century and they granted the monks of Paisley the timber rights of the area. Robert I, anxious to consolidate his position after his victory at Bannockburn in 1314, ordered the building of a castle to replace the earlier one, along with a fort on the west loch and one at Cairnbaan in Knapdale. He enlarged and strengthened the castle, building out from the inner bailey with two drum towers overlooking Loch Fyne. There was a gatehouse and at least one tower over an area of more than two acres. Bruce supervised the building of the castle personally and it is

Fortification was in place overlooking East Loch Tarbert in 712. Robert Bruce rebuilt the medieval Tarbert castle. (John Campbell of Kilberry collection.)

perhaps because of that involvement that the record of accounts has survived. The building was completed on 20 July 1326 and had cost £518 13s. 6d. It included all the necessary facilities for comfortable living and ruins to the south of the castle may have been a mill with its reservoirs, mill pond, lades and sluices. There is also a possible underground water system which even in Bruce's days brought fresh water from as far as Barfad. Funding for the castle was raised by local lairds, including the Macleans of Duart and Gilchrist of MacAy, and public figures such as the bailie of Kintyre, the Abbot of Paisley and (the main contributor) Dugald Campbell, Sheriff of Argyll and Bailie of Athole. The castle maintained its royal links: James IV, who repaired the castle and added a tower-house half way along the south eastern curtain wall, used Tarbert as a stopover on his peacekeeping sorties to the islands.

The castle was gifted to the Earl of Argyll when the MacDonald lands were forfeited, and in 1503 a sheriff was appointed by Act of Parliament to sit in Tarbert and Kilkerran (which would become Campbeltown) where the 'pepill ar almaist gane wild'. The Shire of Tarbert existed from 1481, taking in Knapdale, Kintyre, Mull, Islay, Jura, Gigha, Scarba, Colonsay and the smaller west-coast islands. The 'shirefdom of Tarbert and the shirefdom of Argyll' [the

Overleaf. When the 20th-century remains of Tarbert Castle were threatened by development, the Historic Buildings and Monuments Directorate said: "Ruins should be allowed to disappear ..." (Neil and Marie Kennedy collection.)

TARBERT, LOCH FYNE. 6416. J.

latter had been divided between Inverness and Perth] were joined in 1633 to become what is almost modern Argyll. During that century, much blood was shed in and around Tarbert, and after the execution of Charles I the castle was in the hands of the Commonwealth troops. The Earl of Argyll, in his royalist period, tried to recapture the castle, but finding the Commonwealth troops out gathering nuts, relieved the premises of gunpowder, cheese and biscuits, which he had to pay back. When Charles II came to the throne and executed the earl, six lieutenants were appointed to Argyll and Tarbert to keep the peace. They were stationed at Tarbert, in Cowal, Inveraray, Saddell, Craigness and Dunstaffnage. William and Mary brought some stability, and in 1701 the successor to the House of Argyll was given a dukedom; but the MacAlisters of Tarbert were by now financially exhausted and their lands passed to MacArthur Stewart of Milton, Peter Dow Campbell of Kilduskland and other minor lairds. In 1746, the remainder of the estate, including the mansion house at Barmore, was bought by Archibald Campbell of Stonefield. The castle itself, which had been in the hands of the MacAlisters, had suffered because of their lack of revenue and was now in a dilapidated state. It was described as a 'fine old ruin' in the 1790s and it became increasingly so in subsequent centuries. In 1973 the castle's owner offered the castle free to the Ministry of Public Buildings and Works, but the Treasury refused to allow the department to

A sheriff court house stood where the Free Church stands today and the streets of Tarbert were among the first in Scotland to be paved – yet the fishermen lived in squalor. (Maureen Bell collection.)

Tarbert's fishing fleet was at the mercy of the 'silver darlings' and the legislation concerning nets. (Duncan MacMillan collection.)

accept on the grounds that 'the castle was in a remote area where no visitors could be expected in sufficient numbers to justify the expense involved'. This was something of a grand irony: Tarbert had from the mid 19th century been the target of tourists who swarmed to the village on steamers and stayed in properties let to them by local fishermen who cleared out into sheds at the back of their homes. Although by 1973 the heyday of the steamer was over, the new roads made Tarbert accessible and yachting events were bringing a new breed of visitor to the village. In the 1980s, the castle almost suffered the fate of Castle Sween when an application was received by the council to build a holiday bungalow beneath the castle on the unexcavated grounds of the ancient Royal Burgh. This galvanised local people to protest. In 1986, the castle grounds were owned by the Forestry Commission and under the Town and Country Planning Act the castle was listed as a Category B building. The Forestry Commission felt the building was too unsafe to invite the public to visit the site and the District Council had attempted to improve the castle with success. It was suggested, however, that the Council would lease the castle from the Forestry Commission and that a Manpower Services Commission would become involved in improvements. The MSC declined and the Historic Buildings and Monuments Directorate said: 'The law says ruins should be allowed to disappear rather than have inexpert repairs effected'. An estimated £200,000 was required to make the castle safe in the late 1980s and there was a Catch 22 presented to campaigners who wanted to preserve the building: 'It cannot be made less dangerous because it is too dangerous.' The Tarbert Castle Trust was formed and collecting cans were put into local shops. School students wrote to the local papers and many local dignitaries became involved in the campaign to save the castle. Two decades later, the ivy-covered ruin remains a precariously beautiful backdrop to Tarbert. It is apparently being allowed to disappear, however long that may take.

Although the roads into Tarbert from north and south were almost non-existent until well into the 20th century, a road from west to east was constructed in the early 14th century when the castle was being built by Bruce. A fort with stone foundations and wooden walls was constructed at Wester Tarbert at the same time near what today is the junction of the Kilberry and Campbeltown roads, and a road between the fort and the castle was paid for. A Sheriff Court House is believed to have stood where the Free Church stands today and the street leading to it is said to have been one of the earliest paved streets in Scotland. The old cottages which lined this street were demolished in the 1950s and replaced by a modern housing scheme. A stine – the large stone used as a mounting block for horsemen – stood at the doorway of one of the cottages and was lost along with the old houses and the ancient cobbles.

Tarbert retained some of its status, however, because of the extent of the fishing industry. In 1809, Parliamentary Commissioners were told this was 'one of the most considerable places in the Highlands' because of its harbour and locality. The harbour was improved and the thatched cottages with their earthen floors which had been scattered across the hillsides disappeared and in their stead a village was built in modern terms around the harbour. By the 1940s, 40 per cent of the old houses were uninhabitable and 100 new council houses went up. The outer pier had been built in 1866 to bring steamers to the village and the population of 2,000 increased with the addition of new villas and new fishermen's cottages with gardens. The herring were plentiful in the later half of the 19th century, but the work for coopers and fish gutters and packers was to be lost to Tarbert as to the other Loch Fyne harbours. Steamboats brought tourists but steamboats also took the fish straight from the the drift nets put out by the fishing fleet and delivered them directly to Glasgow breakfast tables. The middlemen and women would lose their jobs and the harbour, once alive with the sounds and smells of a busy industry, would fall silent. Today's fishermen go out of Tarbert mainly for seafood rather than herring. Colin M. MacDonald said that by the 1950s, only three per cent of men worked at the fishing and the departure of the Loch Fyne herring from familiar fishing grounds[36] meant that fishing communities were left 'without obvious means of livelihood'. In 1948-9, £200,000 worth of fish were landed at Tarbert. The following year there were 30 boats and 200 men employed in the industry.

Horses from Tarbert took the mail coach back to Campbeltown. (Maureen Bell collection.)

By 1957, there were ten boats and 60 fishermen. The industry has continued to decline and men have gone instead to work in forestry or the hydro-electric industry. Boat-building is a vastly reduced industry from three yards to one, but sail making continues. Another of the lost industries of Tarbert is the cotton mill which stood behind today's Co-op shop. The village had a range of shops which reflected its status, including a butcher with his own slaughterhouse run by Duncan Crawford, who kept sheep and killed them when required, a ship's chandlers run by Neil Black, who also had a coal-ree and two puffers, the *Boar* and the *Bloodhound*, and two carts to deliver the coal round the village. His horses, Punch and Bochdan, were well known to villagers and Punch was one of the last horses to pull the Campbeltown coach.

In the 18th century, fishing and farming were the only industries and they were controlled as always by the local lairds. Archibald MacAlister, Captain of Tarbert in 1748, had a house reflecting his status at Barmore, for which he paid tax on no fewer than 33 windows. This showiness, despite his Knapdale lands producing no real income, no doubt contributed to MacAlister's financial downfall and in 1751, Archibald Campbell, Chamberlain and Sheriff Depute of Argyll, had bought Barmore and renamed it Stonefield – an English translation of the family's Loch Etive property, *Achnacloich*. By 1790, Barmore house had been destroyed by fire and Campbell of Stonefield built what is today's Stonefield Castle Hotel – a mansion designed by Playfair between 1836 and 1840.

The lairds who survived in the late 18th and 19th centuries were those whose agricultural policies were to modernise – which we have seen could mean disaster for their tenants.

The introduction of lime as a fertiliser made a major difference but kilns identified as producing lime at Mealldarroch in East Loch Tarbert were in fact corn-drying kilns. There were, however, two lime kilns above what became Tarbert's golf course. Mealldarroch ('the rounded hill of oak trees') sat at the southern entrance to East Loch Tarbert and was sometime known as Old Tarbert. Above it on a narrow terrace was Beldarroch, an old settlement but not noted on Timothy Pont's map of 1600 along with neighbouring settlements like *Allt Beithe*, or Altbea, some two miles east of Beldarroch. It existed by 1747 when General Roy made his *Survey of Scotland* and was shown on the map as 'Beldarick'. In 1793, the George Langlands map showed 'Muldarroch' as part of the Stonefield Estate. By the end of the 19th century, individual houses were shown on the map with a road leading to them and the wrongly identified lime kiln. The remains of the houses, which are listed as of historic importance, show drystone foundations but no chimneys. Each dwelling had a drain onto the street and the houses were in rows with a well and a kailyard, and a D-shaped enclosure below the settlement seems to have been the corn-drying kiln. Rent was paid by the people of Mealldarroch to Archibald MacAlister of Tarbert in 1750 and the 1841 census shows five households, all Carmichaels, all fishermen, farmers, carpenters and servants. In 1843-4, an assessment list for work on the Tarbert roads showed that six Beldarroch men were absent from work for six days. In 1851, the census return gave no mention of Beldarroch and the 1868-78 Survey of Argyll records Mealldarroch as ruins, formerly a farm steading belonging to G.C. Campbell of Stonefield. In 1892, a number of steadings – Laggan, Altbea, Muldarroch, Breachlarach and Knaock-a-Cathal – had become one farm, known as Muldarroch. Was this just another case of sheep taking over from man? At the inquiry into crofting which was heard in Tarbert in 1892, John MacCougan of Castlehill, Tarbert, a man then in his mid-60s, told the Royal Commission (Highlands and Islands 1892) that some farms in the Eascairt area had been cleared in 1839 but there was never any record of Beldarroch being cleared. Tradition says instead that this settlement was deserted in the mid-1840s in a cholera outbreak which also wiped out Allt Beithe. At Allt Beithe, there was no question about the fate of the people. A report by a descendant of the families who lived there (including the great-great-grandfather of John Smith, the late leader of the Labour Party) in the 19th century[37] suggests that here the houses were built with their gables to the sea for maximum shelter from the gales. They had two rooms and were built of local stone with a chimney in one gable. They are now within the Forestry Commission's plantation. The 1841 census listed John Leitch, a 40-year-old fisherman, six children aged between 14 and two years, and Catherine Leitch, whose age is given as 26 years. There was also a 15-year-old herdsman called

Archibald McLean. There was a second Leitch family headed by Duncan and his wife, also Catherine, and both men were fishermen. This was land where crops wouldn't grow and if the men had any agricultural links it was through buying and raising cattle. But then, the shore beneath Allt Beithe was not a good place for fishing boats either and it is most likely that John and Duncan worked the boats out of Tarbert in the wintertime. The path which led from Tarbert through Allt Beithe and beyond has long since disappeared under conifers but there was once enough of a track to allow a horse and cart to carry a coffin to Tarbert. When people got nearer to Tarbert at *Tobar Phoin* (Jacob's Well), they used to wash the mud from their feet and put their good shoes on. Cholera came to the settlement without any warning and it was when the families had not been seen for several days that two men went out from Tarbert to see what was wrong. They found everyone dead or dying except the baby, Archibald Leitch. He was taken in by his relatives at Bruach na Suith and was raised by them, and it was he who became the great-great-grandfather of the 20th-century political leader. Four older children survived because they were working away from home. A stone to John and Catherine is in Tarbert graveyard, putting the dates of their deaths as 4 and 16 December 1845. When the dead and dying were removed, Allt Beithe was burned to eradicate what they called 'the plague'. Such outbreaks were not rare and a temporary cholera hospital was built in Campbeltown in 1886 by the Glasgow architect Henry Edward Clifford. The corn-grinding quern from the settlement was taken as a memorial and it sits at a house called Breezycliff. Archibald became a carpenter and boat-builder and his sons followed him into the business. It seems certain from the Leitch version of the story that the settlement at Beldarroch did indeed suffer the same fate. The Tarbert women had gone to Beldarroch first and when they found everyone there dead, they followed on to Allt Beithe and made their tragic discovery there.

The Leitch family were also to become sail makers in Tarbert and the business, which survives today, was set up on the site of the Barking House Quay. Barking was a job the fishermen did on Saturdays to prevent their cotton nets from rotting. The nets were taken to the barking house where they were hauled into vats 8 ft by 6 ft by 5 ft which lined the walls and steeped in a concoction made from bark and leaves. The bark mix was heated, and once the nets were immersed, the vats were covered by a tarpaulin to keep the heat in. On Mondays, the bungs were knocked from the vats, the liquid drained away and the nets were taken back to the boats. The arrival of synthetic nets did away with this old method of preserving the natural fibres and the barking house disappeared. It was at Tarbert that the men designed their own ring nets in the 1840s which precipitated a fishing war. A special police station known as 'the Barracks' was built on the site of today's fire station, and the police patrolled in a boat called the *Jackal* to stop the men using these nets, which were banned for several decades and led to questions at Westminster from sympathetic local lairds about the ability of fishermen denied their livelihood to maintain their families. Fishermen from Tarbert, Carradale, Ardrishaig and Campbeltown went to London to plead their case. A man died in the campaign and eventually the nets were allowed, but fishing quotas and net sizes restrict today's fishermen in much the same way as the 19th century catches were controlled.

KINTYRE

Mealldarroch was to become a Natural Nature Reserve in 1983 to preserve the native woodland of oak, rowan, hazel, holly, ash, elm and a variety of flowering plants, moses and ferns. The Forestry plantation surrounds the 500-acre site, where there are also charcoal platforms dating from the days of the iron ore works at Furnace. The old track from Tarbert to Skipness was planted with deciduous trees in an effort to preserve its direction. This rugged coast from Tarbert to Skipness seems inaccessible today. Once it bristled with settlements like Beldarroch and Allt Beithe but the ordinary folk would not have had access to worship at the ancient chapel at Skipness dedicated to St Brendan. It was part of the castle which they say was first built by Somerled or one of his supporters and as such would have been the place of worship for the laird and his family. Skipness Point was an obvious place of vulnerability on the Kilbrannan Sound looking across to Arran, and there must have been defences built here from the earliest times. The extent of the deterioration of the castle in Tarbert makes Skipness the largest surviving castle in Kintyre. Unlike Tarbert, perched high above the loch on a rocky promontory, it was built on flat grazing land, but even so held as strategic a position as did Castle Sween, and a charter of 1261 records that the Skipness lands were granted to Dugald MacSween, son of the Sween who built Castle Sween. In 1262, both Castle Sween and the Skipness lands were granted to the Menteith family. The hall-house erected there in the early part of the 13th century had a chapel running its full length and the hall stood two storeys high. This became an enclosed castle at the end of the 13th century and a new chapel was built near to the shore, freeing up the original chapel to be part of the defences. A curtain wall went up at that time which created a courtyard, and towers were built on the

A chapel dedicated to St Brendan was secularised and incorporated into the medieval castle at Skipness. (Author's collection.)

south-east and north-east corners within the new wall. A latrine tower was built at the west corner. There was also a new entrance on the south wall which had a portcullis operated from a vaulted chamber over the entrance archway. The Lords of the Isles gained control of Skipness and held it until the Forfeiture in 1476. At that time the lands reverted to the Crown, but in 1502 James IV granted the charter of Skipness to Archibald 2nd Earl of Argyll.

It was around that time that the building in the north-east corner of the courtyard was extended to become a five-storey tower-house. Later that century, a parapet walk was constructed. The corner turrets survive. When the

2nd Earl was killed at Flodden the Skipness Estates were entailed to Archibald Ban, his middle son. The oldest son, Colin, became the 3rd Earl. Archibald Ban was made Captain of Skipness and the family retained the post until the 19th century. In 1563, a Campbell daughter became heir to the castle, and having married a younger son of the Campbells of Ardkinglass was the founder with her husband of the Campbells of Skipness, Shawfield and Ardpatrick. In 1645, when Alastair macCholla deserted the Montrose Army after the Battle of Kilsyth so that he could wage his own private war against the Campbells in Argyll, fighting centred for a while around Skipness and the castle was under siege for a long period before it could be relieved. The castle's defender was our friend MacNaughton from Dunderave, north of Inveraray, and the siege of Skipness ruined him. The Marquess of Argyll's rebellion in support of Monmouth in 1685 – the last straw as far as the Royalists were concerned and the action which led to his execution – resulted in an order for Skipness castle to be razed to the ground. The Captain of Skipness then was Walter Campbell, and he stood accused of supporting the Marquess. To save himself and the castle, he told the Privy Council that he was going to leave Kintyre and live in Bute. In 1756, when the troubles waned and the executions were over, the Skipness estates were re-inherited by Campbells of Shawfield and Islay. On the death in 1816 of Walter Campbell, the 3rd laird of Shawfield and Islay, the property went to his son Robert. But after 350 years in the family, the estates had to be sold in 1867 because of severe financial difficulties. The 15,000 acres were not producing an income and the Campbells of Auchindarroch kept them financially afloat. The castle had been abandoned in the 17th century and in the mid-19th century, the Campbells were living in a Georgian mansion which became the home of the Graham family. The architect John Honeyman was commissioned by Robert Chellas Graham to build a Scottish Baronial mansion on the site of the Campbells of Skipness House. Skipness House was a three-storey building with an attic keep. The wings had two storeys with round towers and corbelled angle-turrets. By the 1960s, Skipness House was owned by C.A.M. Oates, who lost his life trying to save others when the building was destroyed by fire. A new house was built on the foundations of this one and today the estate is a working farm and tourist venture which offers seafood specialities.

Across the peninsula at Tayinloan, Largie Castle was the seat of the MacDonalds of Largie, a family which claimed direct descent from Somerled. In medieval times they built a modest fortified house which was later incorporated into a farmhouse, while the modern Largie Castle was built in the 19th century. It was designed in the style of a European tower-house on an L-shaped plan with turrets, and it incorporated an Episcopal chapel. The tower-house was demolished in 1953 and the family moved into a much more modest Georgian estate house at Ballure. The MacNeals of Lossit had their seat at Machrihanish, which was destroyed by fire in the early 1800s. A new Lossit House was built a mile from the original site between 1824 and 1830, with a projecting slated roof. Between the 1840s and 1890s, there were additions to the north and south wings which were mainly demolished in 1976, leaving a projecting tower with a balustraded parapet.

It is almost 800 years since Kintyre was re-assigned to Scotland after its possession by the Vikings, yet even now there is a separateness about this part of Argyll. It is not all in the imagination. The geological 'Highland Boundary Fault' which stretches from Stonehaven in the north-east of Scotland through Bute and on to Kintyre in the south-west is where over 400 million years ago an ancient ocean was squeezed and buried; and where some of the oldest rocks in the world come up against some of the much younger ones. The geology of the peninsula created land good for agriculture which the earliest Argyll settlers enjoyed, leaving behind them cairns, flints, cists, standing stones and jewellery. On the tiny island of Gigha alone, there is evidence of seven cairns, seven cists and a standing stone, and although there may have been several climate changes in the intervening millennia, Neolithic farmers perhaps found it as conducive to the growing of crops and domestication of animals as today's agriculturists, whose Gigha lamb is widely renowned.

Balnabraid cairn is one of the most important Bronze Age sites in Kintyre but there are also multiple cist burials under cairns at Trench Point as well as those at Carn Ban on Gigha. A jet necklace, now at Inveraray Castle, was found at the head of Campbeltown Loch and ten others have been found throughout Argyll and Bute. Many urns containing gold bracelets and armlets have

Largie Castle at Tayinloan, traditional seat of the MacDonalds, was replaced by this 19th-century house which was demolished in 1953. (Argyll and Bute Library Service.)

disappeared without trace from sites as far apart as Gigha, Killmaluaig, Trench Point, Bealloch, Killean House (where a gold bracelet was found during the construction of a carriage drive), Largie Castle near Tayinloan and Tangy Hill Moss. Evidence of Iron Age forts and duns survives and many were occupied through to the Early Christian period and even into the Middle Ages.

'Kil' names abound in Kintyre, but there is little structural evidence of the Early Christian ecclesiastical buildings which those names indicate. Many of the carved stones of that period and later medieval times have also been lost. Those which remain show a great variety of styles across all the Argyll schools, but the iconoclasts of the Reformation were particularly vigorous in Kintyre. A slab at Killean shows five crosses on one face and a single cross on the other. It was probably part of an altar or prayer station. Larger crosses at Tarbert on Gigha and at Killean were probably erected as acts of piety or to commemorate particular events. Killmaluaig has a grave-marker dating from the late 6th to the early 7th centuries. Gigha also has an inscribed pillar and other carved stones. Clachan, Kilchenzie, Kilkerran and St Ciaran's Cave may all date to before the ninth century. Later crosses have been found on Sanda off Southend, Balinakill and Tarbert on the Isle of Gigha and some from the 12th and 13th centuries were found in the sea at Southend, at Clachan, Cara and Kilmichael Ballochrog. The Gigha Ogam (depicting the Celtic alphabet) is Irish in origin and others show Irish influence.

Parish churches were built on Gigha, and on the mainland at Kilchenzie, Kilchousland and Killean. These were small chapels, no longer than 40 feet and around 15 feet wide. Their windows were small and often rebated externally. Kilchenzie, Kilchousland and Killean date to the 12th century while St Cathan's on Gigha and Kilkivan were built in the 13th century. Killean and Kilkenzie were lengthened in the 13th century and given richly decorated chancels like those at Dunstaffnage chapel in Lorn. These have not been preserved and the parochial chapels are mainly in poor condition. Ruins can be seen at Southend, on Sanda and at Skipness. Even the post-Reformation churches are all altered from their original early 18th-century state, although at Southend, while the outside reflects the Gothic revival, the interior from 1774 was preserved. Stone carving stopped at the Reformation and most religious depictions were simply smashed. Eventually, some compromises were made and the Campbeltown market cross, with its 1380 Crucifix chipped away, survives as a secular monument.

Kintyre's political and domestic history can rarely have run smoothly. Even the industries taken for granted as part of the traditional scene have their own peculiar histories. In the south of the peninsula, dairy cattle flourish. This was an industry introduced during the 16th-century 'plantations' manipulated by the Earl of Argyll so that he would have political supporters from the Borders and Ayrshire in place in otherwise alien territory. Campbeltown's creamery is a legacy of that manipulation.

This had been MacDonald territory; the mainland outpost of the Lords of the Isles. It was so near to Ireland that the MacDonald cousins could almost reach out and touch each other. It was, of course, the first place where the Irish princes landed in the first centuries of the Christian era. Erc from Antrim put his sons in charge of Lorn, Cowal and Kintyre. It was in the settlement which a millennium later became Campbeltown that Fergus, first king of Scotland, built his parliament house and where the affairs of Scotland were administered until 843. Fergus was not the first to take an interest in 'Cantyre' (*Ceann Tir* – 'head of land'). After the Neolithic tribes had settled here the Romans sailed by, drew the map of where the Epidii tribe lived and even traded with them. The Romans perhaps saw this land as too distant to administer with any authority. It was a problem rulers were to have for another 1,700 years or so: Kintyre was not a place which was easily administered. It was heavily fortified and when Gabhran, ruler of Kintyre, was attacked by Selbhach in 712, he relied on the defences at Dunaverty to maintain his power. The Vikings took over where Fergus and his descendants left off, making their presence known for a couple of hundred years and then, after that master stroke by Magnus Barefoot over the Tarbert isthmus, taking at least nominal control of the peninsula.

It wasn't all warring, of course. St Columba landed at the southernmost tip of the peninsula and made his way north to put views of his homeland behind him. At Southend, his 'footprints' in the rocks leading to a medieval chapel are part of Kintyre's spiritual history as much as the lowering remains of Dunaverty Castle, eventually destroyed in a bloody massacre during the civil war, are part of the peninsula's secular past. St Kieran was another Irish saint influential in Kintyre, and his name was celebrated in the settlement at *Ceann Loch Cille Chiaran* ('head of St Kieran's loch') which was first Kilkerran and then in time became Campbeltown. As we have seen, Early Christian chapels and later medieval ones were scattered the length of the 42-mile peninsula.

There was, however, a constant power struggle here. After Gabhran's son Aidan was consecrated as the first Christian king of Scotland at Dunadd in Mid Argyll in 575, the independence of the Dalriada kingdom was secure for a short time. After his death, however, the Pictish wars, followed by Viking invasion and eventual possession by Magnus Barefoot in 1098, meant ordinary lives were lived out against a violent backdrop. Dunaverty Castle was pivotal when Kintyre was attacked by Selbhach, king of Lorn, in 712. It became still more important when Angus Og, son of the Lord of the Isles who in 1249 first acknowledged the superiority of the king of Scotland over Kintyre, gave Robert Bruce refuge there in 1306. That protection was not rewarded as Angus Og would have liked, and nor was his support of Bruce at Bannockburn in 1314. Dunaverty Castle was not gifted to him but to a nephew of Bruce's, on the premise that a relative offered a safer pair of hands. However, Angus Og's son John gained the Northern Isles through marriage, divorced his wife and married Robert II's daughter. She brought Kintyre with her to the marriage, making the Lords of the Isles all powerful again. The chess-board manoeuvres did not bring permanent power. When more marital alliances gave the MacDonalds lands in Antrim, the king fobbed off John Cathanach MacDonald of Dunnyveg with a knighthood, but Kintyre was put under the authority of the Tarbert sheriffdom and Dunaverty Castle was refortified by yet another king's man. This governor was hanged over the walls of the castle in sight of the king by MacDonald, who of course had then to flee to Antrim and in time was captured and executed. It could not have pleased the MacDonalds, but certainly could not have surprised them, when the 2nd Earl of Argyll was made Crown Chamberlain of the forfeited MacDonald lands and granted Dunaverty Castle along with a new castle at Kilkerran.

At the Reformation in 1560, Alexander Cunningham, Master of Glencairn, was appointed governor in Kintyre, based at Dunaverty Castle. With an Ayrshire name, he was probably a forerunner of the allies brought to Kintyre at the behest of James VI after the Union of the Crowns in 1607 to create support for the authorities where none existed. The MacDonalds had caused problems for the English as well as the Scots, which brought a punishment force under Thomas Ratcliffe, Earl of Sussex, in 1588 to teach them a lesson for meddling in the affairs of the Irish against the English crown. The MacDonalds at that time held Saddell Castle as well as Dunaverty, Machrimore and Islay, courtesy of Mary Queen of Scots who was fighting her own battle against the English throne as best she might. The Earl of Sussex's violent retribution damaged Saddell and Dunaverty and laid waste much of the countryside from Carradale to the Sound of Sanda. After the Union, the MacDonalds were pushed out of strategic lands and posts and pro-Campbell families from the Lowlands replaced them.

In the 17th century, a similar exercise was carried out to gain support during the civil war. Ayrshire and Renfrewshire families such as the Laird of Ralston were moved in and given prime properties. Ralston first occupied the lands around Saddell in 1650 and was then granted lands in the parishes of Kilkerran and Kilcolmkill and Kilblaan, the latter joint parish becoming known

Dunaverty Castle was yet another victim of the Civil War. (Maureen Bell collection.)

as Southend from Reformation times. There was famine in Kintyre caused by a combination of bad weather and the presence of marauding troops. In 1647, Lieutenant General David Leslie led a Parliamentary Army into Kintyre to deal with Royalist Alasdair Colla Chiotach, known as Young Colkitto, who had left his senior commander, the Marquess of Montrose, in order to carry out anti-Campbell tactics in Argyll. MacDonald was surprised at Rhunahaorine near Largie in the north-west of the peninsula and retreated south to Dunaverty, where three hundred fencible men were pulled in to defend the castle against Leslie's troops while MacDonald went to seek reinforcements. Leslie and the Earl of Argyll besieged the castle. The men surrendered, but were then massacred without mercy. The castle was not used again, and by 1685, when the Earl of Argyll raised a rebellion against James VII it provided no shelter.

Peace in the 18th century brought longer leases for Argyll Estate tenants, but also meant combination farms instead of the old runrig system, and many lost their homes and livelihoods. Rents were high. In 1757, Archibald McIlchallum (McCallum) and three others, none of whom could write their names, took a 19-year lease of the farm of Mid Kilmory near Tayinloan on the Killean Estate owned by the Duke of Argyll. They had to pay £21 for two merklands. In 1770, Gilbert McIlchallum from Breachlarach, Carradale, took out a lease of the farm of Crunastil near the village of Muasdale in West Kintyre. These lands comprised four merklands and he had rental of one merkland for 19 years at £18 10s. 7d. plus a boll of bere or barley, and half a boll of meal annually. The farm stayed in the family for 60 years before going to a new tenant. Others simply could not keep up with the rent payments and provision of crops as part of the rent. Widow Christy McCallum went to renew a 19-year lease with her son Duncan Beaton in 1833 on North Beachmore, but when they were told it was £130 a year, they refused to pay, saying the rent was too high. They were evicted and emigrated to Australia. There was no guarantee of succession of leases, and if a tenant couldn't pay, he was turned out. The lease of the farm of Keprigan in Southend was in the MacCallum family from 1729. The rent went up and up and by 1786, Hugh McCallum was paying £25.10s. sterling. At the same time he was paying £60 a year and 55 bolls of meal to rent Machrimore Mill. He built a new mill with a kiln and a slated roof to keep the grain dry. The Duke supplied the timber, stone and lime. The building was moved to higher ground because the mill wheel had not been able to cope with debris during heavy rain. Yet in 1817, despite all his hard work, he was outbid for the lease by Robert Colvill, who offered £90 against Hugh's £70. In 1839, it changed hands yet again.

Machrimore Mill, a mile or so east of Southend, and the mill at Tangy, were the last two water mills to remain in operation in Kintyre, continuing through to the 1950s. The machinery from Machrimore was removed and stored. The new mill built by Hugh MacCallum was a three-storeyed building on a sloping site with its entrance on the east side. It was typical of water-

Saddell Abbey was commissioned by Somerled or his heir. The lay brothers were farmers here for centuries. (Author's collection.)

Sadell Castle. Saddell House and Castle have been reprieved by the tourist industry while the abbey is a crumbling ruin. (Neil and Marie Kennedy collection.)

powered vertical mills of the 19th century and was built of rubble masonry with sandstone dressings and a slated roof. The windows in the lower part of the building had ventilating shutters while above the kiln there was a revolving ridge-ventilator. It was powered from Corrieglen Water, which was brought along a lade from the north through two sluices that regulated the flow and discharged the excess into the burn. There was once a mill pond which augmented the Corrieglen supply but it dried up long ago. A wooden trough took the water onto the wheel, which was iron but had wooden buckets. A system of levers inside the mill controlled speed and water flow. On the ground floor, the gearing for the wheel was housed. It was all made from iron. On the middle floor were the grinding stones, three sets, each 3ft 3ins in diameter, grouped around an upright drive shaft. Each set was in a circular wooden casing with a grain hopper above. The grain was shaken from the hopper to the stone through a pivotal feed-trough which was in permanent motion. This was a modern mill for its day and it must have been a blow to MacCallum to lose it for the sake of £20 a year.

But property was granted to and taken from people from every walk of life. The abbey at Saddell, founded by Cistercian monks around 1150, held lands gifted to it by the great and the good. The Earl of Carrick and his wife gave the monks lands in Ayrshire. Alexander, 3rd Lord of the Isles, gave them Davaar Island in the bay of Kilkerran (later Campbeltown) and the island of Gigha.

Duncan Campbell of Loch Awe gifted them lands around Crinan. There was a school of stone-carving at Saddell (the remnants of fine examples are in a protected area beside today's abbey ruins) and the monks farmed extensively. When the abbey was closed in 1507 on the grounds that it had become too laicised, James IV could not allow such valuable and strategic property to fall into the wrong hands. He decided it should become part of the diocese of Argyll and he gave the lands of Saddell as a barony to the Bishop of Argyll, David Hamilton, who was the illegitimate son of James, Lord Hamilton, and half brother of the 1st Earl of Arran. The Bishop built a new castle half a mile from the abbey. The contemporary barmkin was absorbed into later courtyard buildings but the tower wall miraculously survived. It was built to an elongated rectangular plan which allowed the hall and the kitchen to be grouped together at the first-floor level and there was generous domestic accommodation on the upper floors. A cathedral might well have followed if James IV had had his way. He wanted to remove the power of the diocese from Lismore to Saddell and petitioned Pope Julius to that effect. The letter did not reach Rome (it is now among Henry VIII's state papers) and because James died at Flodden in 1513, he was unable to follow through on the request. The castle, completed in 1512, was to become one of the properties given and taken away in the political games of the coming centuries. David Hamilton set the ball rolling in 1556 by gifting Saddell to his half-brother in return for having his many heavy debts paid for him. James MacDonald, heir to the now non-existent title of Lord of the Isles, suggested exchanging lands which he held in Arran for the Saddell lands. The Earl of Arran agreed on condition that MacDonald paid the feudal dues on Saddell, collected tiends and rents in Kintyre, gave hospitality to the Hamilton family when required and refrained from interfering in Arran matters. Two years later, the Earl of Sussex caught up with MacDonald, burned 'Saudell, a fayre pile and strong', Machrimore and Dunaverty. Saddell stayed in the MacDonald family until 1607, when all their lands went via the Crown to the Earl of Argyll and Argyll gave Saddell to Ralston. By that time, the iconoclasts had had time to destroy many of the Saddell carved stones and crosses, particularly those depicting Christ on the Cross. The newly named Royal Burgh of Campbeltown, created at the turn of the century, was not alone in choosing a secularised cross for its market-place while carvings at Southend, Saddell, Kilkivan, Kilkerran and Kilchousland saw religious icons thrown from their places and sometimes smashed on the rocks or flung into the sea. Meanwhile, the Earl of Argyll was removing the people themselves from their homes. In 1609 he applied for a Decreet of Removal to evict Kintyre tenants. And if the landlord and the church did not wreak enough destruction, Nature

Keil House, a mansion which became a school. Under-insured, it could not be rebuilt when it burned down. (Neil and Marie Kennedy collection.)

had her way, too, sending the plague to Kintyre between 1644 and 1648, leaving many settlements empty. The dying were left to bury the dead and the Earl of Argyll had to repopulate as well as politically manipulate. At least he now had empty property into which he could place his 'plantations' from elsewhere.

In the 1700s, the Argyll Estates were surveyed and the tenants' houses were found wanting. Mud floors, poor thatches and animals inside the houses were typical of the conditions in which tenants were living, yet the Enlightenment was inspirational in pushing the Duke of Argyll to use new machinery, new agricultural methods and even to create a model farm village at Monirua near Southend. There was little that was 'model' about the lives of tenants and it was to remain so for another two centuries, despite the innovations which Kintyre witnessed.

From time to time there was some degree of economic security for the ordinary family: the fishing in the 18th century went through a period of boom which affected people's incomes. But for most it was an uphill struggle: walking miles to cut peats in the summer to keep a smouldering fire going in winter, cultivating strips of land shared with neighbours, ploughing up the ground with crude wooden implements. People drained away from Kintyre in thousands.

There was a desperate need for education, and when Keil House became vacant at the beginning of the 20th century, it was turned into a school to educate a generation of engineers. Keil House dated back to pre-Reformation times, when it was owned by the Omay family. It was sold in 1819 to Dr Colin McLarty of Chesterfield, Jamaica, who improved the farm, and planted trees and gardens. It became the property of James Nicol Fleming, who built a small Victorian house on the site of the previous laird's house and by the 1860s it was reputed to be one of the finest in the Western Highlands. He and his fellow directors of the City of Glasgow Bank had, however, spent their shareholders' money and were responsible for the bank's collapse. Mr Fleming was imprisoned and the house went to Ninian Bannatyne Stewart, another Glasgow businessman. This was the age of steam when it was possible to work in Glasgow and have a home on the the the furthest reaches of the Firth of Clyde. After Mr Stewart's death, the estate was broken up in 1815 and the trustees of the estate of Sir William MacKinnon, a son of Campbeltown and founder and chairman of the British India Steam Navigation Company, bought Keil to meet a clause in Sir William's will; to set up an engineering school for boys from Argyll and the Isles. The Kintyre Technical School trained the boys free, but in 1924 a fire gutted the place and because it was under-insured, the building wasn't repaired and the school was transferred to Dumbarton. Keil was sold in 1926 to James Barbour, a Stirlingshire farmer, but the building was never restored. Nearby stands what was built in 1939 as Keil Hotel, an ugly ruin of a building used in the Second World War as a naval hospital. It had some success as a tourist attraction in the 1960s and 1970s but has lain empty since.

Less visible is the history of the Drumlemble mine, its canal and its railways. It was a long history and an exciting one, involving some of the major figures of the industrial revolution, but today there is little more to be seen than a row of cottages and a stretch of disturbed land which traces the course of a canal. It was in 1498 that James IV sent the collier John Davidson to Kintyre to 'verify if colys may be wonnyn thare'. They were present in the Laggan Moss, a stretch of peat bog between Campbeltown and Machrihanish, and they were mined to heat Kintyre's castles. The coal was not of the best quality, being the last outcrops of the seam running across Scotland and petering out in Antrim, but there was enough to employ miners throughout the 17th century, and at the end of the 18th century the Drumlemble pits were producing 4,500 tons a year. Laird Charles MacDowall of Crichen, who rented his property from the Argyll Estates, wanted to restore the salt pans at Machrihanish as a going concern and needed coal to develop the process. He also saw the potential of developing the market for coal in Campbeltown, but he had transport problems. To solve them, he invited his acquaintance James Watt, the Greenock engineer, who was by the 1770s becoming quite famous. Watt sailed for Kintyre in June 1773 and

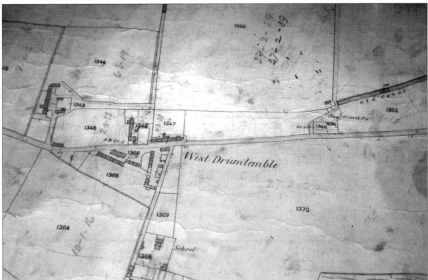

Top. Gutting fish at Campbeltown. (Neil and Marie Kennedy collection.)

Above. Map of West Drumlemble farm where the canal terminus lay. (James and William Wallace collection.)

spent some time surveying a line for a canal from Drumlemble to Campbeltown and discussing flooding problems in the mine. He also went to Carradale to look at the quay there, but this was work which would not come to anything. The canal, however, went ahead in 1783 and was finished by 1791. Once a tax on transporting coal by sea had been lifted in 1794, this could have opened the way for an export trade.

Meanwhile, meeting the needs of a growing Campbeltown was enough for MacDowall of Crichen. The population had grown from 28 houses in 1636 to 5,000 residents in 1791. A century later, that had grown again to 8,235 and there were already industries using coal in the town. Orr, Ballantine and Company had a brewery which they had built in 1770, and in 1772 there were 22 small licensed distillers producing 19,000 gallons of whisky a year. Since 1700 there had been a shipyard in Campbeltown; there was a cooperage where barrels were made for fish and whisky, and fishing nets were manufactured. The repeal of import laws after the Union of the Parliaments in 1707 meant luxury goods like tea, coffee and tobacco could be traded in Scotland as well as England, and while the tobacco barons of Glasgow profited most, merchants set themselves up in Campbeltown too. Whisky and herring made the most money but there was trade in textiles, copper stills and soap. A man like Crichen, providing the fuel of industry, could make his fortune. He had found a 6ft seam and he needed the coal to be transported efficiently and cheaply. Watt's canal was 4.5 miles long and began at what is today West Drumlemble Farm, where barge horses circled at a terminus. There were no locks and it was 9ft wide at the bottom and 4ft 6ins deep. Passing places for the boats were built and the only wooden aqueduct in Britain was incorporated to carry Straw Water. Watt wanted to use the best materials but Crichen said his lease was not long enough to make such finesse worth it. Sadly, he did not live to see his innovative transport system completely finished. He died in September 1791 and the official opening of the canal was in 1794. The coal kept on coming, however, although it fluctuated wildly. In 1788, 31,418 cartloads were mined at Drumlemble. The next year there were 40,987 cartloads, but in 1791 only 34,937. By 1798 there were three flat-bottomed barges operating on the canal, a new seam was opened at Drumlemble and 40 cartloads of coals were being hauled

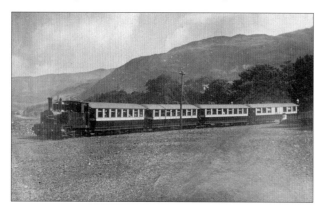

The most remote railway in the country ran from Campbeltown to Machrihanish. (Neil and Marie Kennedy collection.)

Come, behold the swells of the Atlantic Ocean.

The Cantyre Corridor Train-de-Luxe.

OUR LOCAL EXPRESS

Top. The pier and harbour at Campbeltown was an integral part of the town's wealth. (Duncan MacMillan collection.)

Above. The Campbeltown railway carried holidaymakers and miners alike – and the freight wagons transported the coal. (Maureen Bell collection.)

on the boats every day at a cost of seven shillings a ton. This compared with 4,820 cartloads of peat carried from the surrounding Laggan Moss every year, a process which drained the wetlands, created good fertile arable land and was encouraged by the payment of £4 paid to tenants for every acre they brought under cultivation.

The farm at Drumlemble in 1779 was run by 14 families, higher than the average of around ten families to a farm on the Duke of Argyll's Kintyre estates.

Many augmented their income by illegally distilling whisky but this was stopped by the tough legislation introduction in 1823. It was only worth the bigger distillers taking out licences and this became the peninsula's growth industry. It had its demands, and by 1835 the Drumlemble mine was producing 10,950 tons of coal to meet those demands. It was not to last. Two decades later the mine was merely being maintained and the canal was silted up and overgrown. It was abandoned in 1856 and two coal seams closed in the early 1860s. A new pit, opening at Kilkivan in 1866, brought a suggestion of hope for men unable to work, and when new owners took over in 1875, an exciting new era began.

A railway was built: a railway which was the most remote in the country and which boasted Scotland's only narrow-gauge line. It came to a peninsula where Jura carrs, the sledges of birch poles, were still the main means of transporting goods, and the mail went by coach and horses up and down perilous roads from Campbeltown to Tarbert.

Steam was something hitherto confined to the boats which brought passengers and commodities to Campbeltown, Southend and Carradale, and took cattle and sheep and people away to the Clyde ports. Now it was to be seen in the guise of a goods train running across the heartland of Kintyre. The Argyll Coal and Canal Company had first to close the Watt canal and draw up a route for the line. In July 1876, work on the line began at Trodigal. The first stretch was 4.5 miles long. This was extended to 4.7 miles in 1881. It had a gradient of 1 in 35 and the sharpest curve had a radius of 150 ft. Level crossings were replaced by cattle grids and the trains were soon able to meet the distilleries' coal demand of 600 tons a week and the Campbeltown-wide consumption of 1,700 tons a week. On 11 November 1876, a 0-4-0 tank engine named *Pioneer*, manufactured in Kilmarnock by Andrew Barclay, arrived by steamer. On 21 April 1877, the line, at a cost of £900, was complete. Wagons were delivered and the service running the following month, delivering coal which cost domestic users 8s. a ton while dross cost 2s. 6d. The Kilkivan pit was exhausted by 1881 but new works were opened again at Drumlemble and the railway line was extended there. A new locomotive had to be bought in 1885 to cope with the volume of coal. This was the *Chevalier* and it was to be the longest-serving loco in Kintyre. The line cost the company £150 a year to run and when the Campbeltown Coal Company took over in 1897 it had 18 wagons on the tracks. The *Princess* was a third locomotive, not used after 1906. The line had been introduced solely as a freight venture but the concept of a passenger train seemed to make good business sense as more and more visitors arrived by steamer in Campbeltown. The *King Edward* and the *Queen Alexandra* brought day trippers who had to transfer to horse-drawn carriages to reach the beaches and golf course of Machrihanish. A motor car had been seen in Campbeltown in 1898 but there were no roads to speak of and the train was the answer. An application was made to the Light Railway Commissioners in 1904 and a prospectus for 23,000 shares issued. A new terminus was built at Campbeltown in Hill Street and a new link separated out the freight from the passengers. A speed limit of 20 mph was imposed and first-class passengers paid 3d. a mile while third class was a penny a mile (second class didn't exist).

Local people used the train for school and work; it was advertised as the Atlantic Express in the travel industry throughout Britain; and it carried 70,000 tons of coal into Campbeltown in 1905. The train refuelled at Limecraigs, and as there were no stations, the guard blew his whistle to indicate when someone wanted to get off. As a public relations exercise, miners' families took the inaugural trip free and in the first three weeks of its operation, more than 10,000 local people travelled on the new passenger train. There was, of course, no Sunday service until 1930. The tourist express (which took the same time as the regular run) ran until the First World War and then less frequently until 1930. During the Depression of the 1920s, there was no passenger train scheduled if the pit wasn't operating, but eight a day did run during the summer months.

It was a combination of the coal running out and the development of road transport which killed off the railway. Buses were able to compete more economically, and in 1929 the Kintyre railway closed. Although 21,373 tons of coal were transported in 1923, the men left to seek work elsewhere during the hard economic times, and by 1929 the pit was closed too. The day trippers didn't appear again until the early 1930s, by which time the wagons, land and plant were being sold off. Three engines were broken up at Drumlemble, just over half a century after the first one had taken to the tracks.

The economic collapse across Europe in the wake of the First World War had far-reaching effects. Unemployment in a rural area with a small population was just as devastating as in an industrial belt where thousands were jobless. The miners had suffered hard enough conditions when there was work: now there was none. The miners' houses built in 1860 around Coalhill and in Drumlemble were no more fit for human habitation than those in the rural areas. The surveys of tenants' houses in Kintyre carried out for the Duke of Argyll in the late 1700s revealed earth floors and animals sharing the domestic quarters. In 1899, the medical officer of health found conditions little better. In the parish of Killean and Kilkenzie between Kilchenzie and Tangy, one house called 'The Ark' housed three people, a cow, a pig and hens living together in

Water and electricity came too late for men who wanted a bath after hewing coal.
Drumlemble miners' cottages in 1890. (James and William Wallace collection.)

one room under a roof which was in danger of falling in because the damp walls were bulging so much. As with the miners' rows, no improvements were made for another half century. The miners' houses were overcrowded, had no interior doors and their apartments were divided with scraps of material, curtains if they were lucky. They got their water from a pump in the street, had privies at the back of the houses, and in common with most of Argyll, saw no gas or electricity until the 1960s. Most of the miners' houses have now gone and many rural houses are ruins. The Drumlemble pit reopened in 1945 and was worked until the 1960s, producing 3,000 tons of coal a week and employing 250 men. Although in 1954 it produced 80 per cent of the local demand with a production of 130,000 tons, the closure was on the grounds that it was uneconomical. The electricity and water put into the remaining houses came too late for men who wanted a bath after a hard shift hewing coal.

The jobs were by then in Campbeltown and in the 1950s and 1960s, fishing, shipbuilding and distilling were still the industrial backdrop to an attractive town where people sailed from the Broomielaw in Glasgow for a holiday. They were greeted by very familiar buildings because much of the Victorian architecture in the town stemmed from a series of commissions given to Glasgow architects. The now demolished English Free Church, later known as Lochend United Free Church, and opened in 1868, was designed by

Campbell Douglas and Stevenson, and the former Lochhead Distillery in Lochend Street was designed by H.E. Clifford in 1899. Much of the old property in Campbeltown around the Wide Close was demolished to made way for typical early Edwardian 'Glasgow' tenements in Longrow South, designed by T.L. Watson in 1909. But by the middle of the 20th century, Glasgow holidaymakers no longer wanted to feel at home, and steamer trips to Kintyre did not hold the same appeal as flights to sunny Spain. The fish quotas were to curtail the fishing. The shipbuilding would shrink, and even the whisky, which had become Scotland's top export, would no longer provide the jobs and ancillary work of the 19th century. At its height, there were over 20 distilleries in Campbeltown. Today there are three. They turned the old Ben Mhor distillery into a bus station and part of a massive wall of the Glen Nevis distillery can be seen, but there is little to tell the stranger that this was once 'Whisky City'.

Springbank, Glen Scotia and Glen Gyle are the last of a great tradition. From the *Statistical Account* of the 1790s down to modern times, whisky has been seen as the curse of the working man. It was said that a woman accused of running an illicit still told the Sheriff in Campbeltown court: 'I haena made a drap since youn wee keg I sent tae yersel.' Apocryphal or not, it is certain that the wheels of society and industry were oiled with whisky. By 1887, there were 21 distilleries in Campbeltown

As a better quality of whisky was made in Scotland and Ireland, the production eventually ceased in England. Illicit stills continued to be part of the rural scene, but in Campbeltown it was the licensed distilleries which flourished. The Hazelburn Distillery was one of those which started life as an illegal operation but its licensed premises were said to have been built on the site of the old parliament house where James IV emancipated MacDonald vassals. It was built by Greenlees and Colvill on a three-acre site with a 37ft stone frontage. The building stretched back 247ft and differed from the usual plan of the Campbeltown distilleries in that it had two courtyards rather than one. The water for Hazelburn came from Crosshill loch and from two deep wells. The barley in the 19th century was imported from Moray and Perthshire and was carted the quarter mile from the quay to the huge granary doors. There were three granary floors, each 110ft by 31 ft, and five malt barns with tiled or concrete floors. Each granary had a stone steep and there were three 36ft square kilns floored with Hermano's patent wire-cloth and fired with peat. Elevators took the malt from the malting floors to the kilns and below the central deposit for the malt was a mill-room with a pair of metal rollers for crushing the malt. The machinery was steam driven. A 2,500-gallon tank supplied hot water for the mash tun and there was a combined mash and still house. A neighbouring tun room had nine washbacks against the wall, each holding 6,000 gallons and worked by machinery. A furnace under the immense copper wash stills carried heat but no steam. Timber worm tubs connected to the stills had capacities of 6,000, 8,000 and 10,000 gallons respectively. In the outer courtyard, the spirit store held three vats, casks and weighing machinery and the engine department with a 23ft long by 9ins diameter steam boiler and a 14 horsepower engine. Bonded warehouses covered a third of the area of the distillery, and when Alfred Barnard visited in the 1880s he found the bonds holding 302,000 gallons of whisky.[38] Like most of the main distilleries, Hazelburn had a cooperage and carpenters' store and there were excise offices on the premises. In 1885, Hazelburn produced 192,000 gallons of whisky but had a capacity of quarter of a million gallons. Yet there were just 22 men employed there and three inland revenue officers.

Those distilleries which have survived until today are Sprinbank, Glen Scotia and Glengyle. Springbank was built in 1828 and in the 1880s employed 15 people and three excise officers. It stood half a mile from the pier and produced

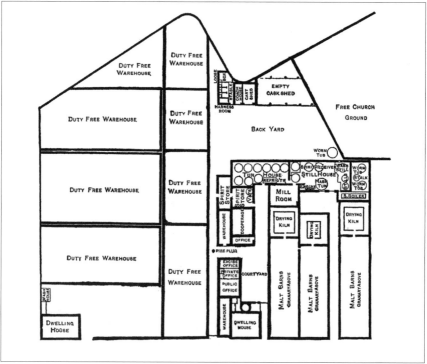

Ground Plan of Hazelburn Distillery, Campbeltown. (The Whisky Distilleries of the United Kingdom, *Alfred Barnard, first published 1887.*)

*Hazelburn Distillery employed 22 men and three revenue officers. (*The Whisky Distilleries of the United Kingdom, *Alfred Barnard, first published 1887.)*

*Dalintober Distillery produced 120,000 gallons of whisky in 1884–85 – one of around 20 distilleries in the town then. (*The Whisky Distilleries of the United Kingdom, *Alfred Barnard, first published 1887.)*

145,000 gallons a year. Dalintober ('valley of the wells', of which there were over 20 in the district) distillery had the finest view of all the distilleries, with its frontage on Kinloch Park, a quarter of a mile from the harbour and the steamboat pier. One of its five warehouses became the biggest in Campbeltown in the mid-1880s but the Dalintober produced just 120,000 gallons in 1884 to 1885. The Benmore Distillery, owned by Bulloch, Lade and Company, was in Saddell Street, a quarter of a mile from the quay, and was the first of a new generation of distilleries which opened up in the last quarter of the 19th century. It had very modern safety precautions for its day and the distillery worked on the principle of gravitation. Ardlussa was another of the new distilleries, while Dalaruan, proprietors David Colvill and Company, was founded in 1824 as the new distilling laws were coming in. *Dalruhadhain* was the name for Campbeltown in the Early Christian period when it was a headquarters of the Dalriada kingdom and even before its names 'Kilkerran' and 'Lochhead'. This distillery employed 16 men and exported, as many of the distilleries did, not only to Glasgow and England but to the colonies. Lochhead Distillery was another to be founded in 1824, while the Glen Nevis, of which part of a wall still stands, was not built until 1877. This distillery was on Gallow Hill facing the main road and had a grand 440-foot frontage, but employed just a dozen men. The Kinloch Distillery was a very early one, built in 1823, and prior to that had provided malt to illicit still operators. Close to the harbour, with its frontage on Kinlochpark, it was modernised in the late 19th century. Burnside Distillery had an interesting name on its list of directors: McMurchy, Ralston and Company. This had to be a descendant of the Ralston 'planted' by the Earl of Argyll, first at Saddell and then at Southend. The Burnside distillery did not stand the test of time. While Saddell Castle, for centuries in a state of disrepair and for many years used as servant quarters, was rescued by a leisure company and turned into an hotel, Burnside Distillery went the way of so many of its contemporary distilleries. The building had its own history: erected in 1825, its malt barn was used as a banqueting hall and ballroom when the then Duke of Argyll came of age. It employed 17 men and produced 96,000 gallons of Campbeltown malt a year. The Glengyle Distillery in Glebe Street has survived from 1873 but the Lochruan was lost. Built in 1835 and extended by new owners in the 1860s, it sat to the north-east of the town 300 yards from the quay. Albyn distillery was also lost. It had been built in Millknowe in 1830 and was still mainly unmechanised in the 1880s, employing 11 people and producing 85,000 gallons of whisky a year for a Glasgow, Ayrshire and London market. The Scotia Distillery had been established by Stewart, Galbraith and Company in 1832 in the High Street and like a number of others got its water from Crosshill

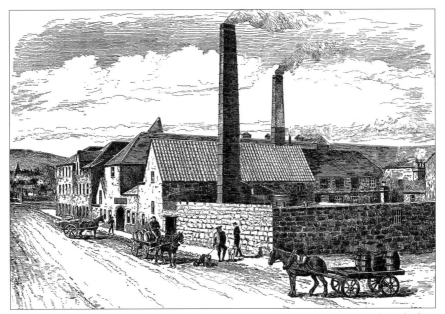

Lochruan distillery was built in 1835, 300 yards from Campbeltown quay. (The Whisky Distilleries of the United Kingdom, *Alfred Barnard, first published 1887.*)

Loch and two wells bored to 80 feet for clear water. It managed to survive while Rieclachan, which went legitimate in 1815 after years of illicit distilling and smuggling, did not. It had been the only legitimate distillery in Campbeltown in the earliest days before being joined by others in 1824. In the 1880s, this Longrow works still had the primitive appearance of the of pot-still days but was employing ten men and producing 70,000 gallons of whisky a year. Glenside, a mile from the harbour, got its barley from Stirlingshire. Longrow Distillery (there were three distilleries in this road at one time) was run by the very elderly and experienced John Ross and reflected the various styles of architecture of the 19th century. Also in Longrow was the Campbeltown distillery, built in 1815 and still using manual labour at the end of that century. The Argyll Distillery in Longrow sold its 40,000 gallons of whisky a year to Glasgow and England while the Springside distillery was the smallest in the town and had a more constricted market.

The popular song of the 1950s 'Campbeltown Loch I wish you were whisky' was almost a reality. Now just three distilleries maintain the old tradition. And Scotland's top alcoholic beverage is not the only drink lost to Campbeltown. Like Oban and Dunoon, Campbeltown produced its own brand of aerated water – 'ginger' to the general populace, 'pop' to the English. Bengullion Aerated Water, advertised in the *Campbeltown Courier* of Saturday,

Bengullion Aerated Water Company manufactured Campbeltown's non-alcoholic beverages, advertising in the Campbeltown Courier in 1902. (Courtesy Murdo MacDonald, Argyll and Bute Archivist.)

7 June 1902, was 'manufactured with the greatest care from the famous Bapley Bannocks Spring with the purest and best ingredients'. the Company had just launched a 'new and delicious drink' called Cherry Cider, and it also sold ginger beer, Kola Champagne, high-class lemonade, Lime-Fruit Champagne, Machrihanish Champagne ('a New, Pleasant, Invigorating Drink') and Sarsaparilla. Potash and Soda waters in bottles and syphons were also sold to complement the town's whiskies. Sadly, such exotic drinks are no longer manufactured in Argyll and the ubiquitous Irn Bru of Lanarkshire long since infiltrated the county.

Blades for wind farms are the industry of the 21st century in the wake of closures of the distilleries, the Jaegar clothing factory, the demise of the fishing industry and the drastic reduction of any boat construction. Once thousands of horses and cattle were shipped back and forth between Ireland and Kintyre and steamers and puffers came to Campbeltown and Saddell daily. The small tenants who raised the cattle and horses were turned out of their homes, like those at the deserted village of Balmavicar Township where ruins of houses,

Carradale could no longer accommodate a fishing fleet when boats were modernised.
(Neil and Marie Kennedy collection.)

outbuildings, enclosures, a corn-drying kiln, a horizontal water mill and evidence of runrig cultivation can still be detected. The fishermen suffered from technological change and government legislation. The author Naomi Mitchison, a Carradale resident throughout much of the 20th century, blamed the lack of investment in the old fishing villages for the demise of the fishing industry. When the old, romantic sail-boats with their cotton nets became unviable, there were no quays built to accommodate the technoboats which are essential to compete in the modern industry. Kintyre, which benefited so much from the technologies of the 19th century, has become a victim of the 21st century's emphasis on road transport. The mindset to use the peninsula's number one commodity – water – has disappeared and left Kintyre high and dry and in desperate need of an entrepreneurial Charles MacDowall of Crichen teamed with an engineer of vision like James Watt, and perhaps coppersmiths like the Armour family, still-makers in the first half of the 19th century, to create a niche market traditional whisky.

CHAPTER 6

COWAL:

THE KERRY CORNER

It was not always so, but today Cowal is the site of the second-largest town in Argyll. Dunoon has become one of the centres of administration and the law and it flows into Sandbank and Innellan: neighbours, which, like it, were once tiny fishing settlements and farming townships on the Firth of Clyde. Fishing, some land to cultivate and some rocky outcrops on which to build defences are no doubt the ingredients which attracted the very first settlers to this corner in the great Clyde estuary, and they made themselves at home in Glendaruel, at Ardnadam on the Holy Loch, at Colintraive and at Low Stillaig near Portavadie. At Ardnadam, settlers from Neolithic to Early Christian times have left their mark and there is now a heritage trail to guide visitors around the site, which includes the remains of an early chapel.

By the 6th century this part of Argyll was called Cowal, a corruption of Comhghall, one of the grandsons of the mighty Fergus who divided up Argyll among his boys. Part of it was also known as Kerry – *ceithir* or quarter – and this was on the western side of Comhghall's kingdom. Chapels were built in the Early Christian era and their names, such as Kilfinan on the Loch Fyne coast, and Kilmun towards the Clyde, reflect the Irish connections. But it was the fortifications which became the important buildings in the centuries ahead.

Dunoon, a name which is most often translated as 'the fort by the river', Barmore in Glendaruel, Inverglen near Strachur and Barr Ionla near Otter Ferry were among the earliest hilltop fortifications. They were necessary buildings: this was land that was fiercely fought over. The battle in *Glenduisk*, 'Glen of Black Water', when the troops of Mekan, king of Norway and son of Magnus Barefoot, met the clans of Cowal, caused the place to be renamed *Glen-da-ruail*, 'Glen of red blood'. From Toward Point, the battle of Largs, which ended Norse rule in the West of Scotland in 1263, would have been

clearly visible as the flames rose from the long-boats. It had been a lengthy foreign presence, and it was followed by squabbles between clans and the attempts to impose law and order by a succession of kings. Cowal soon had a surfeit of ever more sophisticated fortifications.

The castle at Dunoon, of which little remains, was built around 1050, a little earlier than the one at Rothesay on Bute which was built by Magnus Barefoot. A stone castle replaced the one at Dunoon in the 13th century and by the end of the 14th century it was designated a royal castle.

MacDonalds, Campbells and Lamonts were the big names in Cowal. By 1472, the Campbells were already in the ascendancy, although the Lamonts maintained their hold on Kerry. During the civil war, it was Lamonts and Campbells who settled old family feuds. In 1644, the Lamonts massacred around 30 people in Kilmun and Strachur. The Campbells paid them back by attacking the Lamonts' Castle Toward and treacherously going back on an amnesty for prisoners. They were taken to Dunoon and hanged, stabbed or even buried alive despite an undertaking to set them free. The castle on Eilean Dearg ('Red Island') was blown up by the Campbells during the 1685 attempt to put William and Mary on the throne. Over 180 prisoners and much stored gunpowder shared the same fate.

After that bloody century, Dunoon, Innellan, Ascog and Toward Castles (the latter once a fine tower-house with a later hall-house next to it) became too ruinous to repair, and Carrick Castle, a Campbell stronghold at the entrance to Lochgoil dating from the 12th century, was burned down in 1695. On the east shore of Loch Fyne, Castle Lachlan was torched after the 1745 uprising, which the Clan Lachlan chose to support. At Kilmun, the remains of the executed Covenanting Marquess of Argyll are yet another grim reminder that this country has not always been at peace with itself or its neighbours.

Despite the violent backdrop to this quarter of Argyll, however, Cowal and Bute were also playgrounds for kings. The hotel at Colintraive was once a Stuart hunting lodge. Kilmun was made a free burgh of barony in 1490 by James IV and he hunted around the Holy Loch. In later centuries, even while their castles were being blown to smithereens, the Campbells built mansions at Kilmun and at the now deserted village of old Innellan, where just a few stones and broken walls remain, while the Lamonts made their domestic home at Ardlamont House.

And what of the untitled people? Of what did their lives consist when they were not being blown up, hanged or run through for the glory of their lairds? Campbell tenants found themselves on the receiving end of retribution against their clan chief in 1685 during the so-called Depredations on the Clan Campbell. From Hell's Glen alone, 25 cows, 143 cattle, 154 sheep, five horses and some goats were slaughtered in the Duke of Atholl's camp. At Lochgoilhead, 53 mares, 80 cows, 15 sheep, fishing nets and boat equipment were taken or destroyed. In Clachaig, the McKinnys and the Mcinturners [sic] lost a number of horses.

And it wasn't as if the soil of Cowal was rich and could raise much more than black cattle. There were cattle fairs held in Dunoon where beasts from all corners of Argyll came together and were bought and sold. In 1707 there were five such fairs. The cattle were then taken north to a ferry at Ardentinny where they linked with drovers coming from Creggans on Loch Fyne and taken on to Dumbarton and other central markets. Although there was a castle at Dunoon, the land which fringed the Firth of Clyde comprised farming townships, mills and two quarries which provided stone for Dunoon, Innellan (Knockamillie Castle) and Toward castles. As elsewhere, sheep began to take the place of cattle (and people) in the 18th century and the old settlement of Innellan was abandoned. It was resurrected on the shoreline in the 19th century when a still newer industry began to change the face of this coast.

The advent of the steamers meant the advent of tourism. Feus were sold for the site of what would be the new Inellan and in a growing Dunoon. Grand villas went up along the shoreline at Innellan, Toward, Blairmore and Strone. The same thing was happening at Colintraive and at Tighnabruaich, where a man named Arthur Scoular married a local heiress and made a fortune from selling off plots of land to wealthy Glasgow businessmen. He then made a killing by operating the new piers from which those businessmen left in summer at 6 a.m. to get to work in time in the city. The landed gentry no longer held the reins: a burgeoning middle class could afford to buy land from once-grand estates which were now suffering economic crisis after economic crisis. Sheep could no longer keep the lairds in the manner to which they were accustomed and many saw that it was better to reduce the size of their estates than to go under.

In Dunoon, it was a Lord Provost of Glasgow who set the ball rolling and gave his citizens that idea of setting up a second home on the Clyde coast. James Ewing built his Castle House in 1822, just a decade after the *Comet* made its maiden voyage, but he made the mistake of fencing off common land for his garden. Perhaps unusually for the time, the people maintained their rights and today Castle House has become a museum and the common ground around it is a public park. Lord Provost Ewing's enthusiasm for building in Dunoon encouraged others. The wealthy built the big villas and the poorer simply got on a steamer and went 'doon the watter' for the Glasgow and Gourock Fairs. By the end of the 19th century, over 20 piers had been built around Cowal's sea

Tighnabruaich became a village of middle-class villas. (Archie Smith collection.)

Left. Argyll Street, Dunoon with the Argyll Hotel. (Argyll Hotel collection of postcards.)

Below left. Caladh House was eventually blown up after service in World War II damaged the fabric of the building. (Argyll and Bute Library Service postcard collection.)

lochs. The first pier was erected by 1820 and Dunoon's first steamer pier was ready by the 1830s. That was replaced in 1867 by a more elaborate structure which still survives as one of the last Victorian piers still in use. Steamers started running direct from Glasgow in the 1840s. Train links were in place by 1889, taking passengers from Glasgow to Gourock where they boarded a steamer. One of the earliest hotels was the Argyll which dates to at least 1837, when it was known as the Argyll Inn. As holidays in Dunoon became *de rigeur* the Argyll, renamed the Argyll Hotel in 1859, grew more grand, adding a tower designed by the Glasgow architect Alexander 'Greek' Thomson in 1876. The many changes in interior designs for the hotel reflect the changing fortunes of the town. Although it was even nearer than Campbeltown, the Clyde coast could not compete with the cheap Spanish holidays in the 1960s and 1970s any better, but at least it was buffered against the economic loss created by this sociological change with the arrival of the Polaris nuclear submarine base. Two world wars had affected Argyll in many different ways. The boom which was erected across the Clyde Estuary caused a sometimes terminal halt to steamer services: Ardrishaig, Tarbert and Carradale and the smaller piers on Loch Fyne were never to see the same traffic again. But while it was essential to protect the populations on the Clyde Estuary and to safeguard convoys of ships leaving from the Clyde to cross the Atlantic, the old perception of remoteness entered the equation and military and naval operations were carried out in lochs and glens throughout Argyll on the premise that they were too far away to be spotted by the enemy.

Such manoeuvres were to destroy buildings and cultures alike. Castle Toward, a Victorian building extended in the 1920s by Major Andrew Coates, was commandeered by the Royal Navy and served as a naval headquarters throughout the Second World War. Today it is an outdoor centre. A submarine base was set up on the Holy Loch. Yachts and puffers and steamers were requisitioned throughout Argyll by the Royal Navy. Those which were to survive lay in Rhubahn Bay in the Kyles of Bute off Tighnabruaich at the end of hostilities waiting to learn if they would be scrapped or saved. Ardlamont House, once the seat of the Lamont family, was commandeered for troops and the whole estate became a training ground for 25,000 men destined for the Normandy landings. Tenants were moved out and furniture and belongings were stored in the High Church in Tighnabruaich. Caladh House, another of the mansions in the Tighnabruaich area, was taken over by the Royal Navy and renamed HMS *James Cook*. Tighnabruaich House, home of the Scoular family which had sold the feus and turned Tighnabruaich into a thriving 'suburb' of Glasgow, became a military hospital and both Italian prisoners of war and children evacuated from Clydebank were billeted in this once peaceful haven. Caladh House and the High Church suffered irreparably. The former was not maintained and in the years afterwards, when arguments raged over responsibility, it deteriorated beyond repair. It was finally blown up by the Territorial Army as an exercise. The High Church was also in a bad state and was eventually sold to the council as a gym and assembly hall for the local school. Even the local yacht builders became part of the war machine although the world famous Archie Smith boatyard managed to continue after the war. Its original premises were demolished in the 1980s and the firm, still in the family, is repairing boats today.

The Second World War caused a hiatus in the steamer services as it did for all the Clyde ports, and in 1946 a steamer company survey demonstrated that the pre-war services, twelve a day in summer calling at Tighnabruaich and a winter service taking passengers regularly to Wemyss Bay and Gourock to catch trains to Glasgow, were no longer viable. After the 1970s, in the days when CalMac (formerly the Caledonian Steam Packet Company and David MacBrayne) had become king in the world of west-coast ferries, a 'lifeline' service was provided to the islands and peninsulas of Argyll, but pleasure cruising was a thing of the past. Only the paddle steamer *Waverley* continues to ply the Clyde for special holiday cruises. The modern road network and modern holiday aspirations have turned Tighnabruaich into a 'second home' backwater, along with Colintraive, where feus were also sold to Victorians and Edwardians who wanted clear blue Clyde between them and their business world.

For some time, it seemed that Dunoon would suffer most from the socio-logical changes of the 20th century. This was not a retreat for the middle classes but an escape for the working man and his family. It was a place of piers and pubs and paddling pools, a place where Glasgow comics spoke their language in the Pavilion Theatre. After the Second World War the British submarines left and the end of food rationing meant landladies (who had converted the fine Victorian villas into bed and breakfast establishments) could once more offer a full Scottish breakfast: the holiday trade took a turn for the better. It was short-lived. But while other traditional resorts suffered terminally from the cheap flight to Benidorm, Dunoon was given a shot in the arm in the shape of the American naval base.

The Polaris nuclear submarine was not something Scotland welcomed and there were anti-nuclear protests throughout the years the base existed on the Holy Loch. But from the time that the American Navy arrived in 1961 until its departure 31 years later, Dunoon flourished. Houses were built for the officers at Sandbank, flats for ratings went up near the golf course, property prices became very healthy indeed and retailers and those in the service industries prospered, even if it did mean a loss of culture. Intriguing to think that just a century earlier, the local minister was complaining that the accessibility which the steamers brought was destroying the Gaelic culture and that young men

The Pavilion Theatre was a hub of Dunoon's holiday fun but was replaced by a sterile 1960s building after it was burned down. Seen here from Dunoon pier. (Argyll and Bute Library Service postcard collection.)

and women were being influenced by the rather racy clothes and customs of Glasgow and Gourock. The town which in the last quarter of the 19th century had been famous for its skating rink, its convalescent home with 'splendid baths' where 19,000 invalids were restored to health, and which in the 1930s and 1950s had been the epitome of working-class off-duty Glasgow, now became a global village of burgers, transatlantic English, and mixed-race families. There was a strange mingling of tears and joy when the USS *Simon Lake* finally sailed back across the pond. The economic cushion sailed with the mother ship, leaving a Holy Loch badly in need of a clean-up and an economic deficit which the creation of local authority and health board administrative offices haven't quite filled.

Although a £12 million grant was directed at regenerating Dunoon, one thing is certain: there has been no 21st-century investment in the kind of industry which once made Cowal an international centre of export – gunpowder. Perhaps if such plans were mooted, there would be even more vehement protest than was seen against the Polaris submarines. Who wants an explosives factory next to the house in which a lifetime's savings have been invested? Who wants ugly plant spoiling the scenery which provides a backdrop to holiday homes and hotels? Perhaps local people for whom employment comes before view would welcome such work, but today, Cowal is viewed as too remote for industry. In the 19th century, it was that very quality which brought two gunpowder works to Cowal. The Clyde Powder Works at Clachaig in Glen Lean to the north-west of Dunoon was opened in the late 1830s. The remains of this lost industry sit on the south side of the B836 road where the Little Eachaig River forms a narrow gorge. Robert Sheriff, who later opened up the powder works on Loch Fyne, sold Clachaig to Curtis and Harvey of Kent. Thirty people were employed at the works in its first decade, but during the Crimean War many more were taken on to meet the demand for

Even Dunoon's convalescent home became famous for its successes. (Argyll and Bute Library Service postcard collection.)

gunpowder. The year 1855 was a boom year for gunpowder factories, and unfortunately this pun was all too often a shocking reality, as safety came very low on the list of priorities for the proprietors who opened a flurry of new powder mills. The one at Clachaig became a custom-built village with a school that doubled as a church on Sundays and a number of houses for the workers. Even so, many women employed in the mill walked the ten miles from Dunoon to their work. In 1876, Curtis and Harvey bought the gunpowder works at Kames, an even quieter backwater of Cowal.

The Kerry peninsula, running down from Strachur through Strathlachlan and Kilfinan to Ardlamont Point and stretching over to Tighnabruaich and up Glendaruel, had a population of 1,793 in 1755, and the land was already being given over to grazing. Coal-mining had been carried on in a very small way at Kildavaig but was not profitable. Fishing employed around 100 men, and although this number had risen by 1871, at the beginning of the 19th century there were legal difficulties with the nets used and fishing became a part-time occupation along with farming. The gunpowder works at Kames was licensed in 1839, but like so many industries in Argyll, it did not employ many local people. 'Specialist' tradesmen came from England and the 1861 census showed many Glasgow mechanics, engine smiths and coopers working at Kames. Between 1839 and 1921 a total of 410 people were employed – not a huge number over seven decades. These works were set up by Thomas Buchanan of Glasgow and John McCallum from the local settlement of Acharossan. They bought the Lamont land on which the mills were built in 1850. Like the Clachaig works, the Kames and Millhouse gunpowder factory benefited hugely from the outbreak in 1853 of hostilities between France and Russia over Palestinian holy places. Britain became involved in the Crimean war the following year and for for another two years there was a constant demand for gunpowder. Kames added Black Quay to its existing quay to assist the import of raw materials and export of the finished product. This extra investment and the employment of more men put a financial strain on the company after peace was signed, and by 1872 it was in the hands of a Glasgow trust. Curtis and Harvey, the Kent company which by now owned Clachaig, bought out the Kames factory in 1876. As at Furnace on Loch Fyne, the inspectors came to see if the works complied with the 1875 Explosives Act. No doubt having paid £25,000 for the mill, Curtis and Harvey would not have been looking to spend more on safety measures. Between 1846, before Curtis and Harvey's time, until 1922, when the works finally closed, there were 16 deaths from explosion and four men drowned when the company's ship *Guy Fawkes* was sunk in 1864. In fact, by the time Curtis and Harvey bought the place, changes had been made and only three of the 16 factory deaths occurred during their ownership; the third sadly taking place during the clean-up operations after the mill closed in 1921.

As at Clachaig, Curtis and Harvey wanted to make gunpowder mainly for sporting purposes, although it was also used in mining and quarrying. They reopened Clachaig from 1891 to 1903 to manufacture sporting powder. After that, the machinery was removed and the roofs dismantled. The Clachaig site had a high stone wall which ran about 300 yards along the bank of the river. Water power came from a rubble-built dam which spanned the river to the west of the works and from which ran an upper and a lower lade. About 20 buildings made up the Clachaig works, some of them two-storeyed and with hipped and slated roofs. Those in which the most volatile products were stored or manufactured had peat-covered roofs. Like the works at Melfort, Kames and Furnace, there were mixing, granulating, pressing, glazing, dusting and heading houses. There were also offices, stables, a refinery and a laboratory. The afforestation of the area means few of these can be identified. Two brick chimneys like the ones at the Kames-Millhouse works were most likely as boilers used to dry the powder. There were five incorporating mills with a central water-wheel pit at each that was fed by an underground lade. One of these had two pairs of chambers where the pan mills were housed; the others had just one chamber. All five mills had cast-iron wall-boxes to house big timber cross-beams, but the beams did not survive. Rubble-built magazines linked by a horse-drawn tramway were probably built after the reopening of the mills in 1891. The safety measures included baffle walls about eight feet thick. The workers' houses were detached and there were terraced houses along the south side of the public road. There was a single-storeyed five-bay house with a gabled porch inscribed '1863' where the manager lived. There was a quarry nearby which provided rubble for the site. At Sandbank there was a cooperage for the works until 1871, and it was at Sandbank that the raw materials came in and the finished product was shipped out.

The raw materials came to the Kames and Millhouse works from South America. Deep-sea steamships brought the potassium nitrate (saltpetre). Most of the charcoal was also imported but some was produced locally. Millhouse was traditionally a centre of charcoal-burning and there were alder woods surrounding the village. This factory had several very modern steam-powered engines and the buildings were custom made. The saltpetre works were built beside the pier at Kames while the rest of the production was spread around Low and High Mills, South Auchagoyle and part of Millhouse. The buildings had flat corrugated roofs and packed earth or yellow pine plank floors. There

Left. The saltpetre works at Kames, part of the Kames and Millhouse gunpowder manufactory licensed in 1839. (Alan Miller collection.)

Below left. Kirn, one of the string of townships which developed with the arrival of the steamers. (Argyll and Bute Library Service postcard collection.)

was a glazed wall, outside of which hung lamps to light the place for 24-hour production schedules. Production took place inside a seven-foot high wall. Water came to the High Mill via lades and an aqueduct from reservoirs dammed from the Craignafioch Burn. This was not the first water-powered industry in the area; there had been a woollen mill at Mecknock which closed before the powder mill was set up. Millhouse had a narrow-gauge railway with horse-drawn trucks. At Kames, there were one-horse carts which carried nine-barrel loads between the mills and the storage magazine. The men worked 12-hour shifts and between 60 and 70 cartloads of coal, charcoal, sulphur and saltpetre went between Kames and Millhouse every day. Ross and Marshall delivered the weekly 150-ton loads of coal by puffers which were named *Twilight* and *Skylight* and they also took the finished gunpowder away. As the safety regulations continued to improve, packed barrels were taken out from Kames's Black Quay to vessels moored off the Bute coast. The government used Curtis and Harvey's T.S. No. 6 powder specification as the standard for the Martini-Henry rifle and the company was a main supplier. Kames and Millhouse were responsible for producing between 3,000 and 4,000 tons of this gunpowder a year. In 1871, 190 men were working at the Kames and Millhouse works, far more than were ever employed in this corner's other industrial venture at Otter. The Otter Copper Company worked and traded from 1900 to 1914, when the First World War forced its closure. A Canadian company which tried to revive the works in the 1990s found that it was not commercially viable.

Like the landscape of so much of Argyll, Cowal's too had changed greatly. Kilfinan parish never had a market town and according to the *Statistical Account* of 1843, 'strictly speaking, no village'. Although Dunoon had been the residence of the bishops of Argyll during the last episcopacy in Scotland, moving it from its traditional home on Lismore, there were only 30 families living there in 1791. Illicit distilling of whisky had been stopped, an 'Osnaburgh' (linen) manufactory had failed and there was little income to keep any young people from migrating to Greenock. There wasn't even an infrastructure: there were no turnpike roads, quays or harbours except for the quay at Otter Ferry. In 1791, the Statistical Account of the parish recorded that Dunoon and the surrounding villages had 'no creek or safety even for boats at or near this village, which has probably contributed somewhat to its want of improvement'. This lack changed when Dunoon got its first pier, and when Arthur Scoular created a lively village from the sale of feus and the building of piers at Tighnabruaich, and it changed still further when the gunpowder mill opened.

Today, the gunpowder industry is long gone and so too are many of the major mansions, while most castles are in varying states of decay. Not every mansion had as dramatic an end as Caladh House and some survive. The Lamont family had to mortgage the estate in 1862 for £10,900 and tried to sell feus in the style of their neighbour Mr Scoular, but Ardlamont House survives. Like so many other houses, it is much changed. It was first mentioned in 1432 and a charter of James III confirmed Lamont possession of the lands surrounding the barony of Inveryne. The oldest parts of the current house date

Ardlamont House survives in a much changed state. (Alan Miller collection.)

A tranquil Tighnabruaich as it appeared before Arthur Scoular sold off the feus. (Archie Smith collection.)

to the 15th century, but in 1670 two older houses were joined together to form a bigger one. In 1819, Major General John Lamont, the 13th clan chief, paid £1,100 for additions to the house and renovations to the existing building. A large south-facing window was added, together with a front extension. Internally, fashionable plaster ceilings were erected. In 1893, the house was sold to the Watson family, who reroofed it and make alterations in the 1970s after those disastrous war years. The roof was found to be 300 years old.

Innens, the original name of the Tighnabruaich Estate, was owned by Arthur Scoular's father-in-law. It was originally in the hands of the MacLachlans of Strathlachlan and the charter was given on 16 December 1618 to Archibald Dow MacLachlan. It was in that family for 154 years before being bought by John Moody, a writer (lawyer) from Greenock. When he died in 1803, the estate went to Mr Moody's two sisters and was then inherited by Agnes Scoular, Moody's heiress and Arthur Scoular's wife. Scoular built new houses for other members of his family and he contested the boundaries of the Ardmarnock estate. Innens came down and was replaced by a mansion in a rather more 'flashy' Scoular style. Although Mr Scoular's selling off of feus brought many new middle-class families to Tighnabruaich, the old farming tenants had been disappearing: there was a 21 per cent population drop in Kilfinan parish in the second half of the 18th century. By 1871, fishing had eclipsed farming as a stated occupation on the census forms and work at the gunpowder factory topped that.

The lands of Otter and Ardmarnock were owned by Elizabeth Monteith of Merchiston prior to 1494 when they came into the hands of the Earls of Argyll. In 1670, Colin Campbell, second son of George Campbell, a burgess of Inveraray, paid the equivalent of £2,500 for the lands of Otter, which were five miles long, included five farms and supported 42 tenants who sublet to cottars, making a total of around 80 families living in this one small part of Cowal. The death of Major Alex Campbell at the Battle of Holistadt in 1704 meant that the minister of Glendaruel church, the major's younger brother, succeeded to the properties and one of his descendants, George Campbell, moved to Ardmarnock and had a second house at Lower Auchaleck. By the early 1800s, Ardmarnock House had been sold out of the family to a Mr Black of Greenock. His nephew, James McIvor, built a new mansion to replace Ardmarnock House. The estate was sold on yet again in 1855. Otter House is much altered from its original state when the Campbells of Otter lived there. The first mansion, known as Otter House, was built by the same John Campbell who erected the stone quay and inn at Otter. John's daughter Ann married Captain Duncan Campbell of the 18th Dragoons and they sold off the north part of the estate in 1828 to Mungo Campbell, a Glasgow merchant. Ann moved to Auchgoil House, which had been built in the mid 18th century in the style of a similar mansion at Rothesay. This was near Kilfinan, where the original parish church was in the hands of the monks of Paisley as long ago as the 13th century. Ann and her husband renamed their new home Otter House. It was sold by the Campbells to Patrick Rankin in 1852. Mr Rankin drained the land to improve its quality, rebuilt some tenants' cottages and enlarged the ancient Kilfinan Hotel. A school at Kilfinan was open until the 1950s, but with greatly reduced numbers from the days when 80 families from the Campbell property alone attended. In 1893, the Rankins added another storey to Otter House, but in 1958, when so many Argyll properties of note fell foul of high taxes and death duties and increased rateable values, Otter House was demolished, leaving only a semicircular stable yard. According to Michael Davis, the owner of the day, John F.A. Rankin, preserved the interior doors and stained-glass windows.[39] After the original Otter House was sold to Mungo Campbell, he gave it the name of Ballimor House, and in 1832 he brought in architect David Hamilton to build an 'elegant' mansion on the shores of Loch Fyne. In 1899, this property was bought by Major MacRae Gilstrap, who got William Leiper to remodel and enlarge the house in the Scottish Baronial style with gardens designed by Thomas Mawson. A further extension was built in 1914. The much altered house was bought in the late 1970s and restoration work carried out. The purists would say this house, too, was 'lost', but it survives in its evolved state, as does the landscape in which it sits.

The eastern coast of Loch Fyne, once an important thoroughfare, is now one of the quietest backwaters of mainland Argyll. Much of it in the stewardship of the MacLachlans for 700 years, it is the backdrop to the ruined Castle Lachlan, destroyed after the 1745 Uprising. Nearby are the remains of the Celtic chapel dedicated to St Maelrua in the 8th century, which gave the

St Maelrua, the 8th-century chapel which gave the ferry from Brainport its alternative 'Chapel Ferry' name. (Author's collection.)

name 'Chapel Ferry' to the crossing between this shore and Brainport. A pre-Reformation church stood on the site of the present one. It was dismantled in 1790, and its nave is was incorporated into the present church. This is where the bloomeries smelted iron long before the big commercial furnace was set up on Loch Fyne's western shore by an English company. It is where crofts have been stone-robbed to build walls and crofters were turned off to make sheep-walks. Newton was a village built in the 1790s to give some of those evicted crofters a living at the fishing – the laird built the cottages and gave them a fishing boat – while others made their way to America or perhaps to a Glasgow sweat-shop, each as far distant in practical terms as the other. Like so many estates, the MacLachlan lands were partially sold off in the decade after the Second World War and tenants at Newton were strongly encouraged to buy their homes. In 1951 these cottages had no electricity or public water supply. Perhaps because of their delightful position, they have survived all economic changes in the late 20th century and most are now holiday homes. There is

Castle Lachlan became uninhabitable after 1745 and part of the 'new' castle is now rented as a holiday home. (Author's collection.)

257

certainly no more commercial fishing done there, and were any young men to be looking for a job, they certainly would not get one on a luxury yacht for the summer, as was the case between the wars. Two mansion houses survive: a more modern Castle Lachlan and Letters Lodge. Inland from Newton are the remains of those tiny cottages the crofters were forced to leave at the end of the 18th century. To the south of this backwater was Kilfinan parish where the church built in 1759 served the whole community until 1843. It had replaced a medieval church which was so small it was probably little more than a contemplative chapel. There were seven estates in the Kilfinan parish: Balliemore and Otter, which started out, as we have seen, in the hands of the Campbells; Ardmarnock and Crispy; Ardlamont, the historical Lamont stronghold; Auchenlochan, which was once the property of the Malcolms of Poltalloch but never had a mansion house; Glen Caladh, whose final owner was Colonel G.F. Ingham-Clark; and Tighnabruaich or Innens, which came down to the Miller family which linked to the Scoulars. To the north was Strachur, ancient seat of the MacArthur Campbell family. Their estates included Ardgarten and a previous residence, now gone, was at Succoch near the River Cur. John Campbell succeeded as a minor in 1744 and inherited Strachur Park, built in 1713 by General Sir John Campbell. This John had no heirs, and when he died in 1806, his sister Janet succeeded, married her cousin, Colin Campbell of Ederline, and founded a new line. In common with so many lairds in the mid 19th century, this family had to face financial difficulties too, and the estate was sold off in lots. Part went to R.W. Robertson in the late 1890s, the main Strachur estate was sold to Lady George Campbell, a daughter-in-law of the 8th Duke of Argyll, and in turn, in 1958, when still more economic pressures were put on landowners, it was bought by Sir Fitzroy MacLean, who was MP for Lancaster and Under-Secretary for War and who in 1959 stood and won as the member for Bute and North Ayrshire.

To the east of this stretch of Loch Fyne was Lochgoilhead, which was on the direct route from the head of Loch Fyne to Glasgow through Hell's Glen. That notoriously difficult road meant that the coming of a steamer to Strachur was a godsend. Ironically, when road improvements were made throughout Cowal, jobs were lost rather than gained. Miss Augusta Lamont of the Knockdow estate said that there was a direct correlation between rural depopulation and the introduction of motor transport 'which facilitates ever-increasing centralisation'. From ferries to laundries, coal to cobblers, tailors to teachers, jobs were lost. Who could compete with the 50-shilling tailor, the mass produced shoe, the steam laundry, the bus, the centralised schools?

Lochgoilhead is a village which grew around the Church of the Three

Three Bretheren of Kinlochgoil. It was a parsonage annexed to the collegiate church of Kilmun on its foundation in 1441 at the instigation of its founder, Sir Duncan Campbell of Lochawe. Pre-Reformation, the church was an arch deanery and the revenues were considerable. The tithes of other parishes also contributed to support the 'dignity' of the arch dean.[40] The parish minister in 1791, Mr McDougal, said the Reformation had one fault. Under Catholicism, people had easy access to places of worship, '.... but because of the scarcity of protestant preachers and the avarice of the Reformers, particularly laymen, few places of worship are permitted'. Ministers, Mr McDougal said, had difficulty performing their duties within the demography of Scotland – echoes of Dr Samuel Johnson's contemporaneous comment about the Western Isles. The name of Church of the Three Bretheren (*ecclesia trium fratum*) was carried on from pre-Reformation times up to the union of the Church of Scotland and the United Free Church in 1929. The Kilmorich part of the parish round the head of Loch Fyne was bounded by a stream near Dunderave Castle, and on the opposite side by St Catherine's. It contained four villages which, until the late 17th century, were cut off from each other by high hills. The Campbells used a bridle-way known as the Duke's Path, now obliterated. At the head of Loch Fyne was a chapel dedicated to Kilmorich, Morich having been an abbot of Iona who died in 1011, but the settlement became known as Cairndow, a corruption of *Cairn Dhu* – Black rock. This became part of the Ardkinglass estate run by the Noble family – a more positive experience for tenants than the situation under many an Argyll laird. Lochgoilhead was the part of the old Ardkinglass Estate inherited by Andrew Corbett, later Lord Rowallen, who gifted it to the then Glasgow Corporation for the use of its citizens. In the 1950s it had become a recreation ground for Glasgow, visited by thousands of children from the city and by hostellers who used the YMCA camp. Today it has been developed as a much more sophisticated resort with holiday chalets and entertainment centres. Loss of solitude, peace and escape for some – but the gain of many tourists from around the world who are introduced to the Argyll experience through this frontier village.

Carrick Castle, a village on Loch Goil named after the ruined castle, is less well served – its hotel, post office and store are a work in progress. The castle itself was in use at the end of the 17th century, sharing the role with Ardkinglass and Dunderave as outposts of Inveraray Castle. It was originally reached by sea with the help of a drawbridge. Today it is a ruin which falls slightly short of picturesque because of scaffolding. Until after the First World War, there was no road access to Carrick Castle. In the days of the Norse invasions and medieval feuds, the castle was a lowering repellent at the mouth of Loch Goil.

Carrick Castle stood guard at the mouth of Loch Goil. (Author's collection.)

By the 19th and 20th centuries it had become a welcoming landmark for more friendly visitors on steamboats such as the *Ivanhoe*, the *Lord of the Isles*, the *Chevalier* and the *Edinburgh Castle*. Lochgoilhead did not lose its steamers as quickly as other Argyll villages because it was on the right side of the boom put across the Clyde during the First World War. Even between the wars there was still very little road transport (before its modern re-routing, the road through Glen Croe built by General Wade had a hairpin bend which caused early buses to go through a hair-raising reversing manoeuvre and caused many car engines to boil over) and the steamers continued a service to Lochgoilhead throughout the Second World War. By the early 1950s, however, the steamer no longer went directly to Glasgow as it had done in the late 19th century; instead there was a connection with the railhead at Arrochar and there were day and evening cruises from Craigendoran to Lochgoilhead and Arrochar, on a 'railway pleasure steamer'. By then, however, MacBraynes were running a twice-daily bus service from Glasgow to Inveraray through Glen Croe and connecting roads were built via Glen More above Loch Restil and from Cairndow to Dunoon. These were not easy roads, but like Everest, they were conquered because they were there, and the more cars and buses which took to the roads, the less chance the steamers had of survival. With the coming of the forestry to Lochgoilhead, roads were improved and the death knell was already tolling for the *Chevalier* and its ilk.

In 1929, Benmore House had been taken over by the Forestry Commission as a training school for foresters. It ran two-year courses for 30 students and tree nurseries were begun on the estate. From 1935, Argyll National Forest Park

Top left. Kirn pier once landed fish. Now it is history. (Argyll and Bute Library Service postcard collection.)

Middle left. Dunoon Lido could not compete with cheap holidays in warmer climes. (Argyll and Bute Library Service postcard collection.)

Below left. The steamers stopped coming and piers like this one at Strachur became ruined. (Argyll and Bute Library Service postcard collection.)

was initiated, the first forest park in Britain and one which covered 60,000 acres. Within it on the Holy Loch were trees grown for Bryant and May, the match-makers, and at Strachur a sawmill was built with 40 houses to accommodate workers. The development of the forest, which brought jobs and houses (a number were also built at Lochgoilhead), was, as we have seen elsewhere in Argyll, a mixed blessing. The jobs were, of course, intermittent – this cash crop can look after itself for decades at a time – and the forestry workers' houses often became holiday homes. Forest tracks have become a giant playground for walkers and cyclists but the planting and growth of the trees has swamped evidence of past cultures. Runrig farming and lazy beds can be traced over millennia if the land has reverted to its original state or been farmed by modern methods. The planting of trees, which involves rigorous invasion of the soil, destroys such evidence of the past. And nothing is more destructive of a building than a tree taking up residence within the walls. The sawmill survives and is now encouraging the use of biomass heating systems which are an environmentally positive way of using fuel growing on the Argyll hillsides. This could become one of the most viable uses for the trees planted a generation ago with great hopes for generating wealth. In the intervening decades, the value of the timber had plummeted and in some areas of Argyll, including Mull, it is no longer profitable to remove it from the forest.

So many projects started with the best of intentions have come to nothing. Some had their moment of glory in the same way that ancient churches did – like the medieval chapel of Kilkatrine which stood on the site of today's village hall in St Catherine's, was founded by Lord Duncan Campbell, and for which papal consent was granted in 1466 to hold Mass – while some simply struggled to survive even within their own time. Today there is no pier at Kirn, two of Tighnabruaich's piers have gone, the hydropathic establishment in Dunoon has disappeared and the Pavilion theatre in Dunoon burned down in 1958 and was replaced by a far too typical 1960s building called Queen's Hall. There are no regattas off Dunoon, no fishing fleet calling in at Tighnabruaich. The quarry which provided the green schist for Inveraray's new castle certainly had its moment of glory, but is worked no more. The wayfarers' inn at St Catherine's, for which a charter was granted in 1460 giving travellers respite before the journey on to Lochgoilhead, was in 1756 rebuilt as a coaching inn and today has unsympathetic extensions which make the traveller feel the loss of times past. But perhaps in 1460 the traveller would have met with bed bugs and in 1756 there were no doubt some of those drunken wild Highlandman with whom Lord Cockburn seemed so often to tangle.

There are new roads today but fewer ferries. Portavadie to Tarbert is now a convenient car-ferry hop (linking with the Colintraive ferry and then Rothesay to the mainland), having been revived as a route when an abortive attempt to create an oil platform industry at Portavadie failed ignominiously because no-one seemed to have judged the depth of the water through which the monstrous platforms would have had to be towed. The 11 inns which Kerry had in the 1700s have gone or remain as modern imitations of their former selves and there is certainly no longer a yearly fair at Kilfinan in honour of St Finan; yet the tourist industry is flourishing in a very altered state from the 19th and even the 20th century. Walking, sailing, the Botanic Gardens at Benmore, the holiday village complex at Lochgoilhead and plans for better roads on which coach tours can infiltrate to the depths of the Cowal countryside is the metamorphosis wrought by the ever changing social and technological state of our society.

EPILOGUE

So much has disappeared from the Argyll landscape. So much was there simply to meet a passing need. There were once seven primary schools in the Dunoon parish: 90 years previously, in the early 19th century, there had only been a few farms there; today small rural schools are unviable.

Puffers used to be beached once a year on the shores of big estates and small villages alike to deliver the annual coal supply: on 27 May 1881 a boy was absent from Ormsary public school in Knapdale because he was helping to cart coals from the boat to Ormsary House. That was his job. Today, one puffer sits at Crinan waiting for charitable donations to restore it; the school at Ormsary is no more and coal comes by road.

There was a mill at Saddell in 1634 and tenant farmers had to take their grain there to be milled. Today, flour is a supermarket commodity and mills throughout Argyll have been used for other purposes or left to crumble away. In the 1840s, the effects of the potato famine were felt in Argyll. Tenants who were paid in potatoes began to get cash in lieu. Farina factories were set up in Kintyre making potato flour – they lasted little more than a decade. Muasdale

---

THE KINTYRE
~~HOUSE &~~ **DRAIN TILE WORK,**
AT DRUMLEMBLE.

CASH PRICES OF TILES, &c. AT THE WORK.

No. 1, or Common Drain Tiles, . .	27s. -	per Thousand.
2, or Large Drain Tiles, . . .	28s. -	Do.
3, or Small Main Drain, . . .	32s. -	Do.
4, or Middle Main Drain, . .	50s. -	Do.
5, or Large Main Drain, . : .	70s. -	Do.
6, or Extra Large Main Drain; . .	100s. -	Do.

~~House Tiles, 60s. per Thousand; Ridge Tiles, 12s. 6d. per Hundred.~~
Common Bricks £3, and Fire Bricks £5, per Thousand ; Soles to suit the several sizes of Drain Tiles, at one half the price of Tiles.—Ornamental Chimney Cans, &c. &c. on the lowest terms.

~~ROBERT MACGREGOR,~~ Manager.
Donald McDonald

The Kintyre Drain Tile works was selling drainage tiles in 1848. (Courtesy of Murdo MacDonald, Argyll and Bute archivist.)

Farina Company and the Largie Farina Works at Tayinloan had closed again by the mid 1850s. They had served their purpose.

In the days when the pits were prosperous around Drumlemble in Kintyre, and when the Malcolms of Mid Argyll were improving their land, building their mansion and erecting cottages for their tenants, tile works were built locally to provide the raw materials for building. When the construction was done, the tile works disappeared.

Major families have lost their property because they chose to give allegiance to the wrong side, chose to use agricultural methods which were unprofitable, made investments which were unwise. The MacLachlans of that Ilk are believed to have possessed their lands on the east side of Loch Fyne for 700 years – longer even that the Dukes of Argyll have held theirs on the opposite shore. But while the Dukes have their castle, built after all the major troubles in Argyll, the MacLachlans' castle was bombarded and destroyed after they chose to support the Jacobite Uprising in 1745. Barmore estate became the property of the Royal Botanic Garden in Edinburgh – a loss to the landed classes but a gain for science and for tourism. The high rates and social demands on lairds left many mansions empty, some with their roofs removed. In Kintyre, Carskey House, Machanoch and Lephenstrath were unoccupied for years.

Other landmarks and industries have been lost because of modernisation or changes in social behaviour. Throughout Argyll, deserted villages are slowly fading into the landscape. They were bustling communities before the sheep came, the land was enclosed, the cholera came, or the forest was planted. Castles have served their military purpose; mansions have served as a peacock show of wealth and as a reminder that riches come and go.

Factories have produced commodities essential for their era: the pyroligneous acid factories at Crinan Harbour and Tayvallich met the needs of a burgeoning dye industry; the bark house at Tarbert helped prolong the life of cotton fishing nets; the handlooms devised in Campbeltown made cotton nets. With the advent of man-made fibres and the electrification of machinery, neither bark house nor handlooms were needs any more.

Changes in the needs of the merchant navy, the introduction of new materials and the financial constraints on industry after the First World War finished off the Trench Shipbuilding Yard in Campbeltown which had been established in 1877 and in its 45 years employed 300 men, built 116 vessels, the largest of which was the *Roquelle*, 4,663 gross tons and launched in 1918. No more fishing vessels were built in Campbeltown, even though Trench had been an innovative company, installing a motor-engine in a yacht as early as 1906, sparking the idea which became universally accepted of motorising the engines of fishing boats.

But then – there were no more fish. In 1880, 44,788 barrels of white herrings were cured in Campbeltown; 105,155 tons of cod, ling and hake were landed; 639 boats used the harbour; 16,077 fishermen were employed and the value of their nets stood at over £38,000. That is an industry lost to Campbeltown, as is whisky. The financial downturn of the 1950s was bad news for 'Whisky City', and among the closures, the Albyn distillery was transformed into a clothing factory, which in its turn closed in the 1990s. The Lido built in Dunoon in 1937 was no competition for the warmth of the Mediterranean, or even a modern 'flume'.

A railway came and went. A canal has become a conduit of pleasure rather than the industry it was built to serve. Wooden bobbins and lead pipes and slate roofs and gunpowder are not the tools of 21st-century life. Once 40 herring boats sat in Lochgilp with four men in each, waiting to 'chase the silver darlings'. Coopers and fish gutters thronged the quays and piers and harbour walls from Oban to Campbeltown and back up to Tarbert, Ardrishaig and Inveraray. Today, fishing quotas and powerful boats have altered the industry irreversibly. Newton, a fishing village built by the Strathlachlan Estate to maintain workers evicted from their homes to make way for sheep, is now a place of escape for those who have bought the cottages as holiday homes. Daily steamboats called in at Newton, Ardrishaig, Carradale, Tighnabruaich. Ferries crossed lochs and sea routes. A steamboat pier built at Strachur in the 1880s revolutionised communication with Glasgow. Today, motor transport is king of the 2,735 square miles which are Argyll and its 600 miles of coast are seen as remote and inaccessible. By 1955, the Strachur pier, like so many throughout Argyll, was derelict. Copper and coal have added to the sum of Argyll's wealth but now are lost industries. This is now a county – a 'continent' as the Reverend John Smith called it in his 1798 account of agriculture – which is not lost but simply evolving. It has been found by many who are content to seek out its past: the lost Argyll of a 6,000-year-long history.

Fishing fleet off Newton: 'the silver darlings' are protected by fishing regulations and fishing vessels are now highly technical machines. (Dr Alastair MacFadyen collection.)

NOTES

1. *Argyll Inventory of Monuments, Vol. III,* HMSO 1980
2. *Journey to the Western Highlands,* Dr Samuel Johnson, first published 1775
3. *Morvern Transformed,* Philip Gaskell, House of Lochar 1996
4. Murray of Stanhope MSS
5. Royal Commission on the Ancient and Historical Monuments of Scotland, Argyll, Vol. III
6. *The Justiciary Records of Argyll and the Isles 1664-1742, Vol. II, 1705–1742,* edited by John Imrie, The Stair Society, Edinburgh, 1969
7. *Morvern Transformed,* Philip Gaskell
8. *Lost Mansions of Argyll,* Michael Davis, Argyll and Bute Library Service
9. *Curiosities of Art and Nature, An annotated and illustrated edition of Martin Martin's "A Description of the Western Isles"*(first published in 1703), The Islands Book Trust, 2003.
10. HMSO 1980
11. *Ferry Tales of Argyll and the Isles* by Walter Weyndling, 1996, Alan Sutton Publishing Ltd
12. *Lost Mansions of Argyll,* Michael C. Davis, Argyll & Bute libraries booklet
13. *Ferry Tales of Argyll and the Isles,* Walter Weyndling, 1996, Alan Sutton Publishing Ltd
14. *Circuit Journeys, Lord Cockburn, 1837–1854,* published 1888 by David Douglas, Edinburgh
15. *Newsletter No 2,* Appin Historical Society 1996
16. *Lost Mansions of Argyll,* Michael Davis, Libraries booklet
17. *Old Oban,* Michael Hopkin, Stenlake Publishing, 2000
18. *The Islands that Roofed the World,* Mary Withall, Luath Press, 2001
19. *Kist* (publication of Mid Argyll Antiquarian and Natural History Society) No. 55
20. *Argyll,* Vol. 5, Islay, Jura, Colonsay, 1984. Royal Commission of Ancient and Historical Monuments of Scotland
21. Dr David Caldwell, National Museum of Scotland excavation
22. *Pennant's Tour in Scotland,* Vol. II
23. *The Whisky Distilleries of the United Kingdom,* (first published 1887) Alfred Barnard, Birlinn, 2003
24. *Roll of Paupers, Kildalton Parochial Board, 1886–89,* Museum of Islay Life.
25. *Monuments of Industry,* Geoffrey D. Hay & Geoffrey P. Steel, The Royal Commission for Ancient and Historical Monuments of Scotland, 1986
26. *Kist,* November 1972, Duncan McArdle
27. RCAHMS Inventory of Argyll. Vol. VII
28. *Proceedings of the Society of Antiquaries of Scotland, Vols 6 & 7 (1864 and 1870)*
29. *Kist Edition 65*
30. *Lost settlements of Kilmichael* and *Lost Settlements of Kilmartin,* Allan Begg, Argyll and Bute Library publications
31. *Kist* Vol. 34, Sandy Rankine
32. *Proceedings of the Society of Antiquaries of Scotland,* Vol. XXI, 1886–1887
33. *The Whisky Distilleries of the United Kingdom,* (first published 1887) Alfred Barnard, Birlinn 2003
34. *Lost Mansions of Argyll,* Michael Davis, library booklet
35. *Old Inveraray,* Donald Mackechnie, *Kist* Vol. 28, 1984
36. *Third Statistical Account of Scotland, 1961,* HMSO
37. *Kist* 34, 1987 publication of the Natural History and Antiquarian Society of Mid Argyll
38. *The Whisky Distilleries of the United Kingdom,* (first published 1887) Alfred Barnard, Birlinn 2003
39. *Lost Mansions of Argyll,* Michael Davis, Argyll and Bute Libraries Service
40. *Statistical Account of Argyll 1791, Lochgoilhead Parish,* by Rev. Mr Dugal McDougal

BIBLIOGRAPHY

First (1792), Second (1848) and Third (1961) *Statistical Accounts of Argyll*, HMSO.

The Royal Commission for Ancient and Historic Monuments Scotland; *Argyll Inventory of Monuments*, Volumes III, V, VII, HMSO.

Poorhouse registers; census accounts; trial documents; estate records. Murray of Stanhope Papers.

Journey to the Western Highlands, Dr Samuel Johnson, first published 1775.

Morvern Transformed: A Highland Parish in the Nineteenth Century, by Philip Gaskell, House of Lochar, 1996.

Justiciary Records of Argyll and the Isles, 1664-1742, Vol. II, 1705-1742, edited by John Imrie, The Stair Society, Edinburgh, 1969.

Napier Commission Reports.

Lost Mansions of Argyll, Michael Davis, Argyll and Bute Library Service.

Curiosities of Art and Nature; an annotated and illustrated edition of Martin Martin's 'A Description of the Western Isles' (first published in 1703), The Islands Book Trust, 2003.

Ferry Tales of Argyll and the Isles, Walter Weyndling, 1996, Alan Sutton Publishing Ltd.

Circuit Journeys 1837-1854, by Lord Cockburn, published 1888 by David Douglas, Edinburgh.

Appin Historical Society publications.

Old Oban, by Michael Hopkin, Stenlake Publishing, 2000.

Mid Argyll Antiquarian and Natural History Society publications (Kist).

Roll of Paupers, Kildalton Parochial Board, 1886–89, Museum of Islay Life.

Monuments of Industry, Geoffrey D. Hay and Geoffrey P. Steel, The Royal Commission for Ancient and Historical Monuments Scotland. HMSO

Ordnance Gazetteer of Scotland, 1885.

Proceedings of the Society of Antiquaries of Scotland, Vols VI and VII, 1864 and 1870.

Lost Settlements of Kilmichael Parish and Lost Settlements of Kilmartin Parish, by Allan Begg. Argyll and Bute Library Service.

The Whisky Distilleries of the United Kingdom, Alfred Barnard, Birlinn, 2003 (first published 1887).

INDEX

Illustrations appearing in the book are highlighted in bold type.
Names of boats, ferries and steamers are in italic.